LITERATURE AND DOMESTIC TRAVEL IN EARLY MODERN ENGLAND

In the early modern period, the population of England travelled more than is often now thought, by road and by water: from members of the gentry travelling for pleasure, through the activities of those involved in internal trade, to labourers migrating out of necessity. Yet the commonly held view that people should know their places, geographically as well as socially, made domestic travel highly controversial. Andrew McRae examines the meanings of mobility in the early modern period, drawing on sources from canonical literature and travel narratives to a range of historical documents including maps and travel guides. He identifies the relationship between domestic travel and the emergence of vital new models of nationhood and identity. An original contribution to the study of early modern literature as well as travel literature, this interdisciplinary book opens up domestic travel as a vital and previously underexplored area of research.

ANDREW McRAE is Professor of Renaissance Studies in the Department of English at the University of Exeter. He is the author of *Literature, Satire and the Early Stuart State* (Cambridge, 2004) and *God Speed the Plough: The Representation of Agrarian England, 1500–1660* (Cambridge, 1996).

LITERATURE AND DOMESTIC TRAVEL IN EARLY MODERN ENGLAND

ANDREW McRAE

CAMBRIDGE
UNIVERSITY PRESS

CAMBRIDGE UNIVERSITY PRESS
Cambridge, New York, Melbourne, Madrid, Cape Town, Singapore, São Paulo, Delhi

Cambridge University Press
The Edinburgh Building, Cambridge CB2 8RU, UK

Published in the United States of America by Cambridge University Press, New York

www.cambridge.org
Information on this title: www.cambridge.org/9780521448376

First published 2009

Printed in the United Kingdom at the University Press, Cambridge

A catalogue record for this publication is available from the British Library

ISBN 978-0-521-44837-6 hardback

For Jane

Contents

List of illustrations	*page*	ix
Acknowledgements		x
Abbreviations		xi
Introduction		1
John Leland: travels and connections		3
The importance of domestic travel		7
Scope and structure		14
PART I: ROUTES		19
1 Rivers		21
The politics of rivers: real and imaginary journeys		24
The river poem: connection, power and nationhood		33
River improvement and the poetry of the waterman		44
Place, prospect and commerce in seventeenth-century poetry		54
2 Roads		67
Networks: highways and the nation		70
Never out of their way: commoners on the road		91
3 Inns and alehouses		122
Economies of mobility		124
Inns and alehouses on stage		128
Anxieties of mobility: Jonson's *New Inn*		134
PART II: TRAVELLERS		143
4 The progress: royal travellers and common authors		145
Elizabeth and the politics of place		147
Progress texts and common authors		157
The wandering king		164

5   Tourism: Celia Fiennes and her context   174
      Models and motivations   177
      Journey poems   185
      Travel journals   192

6   Traffic: John Taylor and his context   210
      The challenge of traffic   212
      The industrious traveller   220
      Taylor's nation: the spaces of circulation   226

    Epilogue: Defoe's *Tour*   235

Index   243

Illustrations

1.1 Map of Essex, from Christopher Saxton, *Atlas of England and Wales* (1580). Reproduced by permission of the Folger Shakespeare Library.   *page* 30

2.1 Map of the post-road network of England and Wales, from John Ogilby, *Britannia* (1675). Reproduced by permission of the Folger Shakespeare Library.   78

2.2 Road-map from John Ogilby, *Britannia* (1675). Reproduced by permission of the Folger Shakespeare Library.   80

2.3 Distance table for Devonshire, from John Norden, *England: An Intended Guyde For English Travailers* (1625). Reproduced by permission of the Folger Shakespeare Library.   83

2.4 Detail from John Adams, *Angliae totius tabula cum distantiis notioribus in itinerantium usum accommodata* (1677). Reproduced by permission of the British Library.   84

2.5 Proposed road-building designs, from Thomas Procter, *A Worthy Worke Profitable to this Whole Kingdome* (1607). Reproduced by permission of the British Library.   88

2.6 'The North Road from London to Barwick', from John Ogilby, *English Travellers Companion* (1676). Reproduced by permission of the British Library.   107

2.7 Detail from William Berry, *The Grand Roads of England* (1679). Reproduced by permission of the British Library.   108

5.1 Map of Oxfordshire in Robert Plot, *Natural History of Oxford-Shire* (1677). Reproduced by permission of the Folger Shakespeare Library.   184

Acknowledgements

The origins of this book can be traced to an invitation from Donna Landry, Gerald Maclean and Joseph P. Ward, over a decade ago, to contribute an essay to *The Country and the City Revisited: England and the Politics of Culture, 1560–1840*. For that invitation, which prompted me to think and work along new lines, I am very grateful. The project has developed since then in fits and starts, in different jobs and different countries, interrupted for extended periods by my work on political satire and my editorial work on early Stuart libels. This process has left me with numerous institutions and people to thank.

The project's early stages were funded, in different ways, by the Australian Research Council, the University of Sydney and the British Academy. The Leverhulme Trust, finally, gave me funding for a year to finish the book. Many people have contributed to the development of the research and argument, whether through reading drafts of chapters, providing me with copies of unpublished work, or simply sharing ideas. The list of such people includes: Stephen Bending, John Chartres, Katharine Craik, Jess Edwards, Patricia Fumerton, Andrew Gordon, John Gouws, Felicity Henderson, Steve Hindle, Bernhard Klein, Nick McDowell, Michelle O'Callaghan, David Rollison, Julie Sanders, Philip Schwyzer, Garrett Sullivan, Alexandra Walsham, Paul Young. Early versions of particular parts of the books have been published as: 'Female Mobility and National Space in Restoration England: The Travel Diaries of Celia Fiennes', *Meridian*, 18 ii (2001), 127–38; 'The Literature of Domestic Travel in Early Modern England: The Journeys of John Taylor', *Studies in Travel Writing*, 12 i (2008), 85–100; and 'Fluvial Nation: Rivers, Mobility, and Poetry in Early Modern England', *English Literary Renaissance*, 38 iii (2008), 506–34.

Jane Whittle has done much to ensure that interdisciplinarity means a capacity to engage with historians as well as literary scholars, and much more than that to keep me happy. Books are inevitably remembered by their authors in relation to places and people; for me, this is the book that spanned the creation of a family. I am grateful to Anna and Esther, for being so delightful, and I dedicate the book to Jane, with love.

Abbreviations

BL   British Library

ODNB   *Oxford Dictionary of National Biography: From the Earliest Times to the Year 2000*, ed. H. C. G. Matthew and Brian Harrison, 60 vols. (Oxford, 2004)

OED   *Oxford English Dictionary*, 2nd edn, prepared by J. A. Simpson and E. S. C. Weiner, 20 vols. (Oxford, 1989)

Wing   *Short Title Catalogue of Books Printed in England, Scotland, Ireland, Wales … 1641–1700*, compiled by Donald Wing, 3 vols. (New York, 1972–88)

Introduction

John Leland, gathering his notes together in the mid-1540s after six years of journeys across England and Wales, had an audacious vision. He told Henry VIII that he aimed to produce for him linked texts, describing his land in a visual image and accompanying words. He wrote:

I trust shortly to se the tyme, that like as Carolus Magnus had among his treasures thre large and notable tables of sylver, rychely enameled, one of the syte and description of Constantynople, an other of the site and figure of the magnificent citie of Rome, and the third of the descripcion of the worlde. So shall your Majestie have thys your worlde and impery of Englande so sett fourthe in a quadrate table of sylver ... And because that it may be more permanent, and farther knowne, then to have it engraved in sylver or brasse. I entend by the leave of God, within the space of xii. moneths folowyng, such a descripcion to make of your realme in wryttinge, that it shall be no mastery after, for the graver or painter to make the lyke by a perfect example.[1]

These proposed texts, though very different in terms of form, are underpinned by a common purpose. The 'quadrate table of sylver' and the written 'descripcion' were intended, in an unprecedented and ineradicable manner, to render Henry's realm visible. They would have presented to the King nothing less than a comprehensive, encyclopedic knowledge of his land, all capable to being 'apprehended in a single, unified gaze'.[2]

Leland never realized his vision. He lapsed into insanity in 1547 and died in 1552, leaving, as testament to his dream, a brief text from which the above quotes are taken and a wealth of manuscript notes describing his journeys. The notes assumed a cultural life of their own, circulating among scholars for almost 200 years before eventually being printed in the early eighteenth century as *The Itinerary of John Leland the Antiquary*.[3] This achievement in

---

[1] *The Laboryouse Journey [and] serche of Johan Leylande* (1549), sigs. D5v–D6v.
[2] Philip Schwyzer, 'John Leland and His Heirs: The Topography of England', in *The Oxford Handbook of Tudor Literature*, ed. Mike Pincombe and Cathy Shrank (Oxford, 2009), p. 245.
[3] Ed. Thomas Hearne (9 vols., Oxford, 1710–12).

itself marked Leland as arguably the most important author of domestic travel-writing before Daniel Defoe: far more important, in fact, than the belated effort to pigeon-hole him as an 'antiquary' might suggest. Yet there is cause to dwell on Leland's failure as well as his unquestionable achievement. The seductive image of nationhood as wholly visible, suspended from time and process, was clearly an 'impossible object' to realize.[4] Moreover, it was founded on a curious paradox, which may be instructive in the present context. For, while Leland repeatedly stresses, in his letter to Henry, the author's 'laborious' commitment to his task, the effect of his imagined achievement would have been to render those labours invisible. These twinned texts would have offered not narratives of individual journeys, but rather descriptions of the nation's myriad notable sites. They would have provided information about the position of these sites in relation to one another, but would not have traced lines of connection between them. They would have inscribed a knowledge not of travel but of place.

Leland's *Itinerary*, to which I will return in the following pages, thus signals the problematic status of domestic travel in the early modern period. This compilation of notes describes journeys which the author himself appreciated as anomalous; indeed his travels are intended to render similar exercises virtually redundant. In the present book, I want to look beyond Leland, to consider the wider meanings of domestic travel in early modern England. The book is based on the premise that human mobility, within the space of the English nation, posed fundamental challenges to the period's predominant models of social order. Those models assumed a nation within which people were fixed in place not only socially but also geographically, allowing little scope for the undeniable realities of movement in its various forms. How, then, did contemporaries make sense of domestic travel? How did they register the increasing incidence of mobility and the development of new forms of travel? How did they accommodate mobility to existing models of nationhood? And how did literature participate in these processes? The book thus embraces the proposition that human mobility was one of the period's most dynamic forces of change, and endeavours to delineate the cultural dimensions of the profound debates and ideological struggles attendant upon these changes.[5]

Leland and Defoe serve as book-ends. In the Epilogue, I suggest that Defoe's *Tour thro' the Whole Island of Great Britain* realizes a model of

[4] Schwyzer, 'John Leland and His Heirs', p. 244.
[5] David Rollison, 'Exploding England: The Dialectics of Mobility and Settlement in Early Modern England', *Social History*, 24 (1999), 2.

national connectedness that stands, in many respects, as the antithesis of Leland's vision. Nationhood, for Defoe, is brought into being by mobility. But the book as a whole is not principally driven by a chronological narrative. It is concerned rather with an extended period of uncertainty and flux, arguing that men and women in the sixteenth and seventeenth centuries, in the face of severe cultural constraints, developed radically new ways of appreciating their relations with national space, and accordingly new models for representing the contours of nationhood. The present Introduction is intended to establish a framework for this investigation. In the following discussion of Leland I discuss his *Itinerary* in more detail, considering its uneasy oscillation between different models of national space and human mobility. The subsequent section positions the book in relation to various related studies of the period, and introduces the theory and methodology which underpin the argument. The final section outlines the shape and parameters of the project.

JOHN LELAND: TRAVELS AND CONNECTIONS

Set alongside his vision of an immediately visible tablet of knowledge, Leland's *Itinerary*, by contrast, dilates uncontrollably into a mass of 'elusive and ungraspable detail'.[6] Indeed the *Itinerary* is characterized by its sheer excess of purpose. It not only includes a miscellany of information about the geographical structures and human uses of the land, but also moves incessantly back through time, bearing witness to the project's origins in a survey of the contents of monastic libraries. Leland's 'topic is nothing less than "Britain"', and he approaches this topic with no overarching model or set of guidelines, simply because none existed.[7] As much as he struggles towards a sense of coherence, and experiments along the way with different methods of organizing his information, the text remains disordered and indiscriminate. Yet I want to suggest that these volumes, in their unfulfilled gestures towards form, register critical tensions between different models of the nation, and variant ways of appreciating relations between its subjects and the spaces they inhabited. As much as Leland seeks to capture an image of his land removed from the exigencies of time and human endeavour, these forces press themselves upon the text regardless, suggesting in the process very different forms of nationhood.

---

[6] James Simpson, *Reform and Cultural Revolution, The Oxford English Literary History*, Vol. II: *1350–1547* (Oxford, 2002), p. 14.
[7] Simpson, *Reform and Cultural Revolution*, p. 12.

In the wake of the Reformation, which effectively trashed his effort to survey the nation's literary archives, Leland 'transposed his grand project from a bibliographical to a topographical key'. But what happens when space, in Philip Schwyzer's words, is 'called upon to stand in for history'?[8] One consequence is that the fantasy of all knowledge ultimately being capable of presentation to the monarch, as the one person in the land privileged to perceive and comprehend it all, disintegrates. In the *Itinerary*, spatial knowledge is more elusive, and also essentially more demotic, than that fantasy allows. Hence the text records instead the experience of its author gathering his knowledge. From the opening pages the first-person pronouns are insistent: 'I saw in the quire'; 'These thinges brevely I markid'; 'In this chirch … I saw the tumbe', and so forth. These instances, all taken from a single page of the modern edition, are intertwined with acts of interpretation: 'So that I think'; 'This Richard I take to be the same'.[9] Moreover, the text acknowledges the degree to which knowledge of the nation is located not just in libraries, but equally in the minds of commoners. While the text typically suppresses what must have been daily discussions with locals over distances and directions, it occasionally records the value of popular knowledge and memory. In Bedfordshire, for instance, a miller tells Leland of a bridge over the Ouse that he is not able to see, while in Yorkshire he records the 'commune opinion' about the changing course of the Derwent (I.102, I.45). The effect of such notes is to suggest an almost infinite expansion of the nation's stocks of knowledge, not only spatially but also socially. One reason the project is essentially unrealizable, in fact, is this recognition of diffusion, which threatens to reduce Leland to the status of a conduit for 'commune opinion'.

Furthermore, spatial knowledge is demonstrated to be not merely a matter of information about places, but equally a matter of associations and connections. Leland experiments with various ways of structuring his notes. Perhaps the most conventional approach, for the eyes of a modern reader, is to arrange sections by county, with subheadings for that county's notable features. Hence, for example, he gives details of the market-towns, castles, rivers, and forests and chases in Worcestershire (V.8–11). This model, founded on the imaginative breakdown of the nation into administrative units, would be enshrined by the following generations of cartographers and chorographers, including men such as Christopher Saxton and

---

[8] Schwyzer, 'John Leland and His Heirs', p. 242.
[9] *The Itinerary of John Leland in or about the Years 1535–1543*, ed. Lucy Toulmin Smith, 5 vols. (London, 1906–10), all quotes at I.15.

William Camden. More commonly, though, the text records trajectories. These trajectories are across time as well as space, since the *Itinerary* acts in part as a storehouse of historical and genealogical data and anecdote. A visit to a village church, for instance, may prompt a narrative of the fortunes of the local landowning family. But they are most memorably acts of individual travel, that suggest connections between one place and another, and ultimately between all of the various 'regions through which he travels'.[10] These trajectories privilege the experience of the traveller, struggling along the way with the nation's often intransigent geography. Consequently, to take one example of his practice, while he occasionally describes the courses of particular rivers from source to mouth, as though tracing routes along the surface of a map, his attention is more urgently drawn to bridges, which are so essential to the experience of a traveller. As John Scattergood observes, for Leland rivers are essentially significant as 'channels to be negotiated' rather than as lines of connection.[11]

This characteristic of the text aligns Leland's journeys with more common experiences of travel. Indeed, while Leland is determined to represent his own knowledge as unique, and ultimately sufficient to submit to the gaze of the King, the *Itinerary* constantly reminds its reader of the extent to which he was following routes established and rehearsed daily by countless numbers of English men and women. Not only is he on occasion forced to rely on 'commune opinion', he is therefore also positioned, as though against his own will, as another commoner treading common paths. This effect is most striking on the occasions when he inserts tabular itineraries of distances, in the form that would become familiar in a range of printed texts over subsequent decades.[12] In the course of a journey through Gloucestershire, for instance, he includes the following:

> The way lyith this from Cirencestre to London:
> To Fairford vi. miles.
> To Farington viii.
> To Abbingdon ... miles.
> To Dorchestre v. miles.
> To Henley ......
> To London ......

(I.130)

[10] Cathy Shrank, *Writing the Nation in Reformation England* (Oxford, 2004), p. 86.

[11] 'John Leland's *Itinerary* and the Identity of England', in *Sixteenth-Century Identities*, ed. A. J. Piesse (Manchester, 2000), p. 67. See also Jennifer Summit, 'Leland's *Itinerary* and the Remains of the Medieval Past', in *Reading the Medieval in Early Modern England*, ed. Gordon McMullan and David Matthews (Cambridge, 2007), p. 164.

[12] See below, pp. 76–7.

It is not clear that Leland actually followed this itinerary. His ellipses indicate gaps in his knowledge, and possibly also in his experience, while the text itself subsequently moves on at a more leisurely pace through Gloucestershire. Yet this route, like many of the others that he tabulates in this manner, was certainly well trodden by the numerous cloth traders responsible not only for making Cirencester's market 'the most celebrate ... in al that quarters' (I.129), but more generally for driving forward the economic strength of the region and the nation. Cirencester, as David Rollison argues, was in part a product of its 'traffic', and its status typified the growth of the English cloth industry.[13] It is therefore fair to say that this particular itinerary was better known to commercial carriers than to Leland himself. As happens at so many other points in this text, it thus gestures outward – implicitly and perhaps involuntarily, but also as a matter of undeniable practical necessity – to the experience and knowledge of commoners accustomed to traversing the land.

As becomes apparent through such instances, the *Itinerary*'s appreciation of the practical details of human process undermines the professed goal to define a static model of nationhood. This is not a new argument; others have commented that Leland 'describes a remarkably fluid landscape', or 'an England whose identity is fluid'.[14] Such readings, however, have focused on the text's registering of the massive transformations wrought upon the land by the dissolution of the monasteries. The land, as Jennifer Summit states, was 'in a state of passing ... from one point in time to another'.[15] But this was not just a matter of change through time; equally, it was a product of the movements of individuals through space. This point is apparent in the text's recurrent narratives of the genealogies and fortunes of families. The history of the Rainesford family, 'Of Tew in Oxfordshire', for instance, is a narrative of expansion across the land, as the son of 'Old Rainesford' virtually doubles the family's landholdings in the region (IV.76). On a broader scale, Leland often considers the rises and falls of towns as a result of their commitment to particular industries which have either failed or flourished. Of Beverley, Yorkshire, he notes: 'Ther was good cloth making ... but that is nowe decayid'; at Reading, by contrast, the 'waters be very commodious for diers', and as a result 'the toune chiefly stondith by clothyng' (I.47; I.111). Such comments record the uncertain yet insistent

---

[13] Rollison, 'Exploding England', 10; Rollison, *The Local Origins of Modern Society: Gloucestershire 1500–1800* (London and New York, 1993), pp. 45–63.

[14] Summit, 'Leland's *Itinerary*', p. 163; Scattergood, 'John Leland's *Itinerary*', p. 72.

[15] Summit, 'Leland's *Itinerary*', p. 163.

development of trade and industry, which entailed, as essential and definitive factors, the movement of people and goods across the country. Uses of
land involve, of necessity, movements through land.

In the course of the *Itinerary*, then, the author who sought to establish
himself as a unique gatherer of a finite stock of information to present to the
King threatens to metamorphose into merely another subject travelling the
roads and rivers of his nation. In the process, the text sketches the outlines of
a very different model of nationhood to the one Leland proposed to Henry.
This is a nationhood defined by connections across space: given shape by
routes, and enacted by the subjects travelling them. As Schwyzer argues, the
Itinerary 'does not so much discover a unified nation already present on the
ground as, through the figure of the itinerant, bring one into being'.[16] This
is not a model that Leland intended to produce, but it was an inevitable
consequence of his decision to gather information through acts of travel. I
want to suggest here that it is a model that remained a shadowy presence in
discourse on space and nationhood throughout the early modern period. It
posited a form of nationhood utterly different from the period's orthodox
model of placement, yet a form that was increasingly promoted in various
forms by a wide range of texts and authors. Leland's project, one might
argue, was undone by the tension between these different ways of appreciating national space. Over the following 150 years or so, I want to argue,
those tensions would give shape to debates over mobility and nationhood.

THE IMPORTANCE OF DOMESTIC TRAVEL

This book considers, in broad terms, early modern struggles to make sense
of mobility. It is thus concerned not with particular kinds of travel, such as
the narratives of tours produced by Leland and Defoe, but with mobility
per se. The project is founded on an awareness of the significance of mobility –
of people, goods and information – to the English nation. Such processes of
mobility lent shape to some of the definitive transformations of the era: from
the shift towards capitalism, through the ongoing spatial redistribution of the
population, to the political reconceptualization of passive subjects as active
citizens. To study the ways in which contemporaries understood mobility is
therefore to better appreciate the formation of the modern English nation.
The book's task is to identify where – and, more importantly, how – new
perceptions of mobility were conceived.

---

[16] 'John Leland and His Heirs', pp. 247–8.

As suggested in my analysis of Leland, the book is founded on the proposition that a commitment to values of place underpinned a powerful model of social and spatial organization in early modern England. This model assumed that the nation was organized into stable and relatively self-sufficient communities, whether in villages or towns, and it informed thought across the social spectrum. James I was perhaps the most vocal of the nation's rulers, though by no means unrepresentative, in his impassioned exhortations that the gentry should preside over an harmonious social order on their rural estates. 'Therefore as every fish lives in his owne place, some in the fresh, some in the salt, some in the mud', he argued in 1616, 'so let every one live in his owne place, some at Court, some in the Citie, some in the Countrey'.[17] Within villages themselves, meanwhile, social interaction was commonly characterized by 'intense localism', or even 'parochial xenophobia'.[18] The commitment to place was also reinforced by extensive legal structures. The Statute of Artificers, it has been said, 'wrote into law the model of a settled population where each laborer had his superior'.[19] The Elizabethan Poor Laws, which effectively remained in place through to the eighteenth century, encoded the presumptions that paupers had identifiable homes and that their relief was the responsibility of their neighbours.[20] And the laws on vagrancy, to which I will return in Chapter 2, were especially harsh on those who had been displaced from particular settlements.[21] The Elizabethan commentator William Harrison was thus entirely in accord with his age in expressing his disgust at the spectre of 'the vagabond that will abide nowhere'.[22]

These attitudes and assumptions have in turn informed historical and cultural analysis of early modern life. 'The myth of the relatively isolated, self-contained and static rural community', as Keith Wrightson writes, 'is a powerful element in our conception of the past.'[23] Nonetheless, a range of important historical work has challenged this myth, thereby establishing valuable contexts for the present study. The tradition of transport history, which flourished particularly in the early to middle decades of the twentieth

---

[17] King James VI and I, *Political Writings*, ed. Johann P. Sommerville (Cambridge, 1994), p. 227.
[18] Steve Hindle, *On the Parish? The Micro-Politics of Poor Relief in Rural England c.1550–1750* (Oxford, 2004), p. 305.
[19] Joyce Oldham Appleby, *Economic Thought and Ideology in Seventeenth-Century England* (Princeton, 1978), p. 29.
[20] On the history of these laws, see esp. Hindle, *On the Parish?*; and Paul Slack, *Poverty and Policy in Tudor and Stuart England* (London and New York, 1988).
[21] See below, pp. 93–5.   [22] *The Description of England*, ed. Georges Edelen (Ithaca, 1968), p. 180.
[23] *English Society 1580–1680* (London, 1982), p. 41. See also *The Self-Contained Village? The Social History of Rural Communities 1250–1900*, ed. Christopher Dyer (Hatfield, 2006).

century, did much to demonstrate the mechanics of mobility.[24] More recent developments have attended in various ways to its social and economic dynamics. Research into internal migration, for instance, has revealed not only the importance of such movement, but also its characteristic patterns and types. Much migration was conducted across relatively small distances; however, some migrants covered much greater distances, tracing unpredictable arcs across the country, for causes that might be characterized in terms of 'betterment', 'subsistence', or something in between.[25] Other historians have sought to recover the category of the 'labouring poor', which caused early modern commentators such concern. These were people 'able and willing to work', but unable to support themselves within the confines of their 'home' villages, and often forced as a result into marginal and mobile existences.[26] In contemporary parlance, they were 'living by the shift'.[27] Moreover, in extreme cases they were reduced to lives of vagrancy: a category that has rightly been subjected to scrutiny, but which nonetheless retains a certain integrity for understanding some of the most difficult of early modern lives.[28]

Other studies have analyzed the effects of changing practices and understandings of marketing. Alan Everitt, for instance, begins his analysis of 'The Marketing of Agricultural Produce' by commenting: 'By the year 1500 England had moved a very long way from the era of fully self-supporting rural communities. In all probability such arcadian conditions had never existed.'[29] Indeed internal trade, it has been estimated, handled 'perhaps a quarter or a third of G.N.P. in the sixteenth and seventeenth centuries', and this propelled the associated development of modern practices of consumerism.[30] These developments in turn challenged existing models for the

---

[24] See esp. J. Crofts, *Packhorse, Waggon and Post: Land Carriage and Communications under the Tudors and Stuarts* (London, 1967); Cyril Hughes Hartmann, *The Story of the Roads* (London, 1927); W. T. Jackman, *The Development of Transportation in Modern England*, 3rd edn (London, 1966); Sidney and Beatrice Webb, *English Local Government: The Story of the King's Highway* (London, 1913); T. S. Willan, *River Navigation in England 1600–1750*, 2nd edn (London, 1964).

[25] See esp. *Migration and Society in Early Modern England*, ed. Peter Clark and David Souden (London, 1987). The classification of migration as 'betterment' or 'subsistence' is derived from Peter Clark, 'The Migrant in Kentish Towns', in *Crisis and Order in English Towns 1500–1700: Essays in Urban History*, ed. Peter Clark and Paul Slack (London, 1972), p. 138.

[26] Slack, *Poverty and Policy*, p. 27.   [27] Hindle, *On the Parish?*, esp. pp. 92–5.

[28] See esp. A. L. Beier, *Masterless Men: The Vagrancy Problem in England 1560–1640* (London, 1985).

[29] 'The Marketing of Agricultural Produce', in *The Agrarian History of England and Wales*, Vol. IV: *1500–1640*, ed. Joan Thirsk (Cambridge, 1967), p. 466.

[30] J. A. Chartres, *Internal Trade: England 1500–1700* (London, 1977), p. 10. On the development of consumerism, see esp. Margaret Spufford, *The Great Reclothing of England: Petty Chapmen and their Wares in the Seventeenth Century* (London, 1984); and Joan Thirsk, *Economic Policy and Projects: The Development of a Consumer Society in Early Modern England* (Oxford, 1978).

conceptualization of economic relationships. In the early seventeenth century, Joyce Oldham Appleby writes, 'the men who wrote on economic life had no analytical framework for discussing the shaping force of the market'. Indeed this was something, she argues, that was largely developed in the course of that century.[31] More specifically, as Jean-Christophe Agnew has argued, early modern writers were gradually learning to conceive of the market in abstract terms, thereby gradually separating 'the generality of a market *process* from the particularity of a market *place*'. Such writers, Agnew observes, were giving 'practical and figurative form to the very principles of liquidity and exchangeability that were dissolving, dividing, and destroying form and that, in doing so, were confounding the character of all exchange'.[32] They recognized, however uncertainly, that an abstract national market would create new relationships between places and people across the nation.

Scholars of literary and cultural history have added depth to these appreciations of the past, particularly by attending to the power of language to ascribe order to shifting and uncertain circumstances. Discourse can create meaning out of confusion; particularly resonant texts can condense debates into the space of a page. Crucially, Richard Helgerson's analysis of what he terms 'the writing of England', evident in Elizabethan texts as diverse as maps and plays, has influenced a range of further analyses of the meanings of place and space in the period, attending especially to the shift from feudalism to capitalism.[33] In some respects, the present book also benefits from the insights of those who have examined the period's rich literature of foreign travel, demonstrating the ways in which encounters with cultural difference prompted reflection upon the meanings of England and Englishness.[34] Further, the book's concerns align, at a number of key points, with cultural and literary histories of mobile commoners. Numerous

---

[31] Appleby, *Economic Thought*, quote at p. 21.

[32] *Worlds Apart: The Market and the Theater in Anglo-American Thought, 1550–1750* (Cambridge, 1986), pp. 41, 9.

[33] *Forms of Nationhood: The Elizabethan Writing of England* (Chicago and London, 1992). See further Jess Edwards, *Writing, Geometry and Space in Seventeenth-Century England and America: Circles in the Sand* (London, 2005); Bernhard Klein, *Maps and the Writing of Space in Early Modern England and Ireland* (Basingstoke, 2001); Andrew McRae, *God Speed the Plough: The Representation of Agrarian England, 1500–1660* (Cambridge, 1996); Garrett A. Sullivan, *The Drama of Landscape: Land, Property, and Social Relations on the Early Modern Stage* (Stanford, 1998).

[34] See esp. Richmond Barbour, *Before Orientalism: London's Theatre of the East, 1576–1626* (Cambridge, 2003); Chloe Chard, *Pleasure and Guilt on the Grand Tour: Travel Writing and Imaginative Geography 1600–1830* (Manchester, 1999); Andrew Hadfield, *Literature, Travel and Colonial Writing in the English Renaissance, 1545–1625* (Oxford, 1998); Robert Markley, *The Far East and the English Imagination, 1600–1730* (Cambridge, 2006).

studies have seized upon the challenges posed to orthodox socio-political theory by the image of the 'masterless' man or woman.[35] Most importantly, Patricia Fumerton, in a book focused upon the diary of one man who spent much of his life at sea, has argued for forms of analysis that abandon 'traditional notions of place' in favour of engagement with the period's 'new, fluid economy'. Fumerton's conception of an 'unsettled' or 'unbound' subject, existing within an 'emergent economy characterized by mobility, diversity, alienation, freedom, and tactical craft' is particularly influential upon my discussion of common mobility in Chapter 2. Her conceptualization of her approach, as a study of the relations between subjects and spaces, resonates throughout this book.[36]

Space itself, however, remains a problematic concept, in need of theorization. The most influential recent figure in this context, Henri Lefebvre, challenged preexistent perceptions of space as a mere frame or neutral container for social relations and lived experience, focusing instead on what he called 'the production of space', a process dialectically related to changes in the social relations of production.[37] As a result of this fundamental insight, space is freshly politicized. 'Space has been molded from historical and natural elements', Lefebvre writes, 'but this has been a political process. Space is political and ideological. It is a product literally filled with ideologies.'[38] Lefebvre also charted broad historical transitions in the production of space. Absolute space, in this model, is a concept at once imagined and real, which offers a mechanism for grasping the meanings of space at a time before the great historical forces of modernization and capitalism transformed it almost beyond recognition. Absolute space, Lefebvre writes, was 'a product of the bonds of consanguinity, soil and language'.[39] Abstract space, by contrast, is 'the space of the bourgeoisie and of capitalism', and emerged most forcefully in the city-states of the European Renaissance. Abstraction commodifies space, rendering it effectively 'homogeneous' and capable of fragmentation. And abstract space is profoundly shaped by processes of mobility and exchange; it is a space, Lefebvre writes, of 'networks'.[40] The transition from absolute to abstract

---

[35] See esp. William C. Carroll, *Fat King, Lean Beggar: Representations of Poverty in the Age of Shakespeare* (Ithaca, 1996); Linda Woodbridge, *Vagrancy, Homelessness, and English Renaissance Literature* (Urbana and Chicago, 2001).

[36] *Unsettled: The Culture of Mobility and the Working Poor in Early Modern England* (Chicago and London, 2006), quotes at pp. xiv, 4–5.

[37] *The Production of Space*, trans. Donald Nicholson-Smith (Oxford, 1991), esp. pp. 34, 36–7.

[38] 'Reflections on the Politics of Space', *Antipode*, 8 (1976), 31; qtd in Edward Soja, *Postmodern Geographies: The Reassertion of Space in Critical Social Theory* (London, 1989), p. 80.

[39] *Production of Space*, p. 48; see further pp. 229–91.   [40] *Ibid.*, pp. 57, 52, 266.

space, however, cannot be seen as an easy or straightforward process; social space, in Lefebvre's perception, has a multiplicity 'reminiscent of flaky *mille-feuille* pastry', shot through with the tensions and ambivalences of historical process and ideological struggle.[41] For any study of early modern England, this point is critical.

Lefebvre was ambivalent about the impact of cultural influences, such as language and texts, on the production of space. His approach was founded within a Marxist social sciences tradition; the study of texts, he argues, can offer little more than a 'reading' of spaces, in a manner that '[evades] both history and practice'.[42] But since the publication of his book in 1974, a range of developments across the humanities and social sciences has prompted important reassessments of this position, and in the process stretched the field of enquiry, creating a context for a project such as the present one. The work of Michel Foucault has been essential in this regard, with its unrelenting attention to language and discourse. Spatial theorists working in the wake of Foucault have consequently been much more attuned to what Derek Gregory describes as 'the different ways in which the world is made present, re-presented, discursively constructed'.[43] This is fundamentally a matter of attending to representation: the very business, of course, of literary analysis. Moreover, it is notable that mobility has emerged, in a range of work from the post-Lefebvre generation, as a vital theme in the cultural analysis of space. This is impelled partly by interest in postcolonialism and globalization in modern contexts.[44] And it is driven also, in ways that can be suggestive for the analysis of the early modern period, by concerns with the social politics of space. Hence the widespread influence of Michel de Certeau's study of the 'procedures of everyday creativity' expressed in the physical actions of individuals plotting their manifold itineraries through the space of the modern city.[45] These itineraries, for Certeau, subvert orthodox discourses of place; indeed, he declares, 'To walk is to lack a place.'[46] This insight, I suggest, might equally prompt a reconsideration of the meanings of popular mobility in the early modern period.

---

[41] *Ibid.*, p. 86.
[42] *Ibid.*, p. 7. Lefebvre nonetheless admits the possibility of 'as-yet concealed relations between space and language' (p. 17).
[43] *Geographical Imaginations* (Oxford, 1994), p. 104.
[44] See, e.g., James Clifford, *Routes: Travel and Translation in the Late-Twentieth Century* (Cambridge, Mass., 1997), pp. 17–46.
[45] *The Practice of Everyday Life*, trans. Steven Rendall (Berkeley, 1984), p. xiv, and ch. 7, 'Walking in the City'.
[46] *Practice of Everyday Life*, p. 103.

My approach is framed within this broad, and rapidly expanding, theo-retical and historiographical context. I am attempting a form of cultural history: examining struggles over the meanings of space, across the early modern period, as articulated in a range of different texts. The selection of texts may seem, by some standards, somewhat eclectic. The discussion veers from pamphlet literature to poetry, from the discourse of government to that of the Renaissance stage. It also includes some texts that are visual rather than written: maps of England's rivers and roads. Yet the selection is in other respects straightforward: I have been concerned to identify any text, or body of texts, which engages in any substantial manner with issues of mobility. Moreover, the book does not attempt, in the manner of numerous new historicist studies, to draw a line between particular kinds of texts analyzed in order to establish an appreciation of a cultural context, and others reserved for privileged forms of reading within that context. It is essentially an attempt to appreciate a culture rather than a literary canon, and for its purposes a pamphlet on the extension of river transportation, for example, may well be more valuable than a discussion of rivers in a Shakespeare play. Nonetheless, it retains a sense, derived from the study of literature, that particular texts may reward sophisticated forms of analysis, articulating with notable clarity a certain appreciation of space, or drawing into relief the terms of a wider debate. That is why, for instance, Chapter 1 circles around the category of the Renaissance river poem. And that is why the most extended analysis of any text is devoted in Chapter 3 to a Ben Jonson play, *The New Inn*.

This model of analysis positions texts as active agents in the construction of meaning, and consequently within wider processes of historical change. In some cases this interpretative approach directs attention to emergent genres or kinds of texts. Pamphlets narrating peculiarly challenging jour-neys, Elizabethan rogue literature and journals recording experiences of travel are among the more obvious categories. Newsbooks and spiritual autobiographies are perhaps less obvious, though they will be equally valuable. In other cases it directs attention rather to significant develop-ments in the conceptualization of space. Hence the attention devoted, especially in Chapter 1, to circulation. There is no obvious or natural connection between the flow of water through river systems and the trans-portation of merchandise throughout the nation. The point, developed in this chapter, is that an emergent discourse sought to encode just such a link. Similarly, the effort to represent the national road system as a coherent and unified network, evident through a wealth of maps and written texts, provides a crucial model within which contemporaries could justify and naturalize the movement of individuals, commodities and information. Such developments must be appreciated as complex and fraught rather than clearly linear, yet they emerge as fundamental within any effort to appreciate the cultural history of English space.

SCOPE AND STRUCTURE

Of the terms in the book's title, hopefully my use of 'literature' has already been clarified; the others, however, might benefit from further attention. The key term, 'domestic travel', is an anachronism, since in the early modern period to 'travel' typically meant to leave the nation's shores. People did not 'travel' within England; they might 'travail', experiencing the land in various ways in the course of their daily labours, but that was a different matter. For this reason, as considered above, it is possible to say that Leland was doing something at once extraordinary and utterly mundane. In moving through his nation's space he was doing no more than countless numbers of his fellow English men and women were doing; however, in treating his journeys as acts of travel he was seeking, however ambivalently, to transform existing meanings of mobility. Working from this foundation, the book aims to explore the ways in which it became possible to speak and write about travel as something a person might do within his or her own land.

The book is concerned with any form of movement within the borders of England. While economic historians have pointed out that much of the nation's internal trade was conducted along coastal shipping routes, the imaginative significance of movement across the land can hardly be over-emphasized.[47] The early modern literature of domestic travel was thus predominantly, though not exclusively, concerned with overland journeys. The decision to concentrate on England perhaps requires more justification, particularly at a time when so much critical attention is being devoted to broader categories, such as Britain or the British 'archipelago'.[48] But the usage, I would contend, is not something imposed on my sources, but rather something derived from them. In terms of history and culture, the category of 'Britain' unquestionably impressed itself upon early modern minds; however, in terms of space and place, it becomes apparent that people commonly imagined a more constricted nation. For the average

---

[47] See esp. T. S. Willan, *River Navigation in England 1600–1750*, 2nd edn (London, 1964), p. 5.
[48] See esp. John Kerrigan, *Archipelagic English: Literature, History, and Politics 1603–1707* (Oxford, 2008).

English man or woman, therefore, a journey to Scotland was a voyage into a foreign land. Even Defoe, two decades after the Union Act of 1707, could not help but approach Scotland as culturally and economically different.[49] Wales was a significantly different case, since it was politically incorporated into England throughout the period, though distinct in so many ways.[50] Here, I will again endeavour to follow the sources, considering descriptions of journeys in Wales when they are less concerned by those points of distinction, and more concerned to appreciate this most uncertain of British nations as essentially domestic.

The definition of 'early modern' is notoriously hazy: comfortably malleable, in fact, to the shape of any particular line of enquiry. My interest in the early modern period, as suggested above, is centred on processes of upheaval and transition. Lefebvre's categories of absolute and abstract space provide a useful conceptual framework, to which I will refer on occasion; however, they are best approached as pure and extreme models, which break down as soon as one engages with the complexity of texts and discourses. Given these concerns, the period from around the middle of the sixteenth century until the turn of the eighteenth century has a certain coherence. This was a period of unprecedented social, economic, political and ideological change. It was also a period in which people were experiencing domestic travel in identifiably new ways. I stop just short of Defoe – considering him in the context of an epilogue – because I believe that his *Tour* signals a significant shift in its representation of a nation founded upon mobility. It is a product of a decidedly different culture than that of Leland. Much more important, throughout the book, are various lesser-known figures who grappled with the tensions and contradictions of their age. One such person, whose work is considered to some extent in almost every chapter of the book, was John Taylor: a Thames waterman, prolific pamphleteer, outspoken advocate of the improvement of river transportation, and pioneer of domestic travel writing. The achievement of such writers was to give mobility new meanings, within the context of a culture fundamentally anxious about the phenomenon.

This is a book that could have been organized in any number of ways. I have, however, broken it into two parts, concerned firstly with the natural and artificial structures that made domestic travel possible, and secondly

---

[49] *A Tour Thro' the Whole Island of Great Britain*, ed. G. D. H. Cole, 2 vols. (London, 1927), esp. II.689–91.
[50] On the relation between Wales and England in the construction of British identities, see esp. Philip Schwyzer, *Literature, Nationalism, and Memory in Early Modern England and Wales* (Cambridge, 2004).

with certain important models of travel. Part I, 'Routes', contains chapters on rivers, roads, and inns and alehouses. Discourse on rivers, I argue in Chapter 1, brings into relief conflicting perceptions of the land as property on the one hand, and the nation as potentially knitted together by vital lines of connection on the other hand. Arguments in favour of the improvement of rivers for purposes of transportation were not universally accepted; however, they increasingly introduced new perceptions of human and mercantile mobility, centred on the figure of circulation. Roads, by comparison, are pathways of movement wrought upon the landscape by human use and labour. They prompt reflections, across the period, on the organization of space into networks: from the shadowy presence of the Roman roads, to the national systems rendered cartographically in the Restoration. Given the range of people using them, they also raise the question of the politics of spatial knowledge. How might we understand the relation between a map of a national network and the more immediate experience of commoners using the roads? Chapter 3 considers the nation's sites of commercial accommodation, and argues that these prompted some of the period's most sophisticated representations of changing patterns of travel. The three chapters in this section also centre attention, in turn, on different genres. A desire to contextualize the tired category of the Renaissance river poem underlies Chapter 1; attention to drama, which seizes on inns and alehouses as spaces of encounter, gives shape to Chapter 3; while Chapter 2 is more generally drawn to forms of prose.

Part II, 'Travel and travellers', identifies three particularly significant cultural models of travel. The first, examined in Chapter 4, is the progress. This is not a chapter about Elizabethan royal progresses, but rather an exploration of the ways in which the form of the progress was established under Elizabeth, then variously challenged and appropriated over the following decades. As a result, it is a chapter centred on the politics of space, tracing the ways in which the absolutist principles underpinning Elizabeth's journeys gave way in the fraught conditions of the mid-seventeenth century – especially at moments when Charles I became a fugitive within his own land – to more radical claims. The second, considered in Chapter 5, is the tour. Travelling one's own land for pleasure, or in the interests of acquiring knowledge, was one of the most peculiar things that a man or woman could do in the sixteenth and seventeenth centuries. Those who did so were thus forced to justify their actions, fashioning in the process various rationales for domestic tourism. Some works associated with this loose movement, such as seventeenth-century journey poems, betray an underlying anxiety through the use of clubby erudition and the social violence of burlesque; others, such as the remarkable journals of Celia Fiennes, seek more forthrightly to establish an agenda for the domestic tourist. The third, discussed in Chapter 6, is traffic. Whereas 'trade' was generally understood in terms of exchanges conducted across national borders, 'traffic' was the more common term for internal trade. This was the most vital force impelling acts of travel throughout the period, and is discussed to some extent in virtually all of the chapters. At the end of the book, however, it is worth dwelling upon debates over traffic at greater length, and to focus attention on the extraordinary travel pamphlets of Taylor, who did more than anyone else to theorize and legitimize commercial mobility.

PART I

Routes

CHAPTER I

Rivers

In 1665, Sir Edward Turner, Speaker of the House of Commons, addressing the King and a joint-sitting of the houses of parliament, reflected on the function of rivers within the nation:

Cosmographers do agree that this Island is incomparably furnished with pleasant Rivers, like Veins in the Natural Body, which conveys the Blood into all the Parts, whereby the whole is nourished, and made useful.[1]

The analogy seems natural enough, suggested by the respective technologies of cartography and anatomy which had flourished in preceding decades. The associated perception of national space, however, is at once innovative and politically radical. Rivers drain water within localized environments; for the Speaker, however, the comparison with the circulation of blood suggests a model of spatial cohesion founded on mobility. Crucially, the 'blood' being conveyed through the veins (upstream, the statement suggests) is more than water; it is human traffic and merchandise. The logic is clarified as Turner continues: 'Therefore we have prepared some Bills for making small Rivers navigable; a Thing that in other Countries hath been more experienced, and hath been found very advantageous.' His model of nature thereby underpins a programme of political intervention, to promote the navigation of inland waterways and the circulation of goods and people.

The uneasy transition in Turner's speech from a vision of the nation as a corporate whole to a more pragmatic concern with specific 'small Rivers' marks the ambiguous status of rivers as routes of human movement. Whereas roads, by definition, carry human traffic, rivers will only do so if the geographical, economic and legal conditions are suitable. As an option for passengers, river travel was uncommon throughout the early modern period.[2] The real advantage of river transportation was for the carriage of goods, since water transport could be ten times cheaper than transport on

---

[1] *Journal of the House of Lords*, 33 vols. (London, 1767–73), XI.675; quoted in T. S. Willan, *River Navigation in England 1600–1750*, 2nd edn (London, 1964), p. 29.
[2] Willan, *River Navigation in England*, pp. 122–3.

land.[3] After a late-medieval decline in the use of rivers for such purposes, interest in the expansion of river traffic gathered pace throughout the Tudor and Stuart periods.[4] Indeed the rhetoric, if not the practical achievements, reached a peak in the years 1662 to 1665, when parliament passed a number of bills authorizing improvement schemes.[5] Yet the very nature of rivers heightened their status in early modern discourse on travel and mobility. Rivers are figures of mobility mapped onto the landscape, at once evocative of place yet curiously placeless. For John Donne, reflecting on transience in *The Anniversaries*, they undermine assumptions of continuity: 'Nor are, (although the river keep the name) / Yesterday's waters, and today's the same'.[6] They imply directions and connections; as Paul Carter argues, they are 'the kind of object that made travelling as a historical activity possible'.[7] But while Carter, in his seminal study of spatial history, writes about the efforts of European settlers to produce space in a colonial context – bringing Australia into the English language and therefore into Western narratives of history – a study of early modern English space is of necessity a study of overdetermination and contestation. And that contestation, in the present context, focuses insistently on the fundamental idea, identified so lucidly in the Parliament of 1665, of circulation.

In this chapter I want to trace the idea of circulation, in discourse on rivers throughout the period covered in the book as a whole. Rarely is this vision stated as clearly and glowingly as in Turner's speech, because rarely are speakers and authors so forthrightly positive about the phenomena of human and mercantile mobility. Indeed, in accord with my central argument in the book, domestic travel presents critical challenges to orthodox models of social, economic and political order, and consequently discourse on rivers is more commonly uncertain and fraught. Rivers, that is, consistently prompt reflections on mobility, as various writers think their way towards positions on the functions and values of domestic travel. Although I am concerned here with a range of textual types and genres, from political and legal discourse to more traditionally literary works, the chapter coheres around different approaches, across the early modern period, to river poetry. Rivers were acceptably poetic, from the time of John Leland in the mid-sixteenth century to that of Sir John Denham in the mid-seventeenth century. The

---

[3] Evan T. Jones, 'River Navigation in Medieval England', *Journal of Historical Geography*, 26 (2000), 61.
[4] On the decline, see *ibid.*, 60–82.
[5] Willan, *River Navigation in England*, p. 28; H. J. Dyos and D. H. Aldcroft, *British Transport: An Economic Survey from the Seventeenth Century to the Twentieth* (Leicester, 1971), pp. 36–9.
[6] 'Second Anniversary', ll. 395–6; *The Complete English Poems*, ed. A. J. Smith (London, 1986), p. 298.
[7] *The Road to Botany Bay: An Essay in Spatial History* (London and Boston, 1987), pp. 48–9.

ways in which they assumed significance, however, and prompted reflection upon wider spatial structures and practices, could differ widely from one poem, or poetic tradition, to another. Given that most river travel was mercantile, the chapter becomes concerned more with the movement of goods than people, drawn into alignment as a result with studies that have outlined an emergent regime of exchange and liquidity in early modern England.[8] But it is concerned above all with the principle of connectedness. What links, say, Bristol and Leeds? Such questions have obvious practical implications, but also profound cultural dimensions, and reflection upon them will lead to fresh perceptions of both individual and national identities in the period. Discourse on rivers, I want to suggest, provided a critical context in which contemporaries could reimagine relations between the nation's subjects and spaces.

The chapter's sections centre attention on four, albeit loose and over-lapping, bodies of texts, charting a rough chronological narrative through the period. The first section considers the politics of rivers, setting carto-graphic and chorographic texts of the Elizabethan and Jacobean eras, which set out to describe the nation's waterways, in the context of contemporary river practices and laws. The evident tensions here, between the ease of connection suggested by an emergent map consciousness on the one hand, and a powerful cultural and legal commitment to property and placement on the other hand, marks a tension that shapes discourse on rivers through-out the early modern period. The second section examines the minor genre of Tudor and early Stuart river poetry, considering the ways in which rivers were incorporated into myths of nationhood. The third section gravitates back towards the parliamentary vision of circulation, considering gathering arguments in favour of river improvement as a context for reading an alternative tradition of river poetry, produced by men actually working on the rivers. And the final section analyzes images of rivers in country-house and prospect poems of the seventeenth century, that helped to construct culturally resonant perceptions of the national landscape. For all its funda-mental conservatism, and its efforts as a result to contain the possible implications of a regime of circulation, the mid-seventeenth-century river poem is nonetheless a very different thing to the Tudor river poem, just

---

[8] See esp. Jean-Christophe Agnew, *Worlds Apart: The Market and the Theater in Anglo-American Thought, 1550–1750* (Cambridge,1986), pp. 17–56; Craig Muldrew, *The Economy of Obligation: The Culture of Credit and Social Relations in Early Modern England* (Basingstoke, 1998); Mary Poovey, *A History of the Modern Fact: Problems of Knowledge in the Sciences of Wealth and Society* (Chicago and London, 1998), pp. 66–91; Jonathan Gil Harris, *Sick Economies: Drama, Mercantilism, and Disease in Shakespeare's England* (Philadelphia, 2004).

as the meanings of rivers in the 1650s are radically different from those of the 1550s. It must acknowledge, even as it typically works to contain, imperatives of improvement and circulation.

THE POLITICS OF RIVERS: REAL AND IMAGINARY JOURNEYS

Before the nation's rivers could be imagined as a coherent network, they first had to be traced and documented, recorded in the pages of Elizabethan and Jacobean books devoted to the description of the land. William Harrison is best known today for his 'Description of England', published as a preface to Raphael Holinshed's *Chronicles* (1577 and 1586). Its value as a source for social and economic history is largely attributable to its preference for analysis over mere description. Harrison, who admits at the outset that he has rarely 'travelled 40. miles foorthright at one journey in all my life', divides the 'Description of England' thematically, and assesses his evidence critically.[9] Yet this text was preceded by a companion-piece (not available in a full modern edition), the 'Description of Britain', which functions in a very different manner. The 'Description of Britain' devotes sixty-eight folio pages (which amounts to over twenty-five per cent of Harrison's total contribution to the Holinshed volumes), to a survey of the island's river systems. By contrast to the magisterial assessments familiar to readers of the 'Description of England', this is throughout less assured, and at times almost apologetic. Harrison openly rues the inadequacy of his sources, presenting not so much a 'full discourse' as 'a mangled rehearsall of the residue set downe and left in memorie' (I.45). Nonetheless, his project, with its underlying goal of comprehensive spatial description, structured around the tracing of river networks, marks a pivotal moment in understandings of the nation's waterways.

Harrison was ruefully aware that he was working just a year or two ahead of the cartographer Christopher Saxton, some of whose maps he evidently viewed before their publication in 1580. Aided by Saxton's work in his description of the Darwent in Kent, Harrison pauses to lament: 'Would to God his plats were finished for the rest!' (I.51).[10] While I return to Saxton below, an initial comparison of his and Harrison's respective projects is instructive in the present context. Both suggest a certain cohesion intrinsic

---

[9] The quote is from Harrison's dedication to Sir William Brooke, which precedes all of his contributions to Holinshed's volumes (*Chronicles*, 3 vols. (London, 1587), vol. I sig. A2v). Unless otherwise stated, all references are to this edition.

[10] By the time of Holinshed's second edition, Saxton's *Atlas* had been published; however, Harrison's text was not amended.

to the land: a cohesion that, for Harrison, encompasses Wales and Scotland, takes little account of county borders, and virtually no account at all of landowners. Nationhood is here coterminous with a demonstrable and internally coherent geographical unit: a notion that would be useful, though never conclusively so, for the Stuart monarchs. Yet Harrison's text, in contrast to Saxton's, favours the descriptive form of an itinerary, and this at once reinforces and extends the map's assumptions of spatial connectedness and accessibility.[11] As he works his way around the coast, exploring river systems from their mouths to their sources, he adopts the conceit of his text as 'the report of an imagined course taken' along all the waterways (I.45). Accordingly, the text is punctuated with personal pronouns and active verbs: 'we rowed', 'we come unto', 'we sailed on', and so forth (I.54, I.51, I.76).[12]

Harrison is not ignorant of the manifold difficulties facing any actual traveller on the rivers; indeed he begins his description by regretting that he has been unable to record such fluvial qualities as 'length, bredth, depth of chanell (for burden) ebs, flowings, and falles', while an early passage worries over incompatible interests on the Medway (I.45, I.46). Yet such pragmatic concerns increasingly give way to the imperatives of what Harrison calls 'our poeticall voiage', in the course of which he 'imagin[es] a journeie ... whither as yet it hath not beene my hap to travell' (I.65, I.81). Underpinning this imagined journey is an assumption of uncontested movement, textually enabled by association with the element of water. In this initial section of the chapter, in order to establish a framework for the debates to be traced throughout, I want to explore the politics of this assumption, setting the interrelated projects of chorography and cartography in relation to the laws and customs of river usage. Without question, the relation between the circulation of water and the movement of people was more fraught than Harrison's conceit allows.

Harrison's approach is tellingly selective. He was doubtless familiar with contemporary theories of the natural circulation of water: that it was drawn from the sea through underground channels, issuing as springs which initiated the flow of rivers.[13] Presumably he was also aware of theories which held that all rivers of the earth were 'tributaries and branches of a

---

[11] Cf. Bernhard Klein, *Maps and the Writing of Space in Early Modern England and Ireland* (Basingstoke, 2001), p. 142.
[12] Some of these phrases are probably attributable to Harrison's verbatim, yet unattributed, use of notes from sources.
[13] For a detailed discussion of extant theories, see Nathanael Carpenter, *Geography Delineated Forth in Two Bookes* (Oxford, 1625), Book 2, pp. 139–59.

great circular system', versions ultimately of the Jordan.[14] Such beliefs lent credence to his imaginary journey, underwriting its assumptions of accessibility and connectedness. Yet he must also have had at least a rudimentary grasp of the barriers that restricted travel on the rivers he traced. The decline in the extent of river transportation during the late Middle Ages was due partly to a decrease in population, but partly also to an increase in obstructions, such as locks and weirs.[15] These served local interests – weirs, for instance, regulated the flow of water to serve mills, and preserved fish-stocks for neighbouring properties – but created inevitable problems for those operating boats. Weirs could be difficult for boats to cross, while the single-gate 'flash-locks' (the predecessors of modern, double-gated 'pound-locks') were typically operated by landowners who might not wish to open the gates and consequently alter the level of water on one side or the other.[16] The perception of such obstacles as unjust restrictions on the rights of the commons was encoded in British law by the Magna Carta, and was regularly invoked in legislation and popular discourse.[17] Harrison himself refers to an 'act of parlament', by the authority of which 'the water-courses ... were surveied and reformed throughout England' (I.106). But the principle of circulation was nonetheless constrained in practice, across the country.

One major reason for this gulf between legal principle and quotidian reality lay in the laws of property. While the imaginary nature of Harrison's 'poeticall voiage' allows him to avoid the question of property rights over rivers, this matter unquestionably exercised the minds of landowners, travellers and lawyers. Who owned rivers? The law recognized three constituent parts of a river – the bed, banks and water – and acknowledged property rights in the bed and banks, and usage rights in water. A crucial distinction, however, was drawn between 'navigable' and 'non-navigable' rivers. Navigable rivers were recognized as public highways, open to transportation in the same way as the open roads. Their beds were owned by the Crown, and while their banks were often acknowledged to lie in private hands, boatmen were nonetheless ceded rights to stop and to unload goods.[18] Non-navigable rivers, by comparison, were recognized as private property, giving the owner of one or both banks control over the bed, banks

[14] David Quint, *Origin and Originality in Renaissance Literature: Versions of the Source* (New Haven and London, 1983), p. 134.

[15] Jones, 'River Navigation in Medieval England', 60–82.

[16] Dyos and Aldcroft, *British Transport*, p. 37.

[17] A. S. Wisdom, *The Law of Rivers and Watercourses*, 4th edn (London, 1979), pp. 70–1; Willan, *River Navigation in England*, pp. 21–2; Jones, 'River Navigation', 70.

[18] H. J. W. Coulson, *The Law Relating to Waters, Sea, Tidal, and Inland*, 4th edn (London, 1924), p. 77.

and rights of access. The owner of such a river could therefore erect weirs or locks, and prevent boats from mooring on his or her land. The crucial distinction between navigable and non-navigable was, *prima facie*, determined by the extent of tidal flow upstream. In the eyes of the law, a tidal river was assumed to be navigable, while a non-tidal river was assumed to be non-navigable.[19] Inevitably, problems arose in the definitional grey areas, such as stretches of tidal rivers which were unsatisfactory for traffic and had been treated as private by the adjacent landowners, or stretches of non-tidal rivers which had nevertheless been used for transport over a period of time or were eminently suitable for such use. Such contested zones brought popular perceptions of circulation into collision with a property-owner's assumptions of rights of containment and exclusion.

The status of running water was more stable legally, though equally vexed in practice. The seventeenth-century jurist Robert Callis compared running water to the sea and the air, and argued:

it should be strange that the Law of property should be fixed upon such uncertainties, as to be altered into *Meam, Team, Suam*, before these words can be spoken, and to be changed in every twinckling of an eye, and to be more uncertain in the proprietor, then a Camelion of his Colours.

But his conclusion is more subtle, as he states that 'there can be no property therein, but as the same is incident to the soil, taking them two for one, it is drawn with the property thereof'.[20] The qualifications in this statement acknowledge, in line with the established legal position, that those holding property rights over banks and beds might temporarily restrict or redirect the flow of a river. This was precisely the problem with weirs and locks. To a boatman forced to wait at a lock, sometimes for days, until the owner was prepared to bend to the interests of traffic over those of locality, the lawyer's comparison between running water and the air might have seemed somewhat strained.[21] Similarly, to one struggling to keep a boat afloat on stretches of river rendered artificially shallow by the actions of landowners, or forced even (in the terms of the period) 'to buy Streams or Flashes of Water of the Millers', the prevailing legal beliefs might have seemed thoroughly provocative.[22]

Early efforts by the state to improve navigation were often successful only in clarifying the lines of dispute. For much of the early modern period the

---

[19] *Ibid.*, p. 79; Wisdom, *Law of Rivers and Watercourses*, p. 59.
[20] *The Reading of That Famous and Learned Gentleman, Robert Callis* (1647), p. 56. Cf. Wisdom, *Law of Rivers and Watercourses*, p. 11.
[21] Charles Hadfield, *British Canals: An Illustrated History* (London, 1950), pp. 16–17.
[22] *Reasons Against Making the River Derwent, in the County of Derby, Navigable* (1695), p. 1.

main instruments of reform were Commissions of Sewers, royal commissions consisting basically of chief local landowners, which had the power to compel clearance projects but no authority to redefine the status of a non-navigable river.[23] For the extension of river navigation, therefore, these were effectively useless. Indeed extant records of enquiries initiated by such Commissions provide ample evidence of the prevailing interests of property and locality. One respondent to an investigation into navigation on the Medway in the early seventeenth century, for instance, argued that weirs were useful 'Fences betwixt Neighbour and Neighboure'; another commented, of the Wye, that fords could serve as important 'waies of husbandry' within a region.[24] More profoundly, some people unquestionably feared on the one hand 'the exportacion of the native and necessary comodities of [their] country', and on the other hand the 'ymportacion of things unnecessary as wynes, frutes spices &c'.[25] While it might seem easy enough to dismiss such voices on the grounds of self-interest, they articulate with some clarity a culturally authoritative perception of the relation between the individual and space, fundamentally rooted in locality. They invoke a discourse of place and custom, which privileges personal relationships between neighbours, valorizes methods of husbandry that are perceived as traditional, and resists the expansion of trade beyond known local borders. Simply put, in the terms of this discourse it is more important to be able to cross a river in order to get to a local marketplace, than to send produce down the river in order to participate in a national or international market.

Within this discursive context, those people who were actively involved in river traffic were translated into objects of fear. In London, the Watermen's Company was the only trade company formed by act of parliament in order to control its members' behaviour.[26] The act of 1555, establishing the company, described existing watermen as 'ignorant, and unskilful', and for the most part 'masterless men, and single men'. Their essential placelessness was perceived, further, to frustrate efforts to press them into service in the navy during times of war; 'for that they have no known place of abiding', the act claims, they 'do, for the most part, absent and convey themselves into the country, and other secret places'.[27] In the course of the early modern period these terms of denigration echoed

[23] Willan, *River Navigation in England*, p. 16; Coulson, *Law Relating to Waters*, p. 491.
[24] BL Add. MS 34218, fol. 37r; BL Add. MS 11052, fol. 101r.   [25] BL Add. MS 11052, 101v, 116v.
[26] Laurie Ellinghausen, 'The Individualist Project of John Taylor "The Water Poet"', *Ben Jonson Journal*, 9 (2002), 149.
[27] Quoted in Henry Humpherus, *History of the Origin and Progress of the Company of Watermen and Lightermen of the River Thames*, 3 vols. (1874–86), I.101.

across the country. Despite the efforts of the Tudor governors, watermen remained, in the popular imagination, radically unplaced, occupying that which is not property, and making their homes on the flowing streams of the nation's rivers. Defined by mobility, their very existence threatened assumptions of placement and local identity. Time and again in contemporary polemic they are dismissed as drunkards and thieves: 'the worst and meanest sort of people', according to one representative statement.[28] Another early seventeenth-century petition complains that, through their use of tow-paths,

They have been the occasion of much strife betwixt neighbour and neighboure, in that they have (with their rowinge alonge the Ryver) troden downe the Fences betwixt them, and have letten in the Cattell of one man, into an other mans meadowe, and sometyme into the Corne.

Moreover, they have bought oxen to pull barges, which would otherwise have been used to plough fields. 'They are', as a result, 'the decay of husbandry'.[29] Within the terms of the period's orthodox models of social hierarchy and community, watermen – like other men and women involved in the transportation of goods, such as pedlars or sailors – personified the potent challenges of spatial transience and independent labour.[30]

To return, in this light, to the project of describing the nation's waterways, there is an instructive contradiction between the 'poeticall voiage' that Harrison shared with his readers and the prevailing loathing directed against those involved in actual river voyages. While Harrison's 'Description' 'gestures at the multiplicity of possible journeys across the map of the nation', the pleasures of spatial knowledge are predicated, for author and reader alike, on a commitment to placement.[31] Indeed the specifically textual experience of space is proffered as a preferable alternative to travel itself. This contradiction, I would suggest, is inherent in Harrison's text, and in turn underpins the two related modes of spatial representation born, effectively, at the same moment as Harrison's 'Description', cartography and chorography. As others have recognized, the wave of cartographic and chorographic works published in the reigns of Elizabeth and James marks a watershed in the spatial history of the nation. A. L. Rowse wrote of 'the

---

[28] *Commons Debates 1621*, ed. Wallace Notestein, *et al.* (7 vols., New Haven, 1935), VII.45.
[29] BL Add. MS 34218, fol. 37r–v.
[30] On sailors, see Patricia Fumerton, *Unsettled: The Culture of Mobility and the Working Poor in Early Modern England* (Chicago and London, 2006), esp. pp. 84–107; on pedlars, see below, pp. 101–11.
[31] Klein, *Maps and the Writing of Space*, p. 142.

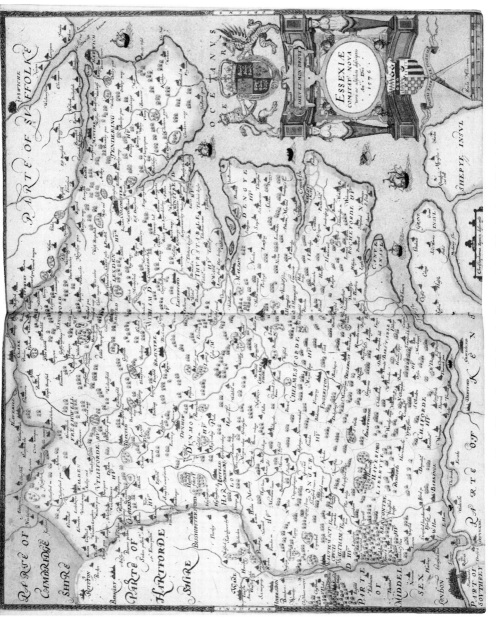

Fig. 1.1 Map of Essex, from Christopher Saxton, *Atlas of England and Wales* (1580).

Elizabethan discovery of England', while Richard Helgerson recognized that 'The function of such books is precisely to make the land visible', in a way that it had not been before.[32] But while they made subsequent perceptions of circulation possible, their own social and spatial politics were invariably more conservative.

As discussed above, Harrison's project proceeded in parallel with that of Saxton, whose *Atlas* initiated modern English cartography. Unlike Harrison's 'Description', Saxton's maps were unquestionably the product of travel; their author, in fact, must stand as one of the most widely travelled Englishmen of the sixteenth century. He was, Bernhard Klein comments, 'the only person in sixteenth-century Britain whose real-life visual experience approximated the comprehensive utopian view of the atlas'.[33] Yet this authorship, as understood in modern terms, is relentlessly effaced from the volume. Instead, as Helgerson has demonstrated, the *Atlas* is presented as a manifestation of a patronage system controlled by Queen Elizabeth, and the land itself is figured largely as a product of royal power.[34] The point is made in the frontispiece, with its portrait of Elizabeth flanked by figures of cosmography and geography, and reiterated by the use of royal insignia on the individual county maps.[35] More importantly, in the present context, the routes of travel which made this monumental work of mapping possible are equally effaced. These maps, establishing a model that would last for 100 years, do not mark roads (Fig. 1.1). The folio volume is intended for display rather than for any practical use; it prioritizes, above all, 'emblems of a settled landscape, ruled through the institutions Saxton used to represent the settlements: churches, cathedrals, gentry estates and nobles' castles, and private parks'.[36]

While rivers are the most prominent natural features on Saxton's maps, as on those of his early Stuart successors, it is possible to exaggerate their apparent promise of connection. These disproportionately engorged lines, snaking their way across the face of the county-maps, appear to invite imaginary, if not real, journeys. For Klein, Saxton's rivers are 'the pulsating "veins" of the country', which lend it 'the fluency and progress it otherwise lacks'.[37] Yet, at a time when the vast majority of the nation's waterways were

---

[32] *The England of Elizabeth* (London, 1950), pp. 31–65; *Forms of Nationhood: The Elizabethan Writing of England* (Chicago and London, 1992), p. 145.

[33] *Maps and the Writing of Space*, p. 99. [34] *Forms of Nationhood*, pp. 107–12.

[35] As Helgerson demonstrates, however, the royal arms competed for precedence with the arms of Saxton's patron, Thomas Seckford (*Forms of Nationhood*, pp. 110–11).

[36] David Rollison, 'Exploding England: The Dialectics of Mobility and Settlement in Early Modern England', *Social History*, 24 (1999), 4.

[37] *Maps and the Writing of Space*, p. 102.

legally non-navigable, perceptions of 'progress' were always somewhat ambiguous. Indeed I would argue that one undeniable quality of Saxton's maps is that they register the spatially discrete relations between the nation's myriad places. For all the maps' apparent promise of potential connections, places are represented in varying states of isolation, surrounded by emptiness. The inert space between places – space, that is, that sets places apart and as a result makes them distinct – is thus just as important as the possible routes that might be imagined to connect these places. In Henri Lefebvre's terms, maps come increasingly throughout the early modern and modern eras to serve the interests of 'abstract space': 'the space of the bourgeoisie and capitalism'. Abstract space, he argues, dissolves local identities; it tends towards homogeneity, and is characterized by 'exchange and communications', and therefore by 'networks'.[38] But spatial history, as Lefebvre himself stresses, is a history of multiplicity and struggle. Saxton's *Atlas*, like Harrison's 'Description', bears the signs of this struggle.

Chorography proved still more resistant to the imperatives of abstraction. Heavily endebted to the twinned publications of Harrison's 'Description' and Holinshed's *Chronicles*, chorography sought to understand the nation and its constituent counties by fusing spatial and historical modes of description. For the first generation of chorographers, for whom the six successive editions of Camden's *Britannia* marked at once a model and an epitomizing achievement, the form of historical enquiry was predominantly antiquarian.[39] Above all, Britain was understood as a product of its Roman past, the marks of which might be traced upon the early modern landscape. As such, it was perceived as a relatively coherent whole: a nation. Yet the trajectory of the short-lived chorographical tradition asserted a rival form of historical knowledge, genealogy, which defined the land rather by tracing the family lines of its current owners. This shift is already evident in the *Britannia* itself – as Camden increasingly packed his text with genealogical information as it expanded from edition to edition – and is compounded in volumes such as William Burton's *Description of Leicester Shire*, Sampson Erdeswicke's *Survey of Staffordshire* and John Coker's *Survey of Dorsetshire*. Many of these authors also lacked Camden's interest in national publication, and circulated their works instead in manuscript among coteries of local county gentry.[40]

---

[38] *The Production of Space*, trans. Donald Nicholson-Smith (Oxford, 1991), pp. 57, 266.
[39] *Britannia* was published in six Latin editions between 1586 and 1607, and translated into English by Abraham Holland in 1610.
[40] Burton, *Description of Leicester Shire* (1622); Erdeswicke, *Survey of Staffordshire* (1723); Coker, *Survey of Dorsetshire* (1732).

Therefore, while Camden, Burton, Erdeswicke, Coker and others adopt from Harrison the use of rivers as structural devices, their works remain committed more to acts of distinction than a logic of abstraction. As Coker notes, when explaining 'The Method Observed in this Survey of Dorset', rivers are useful since they offer a means of virtual navigation between significant sites: 'for on these Rivers and their Branches are generallie seated those Places of note, which I shall have occasion to mention'.[41] In the hands of a more eloquent writer, such as Thomas Westcote, author of *A View of Devonshire in 1630*, this model allows scope for imaginative engagements with the landscape.[42] Westcote's 'travelling discourse' embraces notes of both pastoral and georgic, commenting of the Exe, for instance, that it 'presently gives the spring's livery, and clothes our meadows and pastures with a smiling verdure', then of the Creedy that 'he ... never proves ungrateful to the labourer for his pains, nor deceiveth the husbandman's hope of expected or wished encrease' (pp. 134, 95, 131). On occasion, he illustrates his description with extracts of poetry, by authors including William Browne. Yet ultimately his is a book, in accordance with its genre, for the landowners; gentlemen on their estates, Westcote writes, 'are the liver-veins of the common wealth, yielding both good juice and nourishment to all parts thereof' (p. 50).

Whatever their manifold differences, therefore, such exercises in description translate Harrison's 'poeticall voiage' into a discourse of property and exclusion. They fashion images of a nation and its constituent counties founded on social stability and genealogical continuity. Rivers, for such writers, are not veins for the circulation of goods and people, but merely lines on a map inviting the virtual navigation of a landscape parcelled into units of property. Not surprisingly, these carefully qualified images of connectedness accord at once with the predominant attitudes of the landed and the prevailing law of rivers. As demonstrated above, in the Elizabethan era the law turned rivers into property, and frustrated efforts to increase navigation. New ways of thinking, and writing, would be required to challenge these spatial preconceptions.

THE RIVER POEM: CONNECTION, POWER AND NATIONHOOD

In a remarkable passage of William Vallans's Tudor river poem, *A Tale of Two Swannes*, which follows the progress of a regal pair of swans along the course of the River Lea, they pause at Waltham Lock:

[41] *Survey of Dorsetshire*, p. 8.   [42] (Exeter, 1845).

> Among them all a rare devise they see,
> But newly made, a waterworke: the locke
> Through which the boates of *Ware* doe passe with malt,
> This locke containes two double doores of wood,
> Within the same a Cesterne all of Plancke,
> Which onely fils when boates come there to passe
> By opening anie of these mightie dores with sleight,
> And strange devise, but now decayed sore.[43]

As well as being probably the first poetic celebration of an English pound-lock, this is a unique moment in the brief history of the English Renaissance river poem, attending as it does in such detail to the technology that enables river travel. Controversial improvements on the Lea in the mid-Elizabethan period had transformed the London malt trade to a river-based system, moving its centre from Enfield to Vallans's hometown of Ware.[44] These lines epitomize Vallans's interest in the relation between the river and transportation, sitting comfortably alongside not only an earlier glimpse of 'barges lading malt apace' at the docks in Ware, but also an appended letter in which the author argues that in the time of King Alfred the Lea carried 'big and mighty ships' (sigs. B1r, C2r).[45] The preface also admits an autobiographical subtext, since Vallans claims to be 'fully resolved to leave my country (i.e. county, or home)'. The poem thus becomes, among other things, a means of understanding the relation between Ware and the wider region, including the economic connections that bind it so closely to the capital.

These personal and topical comments aside, *A Tale of Two Swannes* is also acutely aware of its place in a minor poetic tradition, which produced a handful of English and neo-Latin poems, and also informed larger works.[46] Indeed it does more than any other text to define that tradition: its narrative structure invoking as a model John Leland's *Cygnea Cantio*, and its preface announcing a desire to 'encourage those worthy Poets, who have written *Epithalamion Thamesis*, to publish the same' (sig. A2r). Whether Vallans had in mind William Camden or Edmund Spenser, or indeed both, is less significant than his sense of writing a particular kind of poetry. (Spenser, in

---

[43] *A Tale of Two Swannes* (London, 1590), sig. B2r.
[44] Dyos and Aldcroft, *British Transport*, pp. 24, 38. On the controversy, which led to a riot and the burning of the lock in 1581 (to which Vallans possibly alludes in the final line of this extract), see Martin Elsky, 'Microhistory and Cultural Geography: Ben Jonson's "To Sir Robert Wroth" and the Absorption of Local Community in the Commonwealth', *Renaissance Quarterly*, 53 (2000), 500–28.
[45] Cf. John Norden, *Speculum Britaniae Pars: The Discription of Hartfordshire* (1598), p. 6.
[46] See esp. Jack B. Oruch, 'Spenser, Camden, and the Poetic Marriages of Rivers', *Studies in Philology*, 64 (1967), 606–24; and Wyman H. Herendeen, *From Landscape to Literature: The River and the Myth of Geography* (Pittsburgh, 1986), pp. 181–339.

turn, nodded back towards Vallans when depicting swans on the Lea in his
'Prothalamion'.)[47] It is a tradition that was not without classical precedent,
but was introduced to English literature only in the sixteenth century.[48]
It reaches back to Leland, gains momentum from the publication of
Harrison's 'Description of Britain', and stretches forward to Michael
Drayton's chorographical epic, *Poly-Olbion*. It might, however, be defined
less by any actual text than by a textual mirage: Spenser's 1580 plan to
produce a 'Booke' titled *Epithalamion Thamesis*, which would 'shewe his
first beginning, and offspring, and all the Countrey, that he passeth thorough, and also describe all the Rivers throughout Englande, whyche came
to this Wedding, and their righte names, and right passage, &c'.[49] Although
Spenser eventually translated this vision into more modest form in his
image of the marriage of Thames and Medway in *The Faerie Queene* IV.xi,
future poets were influenced by both the original goal and the ultimate
achievement. Taken as a whole, this is decidedly not a poetry of locks and
watermen. Nonetheless, individual poems lend subtlety and substance, in
various ways, to the imaginary journeys of chorographers. Crucially, I want
to suggest that attention to the essential dynamism of rivers, however
constrained, brings static and essentialized myths of nationhood into collision with divergent ways of appreciating space. These tensions can be traced
through some of the most influential poems in this tradition, but become
most marked, and also most creative, in the epics of Spenser and Drayton.

Pre-Spenserian river poems – works by Leland, Vallans and Camden –
narrate passages along particular stretches of river, reflecting in the process
upon national structures and values. Leland's *Cygnea Cantio*, a 700-line Latin
poem (accompanied by fifty-eight quarto pages of commentary), traces the
journey of a swan down the Thames, from Abingdon to Greenwich.
Camden's 'De Connubio Tamae et Isis', published in fragments throughout
his *Britannia*, follows the Thames from the source of the Isis, to its birth out
of the confluence of the Isis and Tame, and subsequently downstream to
London.[50] In these poems, geography is subservient to history. Hence, in
Cygnea Cantio, as the swan progresses along the river, the poem lurches
backwards and forwards through sedimentary layers of human history.

---

[47] *Poetical Works*, ed. J. C. Smith and E. de Selincourt (Oxford, 1912), p. 601 (ll. 37–8).
[48] On the influence of classical river poetry, see Jean R. Brink, *Michael Drayton Revisited* (Boston, 1990),
p. 84.
[49] *Poetical Works*, p. 612.
[50] The arrangement of the poem is tabulated in Oruch, 'Spenser, Camden, and the Poetic Marriages of
Rivers', 608.

Within a handful of lines, for instance, we move from the Saxon heritage of Abingdon, to the Danish attacks on Cholsey, to the more prosaic presence of Henley: 'forum popello / Vicino bene cognitum' ('an ancient market-town well known to folk of the region').[51] All the poems, moreover, identify history with monarchy, attending at length to key royal sites, such as Windsor, Richmond and Hampton Court. The principal value of the Thames, in particular, is that it links such sites, providing a narrative structure for discourses of national identity. Leland, and Vallans after him, underscores the point by identifying the journeying swans as monarchical figures. The swan that serves as traveller and narrator in *Cygnea Cantio* is accordingly decked with a 'coronam / Baccatam nitidis' ('garland studded here and there with gleaming gems'), and accompanied in its progress by a dozen attendants (sig. B2r).

These poems, informed as they are by a consistent political conservatism, generally work hard to constrain suggestions of human mobility. A swan is a different kind of narrator than a waterman, even when it encounters Waltham Lock, and their journeys in the works of both Leland and Vallans assume the form of royal progresses. Moreover, these poems consistently arrest the river's natural momentum by centring attention less on the act of movement than on particular sites. Significantly, Leland's poem finds closure at Greenwich, collapsing into a passage of royal panegyric which is presented as a dying, fulfilled swan-song. This manoeuvre halts the poem's momentum, transferring attention from the river, which to this point had served as metonym for England, to the physical presence of the monarch, whose body and realm are so mystically intertwined ('Henrici patriæ patris Britanniæ') (sig. C4v). Camden, working against the centrifugal pull of chorography, focuses on two fluvial sites: the source of the Isis, and its confluence with the Tame. In contemporary theory, the source was the geographical point at which a single underground spring, linked itself to a global system of circulation, emanated from the ground to initiate a river's flow. An obsession with sources became characteristic of early modern literature on rivers, consistently associated, as in the *Britannia*, 'with inquiry into national origins'.[52] In 'De Connubio Tamae et Isis', the source of the Isis is a cave in the Cotswolds, decorated with gems and images of the great rivers of the world:

> sed et his intermicat auro
> Vellere Phrixaeo dives, redimitasque spicis

[51] *Cygnea Cantio* (1545), sig. B2v. Translations are from Dana F. Sutton's hypertext edition www.philological.bham.ac.uk/swansong/
[52] Herendeen, *From Landscape to Literature*, p. 123; see also Simon Schama, *Landscape and Memory* (London, 1995), p. 267.

Clara triumphantis erecta Britannia Gallis, etc. …[53]
Undoso hic solio resident regnator aquarum
Isis, fluminea hic majestate verendus
Caeruleo gremio resupinat prodigus urnam.

(And here bedight in gold,
Among them glitt'reth Britannie with riches manifold
Of goulden fleece; a Coronet of wheat-ears shee doth weare,
And for her triumph over France, her head aloft doth reare, etc. …
In waving Throne here sits the king of waters all and some,
Isis, who in that Majestie which rivers doth become,
All rev'rend, from his watchet lap pour's forth his streame amaine.)[54]

While Leland's poem finds rest at the end of the journey, Camden's finds it here at the beginning, where the regal Isis sits enthroned beneath an image of Britannia herself. Significantly, the land itself – as opposed to the monarch in Leland – assumes precedence, clad in those classically resonant symbols of self-sufficiency and prosperity, 'goulden fleece [and] Coronet of wheat-ears'.[55] The pattern is repeated at the moment of confluence, when the rivers 'tandem descenditur una / In thalamum' ('To nuptiall chamber thus they both / Joinctly descend at last'), and the figure of Britona sings of the foundation of the nation (pp. 92, 95). Like the passage on the source, this again arrests the progress of the river, constructing the story of nationhood on the conceit of confluence. The joining of the rivers serves as an image of union, fertility and regeneration, which is at once ephemeral and everlasting, like the nature of rivers themselves. At the end of the extract, the momentum of a river's flow draws the Thames forward: 'Oceanumque patrem quaerens jactantior undas / Promovet' ('Advanceth forth his streame, and seeks / The Ocean main his sire') (pp. 94, 95). Whereas that momentum suggests a dissipation, or ultimate loss of identity, as the Thames will be absorbed into the undifferentiating mass of the ocean, the poem's key sites have asserted an appropriate counterweight, offering to locate and define key principles of national identity.

Spenser's representation of the marriage of Thames and Medway in *The Faerie Queene* is more ambitious in its speculation on the relation between

---

[53] The ellipses in the text are Camden's, in accord with his claims that the poem (which he never acknowledged as his own work) survived only in fragments.

[54] The Latin text is that of the 1607 *Britannia*; the English is Holland's 1610 translation. For parallel texts, see 'Poems by William Camden, With Notes and Translations from the Latin', ed. George Burke Johnston, *Studies in Philology*, 72 (1975). Quotes are from this source (here, from pp. 88–9).

[55] Cf. the description of Merlin's cave in Edward Wilkinson's quirky effort to anglicize the Ovidian narrative (*His Thameseidos* (1600), sigs. D1r–D2r). Here, the cave is decorated with 'pictures of the best, / And noblest wights that should in *Brittaine* be', from ancient British times up to Elizabeth herself.

one site and the nation.[56] Admittedly, the canto has been read often enough as a closed and satisfying 'fantasy of power', celebrating a 'visionary England ... united in friendly alliance'.[57] More specifically, David Quint argues that Spenser's representation of the Thames estuary imagines it as a point of 'common origin', 'the source and destination of [all] the rivers of the earth'.[58] This reading makes topographical sense out of the central conceit: the meeting of various famous rivers of the old and new worlds, 'Which doe the earth enrich and beautifie', brought together to celebrate the marriage (IV.xi.20). But much as the canto may gesture towards union on such a scale, it notably lacks a moment of joyous consummation, and struggles throughout to contain a contrary momentum towards dissipation, or undifferentiated multiplicity. The choice of the Thames and Medway is significant in this regard. Theirs is not a typical confluence, since the Medway meets the Thames estuary at a point when the river is giving way to the North Sea. (In the words of Izaak Walton in the following century, the Thames 'weddeth himself to the ... *Medway* in the very jaws of the Ocean'.)[59] Alastair Fowler argues that this was nonetheless an appropriate location for a celebration of national strength since the lower reaches of the Medway represented England's 'principal centre of naval ... operations'.[60] Yet it is also a troublingly open and ambiguous space, in which rivers defined as national territory give way to the fluid and contestable arena of the ocean.[61] For a poet overtly committed to celebrating the English nation and its monarch, the choice of site is laden with risk.

Demands of local specificity equally threaten to undermine the overt narrative of union and universality. The canto is framed by notes of anxiety about how Spenser might 'tell the names of all those floods', numbering 'besides three thousand more' than those he manages to list (IV.xi.10, 52). When he comes to the business of naming, the catalogue of 'famous rivers' of the world collapses after a mere two stanzas (just eighteen rivers), to make

[56] *The Faerie Queene*, ed. A. C. Hamilton (London, 1977).
[57] Jonathan Goldberg, *Endlesse Worke: Spenser and the Structures of Discourse* (Baltimore and London, 1981), p. 135; Alastair Fowler, *Spenser and the Numbers of Time* (London, 1964), p. 175. For a review of critical responses to the canto, see Bart Van Es, '"The Streame and Currant of Time": Land, Myth, and History in the Works of Spenser', *Spenser Studies*, 18 (2003), 212.
[58] *Origin and Originality in Renaissance Literature*, pp. 156–7.
[59] Izaak Walton and Charles Cotton, *The Compleat Angler*, ed. John Buxton (Oxford, 1982), p. 208.
[60] *Spenser and the Numbers of Time*, p. 174.
[61] Cf. Bradin Cormack's discussion of early Jacobean debates about the extent of a nation's jurisdiction over the seas (*A Power to do Justice: Jurisdiction, English Literature, and the Rise of Common Law, 1509–1625* (Chicago and London, 2008), pp. 256–75). In relation to The Faerie Queene, cf. Thomas P. Roche's analysis of an act that is at once one of 'union and dissolution' (*The Kindly Flame: A Study of the Third and Fourth Books of Spenser's 'Faerie Queene'* (Princeton, 1964), p. 184).

way for the insistent throng of native streams. Hence the 'fertile Nile' and 'Rich Oranochy' are joined, for example, by the 'chaulky Kenet', 'Thetis gray' and 'morish Cole', the epithets becoming in the process more geographically specific (IV.xi.20, 21, 29). Subsequently, the English rivers assume agency, dividing and connecting:

> There was the speedy Tamar, which devides
>   The Cornish and the Devonish confines;
>   Through both whose borders swiftly downe it glides,
>   And meeting Plim, to Plimmouth thence declines:
>   And Dart, nigh chockt with sands of tinny mines.
>   But Avon marched in more stately path,
>   Proud of his Adamants, with which he shines
>   And glisters wide, as als' of wondrous Bath,
> And Bristow faire, which on his waves he builded hath.   (IV.xi.31)

Camden's *Britannia* probably suggested to Spenser the lines about diamonds ('Adamants') in the Avon, which is in keeping with the celebratory impetus of the verse.[62] The line about the Dart, more likely derived from Harrison, is more surprising, focusing attention on a river struggling to behave as a river, on account of human intervention in the landscape.[63] One curious detail of geography thereby brings national myth into juxtaposition with contemporary human realities of industry and locality. In the process, the poem dilates, extending its vision from one mystified site of nationhood, to more complicated and dynamic models of identity.

The attention to Irish rivers extends the poem's interrogation of the uncertain contours of Elizabethan nationhood. Other readers have examined the pointed allusion to recent conflict contained in the attendance at the wedding of 'balefull Oure, late staind with English blood' (IV.xi.44). Here, as Bart Van Es argues, the poem 'punningly wrenches the reader away from the mythological past to face the harsh reality of our present "hour"'.[64] To the extent that the attendance of the Irish rivers at the marriage, and hence their representation over five stanzas, is founded on the supposed fact

[62] *The Works of Edmund Spenser: A Variorum Edition*, ed. Edwin Greenlaw, *et al.*, 10 vols. (Baltimore, 1932–49), IV.255.

[63] Harrison states that 'thorough occasion of tin-woorkes whereby it passeth', the Dart 'carrieth much sand to Totnesse bridge, and so choketh the depth of the river downeward, that the haven it selfe is almost spoiled by the same' ('Description of Britaine', I.60).

[64] '"The Streame and Currant of Time"', 214. Cf. Andrew Hadfield, 'Spenser, Drayton, and the Question of Britain', *Review of English Studies*, n.s. 51 (2000), 588; and Joan Fitzpatrick, 'Marrying Waterways: Politicizing and Gendering the Landscape in Spenser's *Faerie Queene* River-Marriage Canto', in *Archipelagic Identities: Literature and Identity in the Atlantic Archipelago, 1550–1800*, ed. Philip Schwyzer and Simon Mealor (Aldershot, 2004), pp. 81–91.

that they 'ioyne in neighbourhood of kingdome deare' (IV.xi.40), this pointed allusion to recent conflict demands to be read as another fissure in the very body of the nation. Rivers are 'chockt' in Devon and 'staind' in Ireland. Moreover, the Irish excursion reiterates an understated yet insistent self-referential strain in this canto, bearing reminders of the puzzling trajectories of human mobility. We first glimpse Spenser when he surveys 'the plenteous Ouse' and pauses to hail

> My mother Cambridge, whom as with a Crowne
> He doth adorne, and is adorn'd of it
> With many a gentle Muse, and many a learned Wit.   (IV.xi.34)

He next draws attention to himself when in Ireland he notes '*Mulla* mine, whose wave I whilom taught to weep' (IV.xi.41). Though generally interpreted as an allusion to his other poetic work on Ireland, particularly *Colin Clouts Come Home Againe*, the possessive ('mine') also functions literally, since the Mulla flowed through Spenser's estate, which he had owned since its confiscation from the native Irish after the rising to which he almost certainly refers in his glance at the blood-stained Oure. The effect is unsettling; the realm is marked, the poem concedes, not simply by reliable flows of water, but equally by the unpredictable and uncanny facts of human agency and mobility. The point is underscored in the Mutability Cantos, at the poem's close, when the incessant movement of water is invoked in support of an argument about the predominance in human life of change and uncertainty. Moving directly from a reflection on the inconstant flow of water, Dame Mutabilitie proclaims:

> So likewise are all watry liuing wights
> Still tost, and turned, with continuall change,
> Never abyding in their stedfast plights.   (VII.vii.21)

Despite Nature's more measured conclusion – that 'all things ... are not changed from their first estate / But by their change their being doe dilate' (VII.vii.58) – the challenge of Mutabilitie is critical. The poem concedes at the end, as it had done more subtly throughout, the significance of contestation and change, and invokes water in the process. In this context, the Thames estuary, point of entrance to a nation ruled by an ageing virgin queen, in which the Thames and Medway are subsumed by the North Sea at their point of confluence, becomes an apt figure of nationhood.[65] Unlike

---

[65] For a reading that considers the analogy between the Queen's sexuality and the contested entrance to the Thames, see Rhonda Lemke Sanford, *Maps and Memory in Early Modern England: A Sense of Place* (New York and Basingstoke, 2002), pp. 27–52.

Leland's commitment to the monarch, or Camden's mythologization of sites of origin and confluence, Spenser's poem acknowledges the dynamism, and myriad disruptions, of human engagement with the land. Nationhood becomes, as a result, a matter of constant negotiation and struggle.

Drayton, who saw himself in many respects as Spenser's poetic heir, betrays the multiple influences on his *Poly-Olbion* when he rehearses the marriages of both Tame and Isis, and Thames and Medway. His Spenserian poem is also a chorography, indebted most of all to Camden's *Britannia*. As Helgerson has argued, this conjunction of influences, or 'representational modes', produces, above all, multiplicity.[66] Rivers marry, in accord with the conventions of the Tudor river poem, but they also speak, driving forward many of the poem's jostling narratives. While I have argued that this quality of multiplicity is also characteristic of Spenser's representation of rivers in *The Faerie Queene*, Drayton allows it to subsume and control his poem to an entirely new degree. *Poly-Olbion* represents 'a complete act of faith in the topographical map', bound throughout to the facts of geography.[67] As critics routinely note, this devotion to natural features of the land is bound together with the text's general suppression of contemporary human claims upon it, from those of property owners to those of the King himself. While for prose chorographers rivers often presented useful vehicles for structuring surveys of properties and settlements, in *Poly-Olbion* the priorities are effectively reversed, with towns mentioned rather 'as features of the rivers on which they stand' and interests of property barely acknowledged at all.[68] Rivers, for Drayton, are categorically not owned; rather, they assert their own characters, their own directions, and their own myths.

The representation of rivers in *Poly-Olbion*, coupled with their numerous interjections into the poem, thereby typifies Drayton's equivocal attitude to the activities of humanity within the landscape. Most commonly, rivers underscore the poem's elegiac mood, joining the poem's chorus of criticism about changes to the landscape, especially the depletion of forests due to the 'base Averice' of 'mans devouring hand' (23.19; 2.64). For a forest to lose its integrity, even to be reduced by deforestation to a pastoral 'Neatheards life', is a matter of regret (12.529). Yet the poem's sheer excess of voices problematizes any critical effort to define a consistent vision. The decay of a forest is the expansion of a plain; and Salisbury Plain, for one, bears no sentimentality about the loss of 'barb'rous woods' (3.111). Further, when one

---

[66] *Forms of Nationhood*, p. 143.   [67] Klein, *Maps and the Writing of Space*, p. 162.
[68] Bernard H. Newdigate, *Michael Drayton and his Circle* (Oxford, 1941), p. 166.

Lancashire river challenges another as an 'alien', the latter responds that her birth in Yorkshire in fact 'adds to my renowne' (27.35, 98). This argument, that something is gained by momentum, is expanded in the Trent's claim for 'greatnesse', founded on a name which is supposedly derived from the fact that she is constituted by thirty tributaries (26.187–92). Inevitably, statements such as these invite judgement according to a river's uses. Thus the Wytham claims to be a perfect model of a river:

> No Land-floods can mee force to over-proud a height;
> Nor am I in my Course, too crooked, or too streight:
> My depths fall by descents, too long, nor yet too broad,
> My Foards with Pebbles, cleare as Orient Pearles, are strowd.
>
> (25.267–70)

The aestheticized ideal is founded upon an ease of use, both for movement along and passage across. More pointedly, the poem elsewhere celebrates the value of a harbour fed by 'some goodly Flood … / By whose rank swelling Streame, the far-fetcht forraine fraught, / May up to In-land Townes conveniently be brought' (15.242–4). Specific instances of such 'goodly' rivers in use are afforded by glimpses of 'mighty ships' on the Tyne, 'Fraught with my country Coale', and 'great-burthen'd Ships' passing through the 'valleyes' of the Thames (29.122–3; 16.47).

The constrained dynamism of these occasional references to inland traffic is amplified by the incessant and unrestricted movement of the author's Muse. As the poem works its way across the country, the Muse directs the movement and endows natural features of the land with the power of speech. While those features – and even the greatest rivers – are constrained by location, the Muse herself asserts a continual and unfolding narrative principle underlying the poem. Admittedly, her travelling hardly mirrors the difficult paths taken along rivers and roads by individual travellers; indeed Klein insists on her status as 'a cartographic fiction', her movement translated into 'an effect of the map, not of any direct spatial experience'.[69] Yet it is nonetheless striking that the poem's vocabulary of mobility consistently translates this action into human terms. Hence the Muse 'wanders' across the face of the land (e.g. 26.37). She is 'laborious' and, repeatedly, 'industrious' (e.g. 1.132, 27.1; e.g. 1.65, 6.342, 12.601); she 'flies', but also treads 'with a steady foot', and 'holds' a 'course' (27.'Argument' 3; 25.12; 26.'Argument' 5).[70] Through the figure of the Muse, the poem becomes an understated narrative of travel. As a result, the nation takes shape as a space

---

[69] *Maps and the Writing of Space*, p. 155.   [70] Cf. Helgerson, *Forms of Nationhood*, p. 144.

of potential connections, criss-crossed at once by mundane and more fanciful itineraries.

To argue that the Muse's movement, and the consequent energy and variety of the poem, help to define *Poly-Olbion* as 'a massive georgic poem' risks overstatement.[71] Georgic, the literary mode devoted to the representation and celebration of labour, and by extension to the human uses and transformations of nature, rather presses its way into Drayton's work. In other hands, it could have been a georgic poem; as it stands, it is a poem in which certain aspects of the project, such as the commitment to detail and progression, inject an intriguing counterstrain to the more determinedly reflective and elegiac construction of nationhood. For instance, a survey of the different 'surface(s)' of England repeatedly assesses regions according to their agricultural uses, from the 'batning Mores' of Somerset, through the 'rich soyle' of Warwickshire, to the 'wondrous fruitfull fields' of Yorkshire (23.57, 88, 93, 201). Similarly, a catalogue of fruit produced in Kent assumes a georgic quality by virtue at once of its agricultural detail and its acknowledgement of 'carefull Frut'rers' and 'the Gardiner' who devotes 'his life' to the 'deare increase' of the fruit-tree (18.657–97, 676, 687).[72] More importantly, in such catalogues of local produce, Renaissance values of *copia* converge with the discourse of a national marketplace, which draws together specialized regional commodities. The Colne River boasts that the 'fat soyle' of Essex sends its cheese 'to every quarter' of the country; Pery-Vale claims that her 'goodly graine' is in such demand that 'chap-men' attend her 'How ere I set my price' (19.129; 16.228, 242). While productivity is encoded as a natural function of the land, Drayton admits mercantile claims over rural produce, the emergent paths of traffic suggesting human dynamics of mobility which shadow the unearthly progress of the Muse.

There are no locks in *Poly-Olbion*. In accord with the weight of the tradition of river poetry, this work is not overtly concerned with the business of traffic on the roads and waterways. Nonetheless, as I have argued about this tradition more generally, the very purpose of *Poly-Olbion* makes it complicit in the imagining of routes and connections. Like Spenser's passing acknowledgement of human industry and mapping of his own trajectory onto the landscape, and like the inevitable onward thrust of Camden's Thames after

---

[71] Alastair Fowler, 'The Beginnings of English Georgic', in *Renaissance Genres*, ed. Barbara K. Lewalski (Cambridge, Mass., 1986), p. 118.

[72] Joan Grundy identifies this passage as the poem's '*Georgics*' (*The Spenserian Poets* (London, 1969), p. 140).

the set-pieces at the source of the Isis and confluence of the Isis and Tame, *Poly-Olbion* demonstrates the virtual impossibility, within this tradition, of locating national meaning in fixed and changeless sites. The land, and its rivers more than any other features, draw the poem onward, into narrative and also into the business of contemporary life. In this respect the very nature of river poetry diverges, however slightly, from the more assuredly settled discourse of chorography. Criticizing blockages and imagining extended practices of circulation, however, would be the matter for a distinctly different kind of river poetry, produced by different kinds of poets.

RIVER IMPROVEMENT AND THE POETRY
OF THE WATERMAN

Those travelling the English waterways left few records. Their ventures could not be rendered heroic or exotic, like those of international travellers; domestic travel, as argued throughout this book, registers only rarely in contemporary texts. Yet it is possible to trace, in the face of these cultural constraints, nascent efforts to refashion the prevailing negative images of mobile commoners. Here, I want particularly to situate the poetry of two watermen, whose respective labours on the nation's rivers span a period from the 1580s to the 1650s, in the context of wider debates about the improvement of navigation. These debates reached a peak in the second half of the seventeenth century, and as a result the discussion here will gradually be drawn towards that era of reform. But I am concerned less with historical eventualities than with processes of contestation and change across the period. By attending to the traces left by those actively involved in river travel, however fragmentary or partial these may be, we might more fully appreciate wider cultural struggles in England, as various commentators sought to realize a vision of a nation defined by processes of circulation.

In 1585, John Byshop, a Thames waterman, was troubled by unlawfully erected locks and weirs that were, he claimed, causing deaths on the river:

> I have complayned to many men
> But there is no remedie founde
> ffor clearing of that worthy streame
> but still poore men I see be drowned

His response was to write a 172-line poem, in four-line stanzas of iambic tetrameter verse, with a distinctly patchy rhyme-scheme, presented on a single manuscript sheet as a petition to Queen Elizabeth. (Its survival in the Lansdowne Manuscripts of the British Library suggests that it may at least have got close to its intended recipient.)[73] It is an ingenuous piece of writing, produced by a man quite possibly unaware of elite poetry on rivers, but very much aware of the practical conditions experienced by Thames watermen. Crucially, he focuses on the functional politics of the river:

> Alas for woe yt should be soe
> in sufferinge of such evill thinges
> good lawes be made them to invade
> by manie great and worthy kinges
>
> Mylles weares and lockes men do them call
> that doe annoy that worthy streame
> Againste the lawe they doe stande all
> but still the drownde those symple men.

Though he aligns himself with the 'symple', Byshop is not an ignorant man; indeed he is well aware of the 'good lawes', produced by 'Eleaven kings', designed to prevent the weirs which made life so difficult for watermen. He deploys this knowledge to challenge easy assumptions of connection and mobility. The Thames, far from being a symbol of national greatness, is translated into an index of the tendency for powerful private interests to ignore, and even to endanger, the 'symple men' and the tasks they fulfil.

Byshop's petition-poem represents a concerted effort to situate those men within the nation. It concludes with a list of twenty colleagues who he claims have been 'drowned and slaine on lockes and weares theis Seaven yeres last past … betwene Maydenhead and Oxford'. This very act of memorialization in an address to the Queen endorses the men's value to the commonwealth, while their positioning as victims works further to invert the period's predominantly negative images of watermen:

> One ffarmer hath a lock in store
> That hath made many a child to weepe
> Their mothers begg from dore to dore
> their ffathers drowned in the deepe.

---

[73] BL MS Lansdowne 44/39. Another document, also preserved in the Lansdowne Manuscripts, indicates that Byshop stimulated a degree of debate. The unnamed author of this document does not dispute the deaths, but shifts the blame to the 'manyfest negligence' and 'evill demeanor' of the watermen, dismissing Byshop's allegations as 'outragious' (BL MS Lansdowne 44/40).

The itinerancy of the begging mother here provides an ironic echo of the purposeful travels of the watermen, driven as they are, Byshop suggests, by a fundamentally domestic desire to provide for a family. Their deaths, not their preceding lives, are the cause of displacement. The poem's subsequent image of burial extends the point:

> Then beinge drowned they bury them there
> where dogges and swyne then doe them finde
> their fleshe they eat and all to teare
> which is contrarie to mankinde.

The sins of the propertied are thereby aligned with a dehumanizing realization of eternal placelessness, which is disturbing in spite of its rhetorical excess. Self-interested manipulation of the river is the true crime, Byshop suggests, not the honest labours of the watermen.

Byshop's naive yet incisive voice prefigures developments in the following century, when established lines of complaint about weirs were increasingly translated into arguments for the extension of navigation. Technically, if the improvement of a non-tidal river required the removal of weirs or other hazards, an act of parliament was necessary to initiate the work. As a result, lobbying assumed a national character, and schemes were not only debated in parliament but also amplified in a range of printed tracts. The unfettered flow of water, in even the most minor tributaries of navigable rivers, is commonly figured in such texts as a national imperative. According to Francis Mathew's 1655 pamphlet, *Of the Opening of Rivers for Navigation*:

all such Streams, great or small, which would willingly fall into our said Rivers designed for Navigation, ought to be free, and not to be bound up with Wears, Sluces, Pens for Mills, and the like *imprestures*, which keep up, stop, and divert the Waters from their natural Course. (pp. 5–6)

The key term here, 'free', breaks down discourses of localized identities. The flow of water through the land thus becomes a metonym for the movement of goods and people, across a national space defined by mobility. As another commentator asserted, this was precisely as 'Nature has afforded it'.[74]

Once nature itself was understood as a force of dynamism, proponents of river improvement could also begin to represent human mobility as orderly and purposeful. Conservative discourse on vagrants (which I discuss further in Chapter 2) typically posits the travel of commoners as random and profoundly unsettling. In the face of such anxieties, the image of the natural flow of water in established watercourses – fed by the sea, through

---

[74] R. S., *Avona*, p. 19.

underground channels, and running back to the sea in a constant cycle – provided a keystone to radically new endorsements of circulation. Simon Schama has demonstrated the Platonic origins of fluvial myths of circulation:

> In the *Timaeus* Plato had decreed the circle to be the necessarily perfect shape for creation as it alone formed a line of complete containment. The principle held good for the circulation of blood about the human body and for waters about the earth. So the rhythms of fluvial death and rebirth, the transmutability of water, blood, and wine, described a cycle that, provided the proper remembrances were observed, would be self-regulating.[75]

In England, the orthodox view, presented in Callis's legal tract, was that only navigable rivers may properly be compared to 'the veins of a mans body'.[76] But numerous commentators in the middle decades of the seventeenth century were less discriminating; in their view, the act of '*making small Rivers navigable*' was a means of realizing a natural order inscribed upon the face of the landscape.[77] This effort to apply a Platonic principle to a social and economic context was reinforced by discourse drawn from a continental context. Giovanni Botero's *Cause of the Greatness of Cities*, for instance, argued that 'God created Water, not onely as an element necessarie for Natures perfection; but also as an apt and opportune meanes, for transportation of Commodities from one Countrey to another.'[78] The English travel-writer James Howell, meanwhile, focused attention on the human uses of rivers in the Netherlands, claiming that '*Nature* in the frame of humane bodies, did not discover more *Art*, in distributing the veines and arteries … as she hath shewed here in dispersing those waters so orderly for traffique'.[79]

Moreover, within this context the strict Platonic conception of the circulation of a finite quantity of matter within a closed system was significantly revised, to accommodate more expansive economic theories. By contrast to those who feared the transportation of local produce out of the local marketplace, the more radical proponents of river improvement celebrated a potential multiplication of goods and wealth within an expanded, and distinctly placeless, market. In James Hely's tract on the improvement of the Avon between Salisbury and the south coast, the

---

[75] *Landscape and Memory*, p. 258.
[76] Callis, *The Reading of That Famous and Learned Gentleman*, p. 56.
[77] Cf. R. S. (title-page), 'making Rivers Of this Kingdom Navigable'; my italics.
[78] *The Cause of the True Greatenesse of Cities*, trans. T[homas] H[awkins] (1635), p. 32; cf. Herendeen, *From Landscape to Literature*, p. 149.
[79] *Instructions and Directions for Forren Travell* (1650), p. 91.

enumeration of commodities becomes virtually an end in itself. The easy transportation of metals, for instance, prompts a fevered rehearsal of the uses of

vast stores of Iron of all sorts, not only that which is wrought by Smiths, Cutlers, Gunsmiths, Armourers, and others; but all sorts of cast Iron, as Stoves for drying of Mault; and all sorts of Pots, Weights, Balconies, Anvils, Vises, and divers Engines, and many other things too large to particularize.[80]

Another commentator, R. S., theorized on the interrelated growth of employment and wealth:

Which mutually advancing each other, the employment first begetting wealth, and then that wealth a greater employment, shall establish … a constant motion, excited by it self, and by it self continued and advanc'd.[81]

Each of these statements articulates a surprisingly precise vision of the economic functions of circulation. For Hely, iron, so difficult to transport by land, provides the raw material for a revival of industry, which carries the potential to resituate Salisbury and its locality within a wider economy. He subsequently catalogues consumer items, such as 'all sorts of Grocery' and 'all sorts of Fish'; however, his attention is seized more compellingly by industry and trade, which can 'raise' men 'to greater Estates' (pp. 8–9). For R. S., more explicitly still, the circulation of goods facilitated by improved transport networks underpins a startlingly abstract perception of mercantile exchange. He seizes upon the capacity of circulation not merely to move goods and money from one site to another but to 'beget' wealth through the mystified 'constant motion' of economic exchange. In Michel Foucault's analysis of economic discourse in this period, the relation between money and wealth, traditionally held to be dependent upon the preciousness of the metal or the seal of the monarch, was gradually reassessed, by merchants who appreciated the material production of surplus value through exchange. 'When goods can circulate (and this thanks to money)', Foucault writes, 'they multiply, and wealth increases; when coinage becomes more plentiful, as a result of a good circulation and a favourable balance, one can attract fresh merchandise and increase both agriculture and manufacturing.'[82] Commentators on rivers lent this theory a spatial form, in the process translating the analogy of rivers and veins into a freshly dynamic model

---

[80] Hely, *Representation of the Benefits and Advantages of Making the River Avon Navigable* (1672), p. 8.
[81] *Avona*, pp. 20–1.
[82] *The Order of Things: An Archaeology of the Human Sciences* (London and New York, 1970), pp. 178–9. See also Poovey, *A History of the Modern Fact*, pp. 66–91.

of nationhood. Fluvial networks become valued less for their orderly distribution of natural resources than for their capacity to facilitate economic growth, while space itself becomes valued less for its capacity to be transformed into property than as an arena for circulation. To borrow a term from modern economic theory, the nation's space is valued for its liquidity.

Marrying the abstract vision with practical reality, however, was another matter. In this respect a key figure was John Taylor. I will consider Taylor at greater length in Chapter 6, which situates his domestic travel pamphlets in the context of debates about internal trade. In the present context, however, Taylor demands attention for slightly different, albeit related, reasons. Taylor was a Thames waterman, an occasional employee of state-sponsored river surveys, a proponent of the improvement of rivers, and a prolific poet. One poem, 'in praise of the Element of all Waters', theorizes the 'perpetuall motion' of water, exploring its importance in all areas of human life. Rivers, he comments here, 'make Dame *Tellus* wombe to fructifie, / As blood in veines of men doe life supply'.[83] His most sustained excursion on the theme of river transportation, meanwhile, is contained in *Taylor on Tame-Isis*, a pamphlet he published in 1632 after his involvement in a project to improve navigation on the Thames.[84] The title evokes the sixteenth-century tradition of poems devoted to the Thames; however, in a prefatory poem addressed 'To any Body', Taylor seems uncharacteristically hesitant about his own position:

> Though (for the most part) in the tracts I tread,
> Of learned *Camden*, *Speed*, and *Hollinshead*,
> And *Draytons* painfull *Polyolbyon*,
> Whose fame shall live, despight oblivion,
> These are the guides I follow, with pretence
> T'abbreviate and extract their Quint-essence.   (sig. A5r)

The progenitors are comprehensive in their surveys of the country: from Raphael Holinshed (presumably a reference to Harrison's 'Description of Britain', published with Holinshed's *Chronicles*), through John Speed's Jacobean atlas of Britain, to the prose and poetic exercises in chorography by Camden and Drayton.[85] Taylor's authorial act of 'follow[ing]', by contrast, is immediately more personalized, based on his own experience

---

[83] *Drinke and Welcome* (1637), sig. C4r.
[84] On the context of this pamphlet, see Bernard Capp, *The World of John Taylor the Water Poet, 1578–1653* (Oxford, 1994), pp. 30–1.
[85] Speed's *Theatre of the Empire of Great Britaine* was published in 1611.

of the river. And this approach, with its unashamed emphasis on labour, prompts a reassessment of the river's textual function. Notably, while chorographers tend to glide along the nation's rivers, with all the ease of a finger moving across the face of a map, Taylor privileges the practical and piecemeal spatial knowledge of the traveller. Hence his gaze rests firmly on the troublesome river itself. Again conflating his respective labours with oar and pen, he promises: 'I (from *Oxford*) downe to *Stanes* will slide, / And tell the rivers wrongs which I espide' (sig. B2r).

This vision underpins a reconfiguration of the anthropomorphism employed by earlier river poets. At one point, nearing the confluence of Tame and Isis, Taylor describes a distinctly troubled river:

> Poore *Tame* all heavie and disconsolate,
> Unnavigable, scorn'd, despis'd, disgrac'd
> Having in vaine so many paces pac'd;
> Despairing and quite desperate with these harmes,
> He hurles himselfe unwares in *Isis* armes.   (sig. A7r-v)

The river is 'desperate' because of 'harmes' inflicted upon it, which prevent it from fulfilling its function within an economy of circulation. As so often in Taylor's work, his attention is drawn to blockages. He asks:

> Shall *Thames* be barr'd its course with stops and locks,
> With Mils, and hils, with gravell beds, and rocks:
> With weares, and weeds, and forced Ilands made,
> To spoile a publike for a private Trade?   (sig. B6v)

In almost every instance, he suggests, a blockage may be attributed to human failings, ranging from mere laziness to the sin of covetousness. Taylor impugns 'private persons' who 'for their gainfull use, / Ingrosse the water and the land abuse' (sig. B1v). By contrast, his ideal is of a river maintained 'For use and profit in community', not spoiled by private interests but rather 'cleane and free' (sigs. B1v, B6v). Moreover, in another departure from the work of Elizabethan poets, Taylor defines freedom by reference specifically to the movement of people and goods. For rivers, in Taylor's view, are more than lines of connection on maps. Indeed, however easy its flow and however seductive a path it may appear to trace, within this perspective a river is of no consequence until it becomes a channel of human traffic.

In other works, Taylor applies this vision more broadly across the nation. Taylor's signature-text, to which I return in Chapter 6, was the travel pamphlet, narrating challenging or simply idiosyncratic inland journeys. Yet when describing his travels on rivers, personalized itinerary repeatedly gives way to reformist polemic. He travelled, for instance, to Salisbury, and wrote in an effort to urge the city governors to clear blockages on the Avon. His voyage thus assumed the form of a 'simple Survey', exposing the apparent 'hinderances unto so good and beneficiall a worke'.[86] And, in a remarkable journey late in his life, he travelled up the Thames and Isis as far as Cirencester, then carried his boat on a wagon to Stroud, at the outer reaches of the Severn river system. The journey thus rehearsed the path of an imagined cutting – in modern terms, a canal – by means of which the Thames and Severn (and ultimately also the Wye and other more westerly river systems) could be joined. The potential connections, from the English capital into south Wales, suggest dizzying images of circulation; 'goods', he writes, might in future 'be conveyed by water too & from *London*, in Rivers at cheape rates without danger, almost to half the countyes in *England and Wales*'.[87] For the slightest moment, in fact, Taylor neglects the cumbersome reality of a boat strapped to a wagon, and scans his eye over the surface of the land, like a chorographer tracing river systems across a map. It is a fantasy of human industry bending intransigent natural waterways into a more compliant shape, and thereby realizing in practice water's principle of circulation.

Canals were not unknown in early modern England. Mill-leets and irrigation channels were common enough, while the sixteenth-century Exeter Ship Canal (one of the earliest of its kind) employed a similar model on a greater scale, enabling river traffic to bypass a troublesome stretch of the River Exe. But these were relatively minor achievements, all geared towards the improvement of existing rivers for particular purposes rather than the creation of entirely new routes. The fantasy of connection, by comparison, was compelling. As Taylor's image suggests, the canal offered a technique for seizing on the principle of fluvial circulation and improving it through human ingenuity. Later in the seventeenth century, Francis Mathew extended the vision, proposing not only a link between Bristol and London, but also a connection between the western and eastern extremities of England.[88] Indeed reformers might now imagine the opening of almost limitless lines of connection across the land. As Henry Robinson mused in 1652:

where there are no Rivers neer unto the Towns already built, nor possibility of cutting Navigable Ditches; it will be necessary to see where such Navigable Rivers

[86] *A New Discovery by Sea, with a Wherry from London to Salisbury* (1623), sig. A2v.
[87] *John Taylors Last Voyage* (1641), sig. A7r.
[88] *A Mediterranean Passage by Water, from London to Bristol* (1670), pp. 7–9. Mathew elaborates on the Bristol to London scheme in *Of the Opening of Rivers for Navigation* (1655).

or Ditches may be made, and accordingly have them cut with all convenient expedition.[89]

Water, according to this spatial logic, was not merely circulating according to natural laws, but might be manipulated to serve the requirements of civilization.

In political terms, the act of imagining spatial connections, particularly in the middle decades of the seventeenth century, inevitably prompted reflection on the foundations of economic and political power in the nation. If in Holland the canal signified civic industry, in France it was posited as 'the perfect expression of absolutist control over the waters'.[90] In England, therefore, the stakes were high. Shakespeare famously mocks absolutist fantasies in *1 Henry IV*, when the rebel leaders pore over a map and plan a division of territory using major rivers as borders. Hotspur, whose imagined reward is control of land north of the Trent, objects to the river's northward turn from Burton-upon-Trent. He declares:

> I'll have the current in this place dammed up,
> And here the smug and silver Trent shall run
> In a new channel, fair and evenly.
> It shall not wind with such a deep indent
> To rob me of so rich a bottom here.   (3.1.98–102)

The joke is that, rather than arguing for a border based on landmarks other than rivers, he accepts this principle but proposes changing the Trent's direction. The exorbitant plan underscores his unsuitability for rule. By the Restoration, however, royal control over water, albeit on a more modest scale, might be translated into a supreme demonstration of authority. Hence Edmund Waller, celebrating Charles II's improvement of St. James's Park, proclaims:

> The sea, which always served his empire, now
> Pays tribute to our Prince's pleasure too.
> Of famous cities we the founders know;
> But rivers, old as seas, to which they go,
> Are Nature's bounty; 'tis of more renown
> To make a river, than to build a town.[91]

For Waller, Charles has successfully privatized water, rightly claiming the 'tribute' of the Thames, and by extension of the sea beyond. Despite the

---

[89] *Certain Proposals* (London, 1652), p. 9.   [90] Schama, *Landscape and Memory*, p. 343.
[91] 'On St James's Park As lately improved by His Majesty', ll. 7–12; in *Selected Poems of Abraham Cowley, Edmund Waller and John Oldham*, ed. Julia Griffin (London, 1998), pp. 77–80.

ambition of the final couplet, however, the engineering feat is in practice contained in its significance, specifically for the king's 'pleasure'.

Through the course of the early modern period, however, this author-itarian politics of water was neither dominant nor uncontested. Taylor was a London waterman, and an aspiring author, when the New River scheme was ceremonially opened in 1613, bringing the capital a new source of fresh water. The naming of this twenty-mile aqueduct as a 'river' is suggestive in itself, as though a natural system has merely been bent to the needs of Londoners. In the pageant celebrating the opening, this innovative and fundamentally commercial enterprise, which effectively commodified household water-supplies, was endorsed by the labourers themselves (or else actors representing them) as 'for the public good'.[92] The 'industry, cost, and care' of the scheme's initiator, Sir Hugh Myddelton, thereby brings about a general improvement of life for London's citizens. Taylor, for all the outspoken royalism of his Civil War pamphleteering, similarly assumes the voice of an informed citizen when contemplating the expansion of river traffic across the country. The manip-ulation of waterways is for him a definitive sign of economic prosperity; 'commerce and Trade', he states, 'is the strength and sinnewes of the common wealth, the chiefe and onely subsistance of Cities and Corporations'.[93] Others, perhaps energized by the republicanism of the mid-seventeenth century, were more specific in their arguments about the political and economic underpinnings of canals. Mathew asks: 'Now who should be the *Undertaker* of this great work but the *State* it self? It being too great an expence for any private man or Corporation to lay out; and of too great a Profit for them to receive, being effected.'[94] Similarly, Hely not only stresses the importance of 'the keeping out of Sharers', but also proposes that the state should assert a proprietary right over running water, in a manner that will ensure sufficient supplies for navigation.[95] In principle, this perception is not dissimilar to Waller's vision of waterways created by the monarch; however, the politics could hardly be more different, since Hely's argument is for free and open usage. By contrast, those diverting valuable water from navigable rivers for the purpose of irrigation, he suggests, should be forced to 'rent the Water … yearly, at ten or twenty Shillings the Acre more or less'.[96]

[92] On the commercial and legal bases of this project, see Bernard Rudden, *The New River: A Legal History* (Oxford, 1985), pp. 1–19. The short opening pageant was performed as part of the Lord Mayor's pageant of 1613, *The Triumphs of Truth*, by Thomas Middleton (*Jacobean Civic Pageants*, ed. Richard Dutton (Keele University, 1995), p. 166).
[93] *John Taylors Last Voyage*, sig. B5v.   [94] Mathew, *Of the Opening of Rivers*, pp. 10–11.
[95] *Representation of the Benefits and Advantages of Making the River Avon Navigable*, p. 22.
[96] *Ibid.*, p. 16.

Given the benefit of hindsight, such schemes may seem naive and impractical. Even the New River project, for all the rhetoric of the opening pageant, was dependent upon private investment; as one critic complained at the time, it converted 'that which was intended for a public good ... to a private gain'.[97] The massive expansion of canals in the eighteenth century proceeded more openly on capitalist principles, facilitating the traffic of merchandise but at the cost of privatizing water and transportation. Therefore, those who made an imaginative, and not entirely illogical, leap from the circulation of water in rivers to the potentially unfettered circulation of subjects and their merchandise effectively lost the debate. The 'begetting' of 'wealth' envisaged by seventeenth-century commentators involved as many exclusions as inclusions; common rights on water would be expanded little more than common rights over land. A regime of 'freedom' was thus translated into the freedom to compete. The arguments and perceptions of such writers, however, represent earnest and informed efforts, at a critical moment in the development of inland transportation, to reimagine existing relations between the citizen and national space. Working in a period before the mature development of capitalism, they pursue the spatial logic of circulation to what seem, to them, to be entirely reasonable conclusions.

PLACE, PROSPECT AND COMMERCE IN SEVENTEENTH-CENTURY POETRY

This chapter, in the spirit of the book as a whole, is an exercise in an interdisciplinary form of cultural history, rather than a study within the more conventional parameters of literary history. In fact one underlying goal has been to rethink the rather tired and canon-bound category of 'the Renaissance river poem', setting canonical figures such as Spenser and Drayton within much richer contexts. In this final section I want to consider a further, seventeenth-century tradition of poetry concerned with place and landscape, running from early country-house poems through to the mid-century poem of 'prospect'. This tradition overlaps chronologically with that considered in the second section in this chapter, yet moves decisively away from the influences of Spenser and Drayton. As others have argued, it is fundamentally committed to values of property; it is a poetry of

---

[97] Quoted in William Hardin, '"Pipe-Pilgrimages" and "Fruitfull Rivers": Thomas Middleton's Civic Entertainments and the Water Supply of Early Stuart London', *Renaissance Papers* (1993), 66. Hardin's essay centres attention on the pageant's handling of these tensions.

enclosed place rather than space, and as a result rivers, suggestive as they are of mobility and spatial connections, are rarely accorded prominence.[98] I want to suggest, however, that attention to some of these rare images may underpin a reconsideration of the status of the poems in relation to the ongoing struggles traced throughout this chapter. This may also help us to appreciate changes across the period. I argue that the transition from the Jonsonian country-house poem to the poetry of prospect is in part indicative of a cultural reassessment of the relation between property and nationhood, place and space. In particular, Denham's seminal prospect poem, *Cooper's Hill*, combining traditional political values with a guarded engagement with discourses of economic expansion, suggests an influential new direction for the Jonsonian tradition.

The country-house poem is generally perceived as the archetypal early seventeenth-century literary statement of the values of placement. This minor genre coalesced with early Stuart social policy, which stressed the importance of the gentry and nobility fulfilling their traditional roles in the country.[99] Its central images of festivity and hospitality epitomize a vision of stable and hierarchical community, which is posited in turn as the bedrock of socio-political order in the nation as a whole. Recent historicizing analyses of these poems, however, have valuably situated them within a contested politics of space. Rather than being assured statements of unassailable orthodoxy, they have been exposed as more fraught, all too aware of emergent challenges to the values they espouse. Significantly, such approaches have attended to matters ranging from the broad shifts towards capitalism and bourgeois domesticity, to more local yet equally pressing struggles.[100] At the latter end of the spectrum, for example, Martin Elsky's study of the micro-politics of river transport on the River Lea has exposed crucial tensions in Jonson's 'To Sir Robert Wroth'. Elsky reads this poem in the context of 'the Wroths' changing relationship to the transportation

---

[98] See esp. James Turner, *The Politics of Landscape: Rural Scenery and Society in English Poetry 1630–1660* (Oxford, 1979).

[99] See esp. Leah Marcus, *The Politics of Mirth: Jonson, Herrick, Milton, Marvell, and the Defense of Old Holiday Pastimes* (Chicago and London, 1986); Felicity Heal, *Hospitality in Early Modern England* (Oxford, 1990), pp. 108–14.

[100] See esp. Leah Marcus, 'Politics and Pastoral: Writing the Court on the Countryside', in *Culture and Politics in Early Stuart England*, ed. Kevin Sharpe and Peter Lake (London, 1994), pp. 139–60; Bruce McLeod, *The Geography of Empire in English Literature 1580–1745* (Cambridge, 1999), pp. 76–119; Turner, *Politics of Landscape*, esp. pp. 142–6; Don E. Wayne, *Penshurst: The Semiotics of Place and the Poetics of History* (London, 1984); Raymond Williams, *The Country and the City* (London, 1973), pp. 26–34.

system', and hence to ideas of how local communities connect with the commonwealth.[101] 'To Sir Robert Wroth' becomes, as a result, a less confident, yet considerably more compelling, celebration of the uncertain, shifting values of property. Here, by attending to images of rivers and water, and associated appreciations of human and mercantile mobility, I want to argue that 'To Penshurst', as well as subsequent poems by Thomas Carew and Andrew Marvell, are similarly shaped by the struggle to sustain an idealized model of property relations in the face of social and political change.

Sir Robert Sidney's Penshurst estate on the River Medway in Kent, like Wroth's on the Lea, was the focus of debates about the limits of river navigation. A series of Elizabethan and early Stuart investigations into the Medway repeatedly questioned the extent to which it might be considered navigable, and on at least one occasion a Commission of Sewers stressed the benefit of opening the river as far as Penshurst. This would be in the interests of the King's navy, and 'also for the general … good of his subjects … by the traffic by boats'.[102] The estate is thus imaginatively situated within networks of trade and communications, one unit within a dynamic and expansive commonwealth. By contrast, as though in reaction to such a vision, Jonson's poem determinedly represents an insular and self-contained rural space.[103] Indeed the poem's only mention of the Medway is as an unreliable supplier of food, by comparison with Penshurst's ponds: 'And if the high-swoll'n Medway fail thy dish, / Thou hast thy ponds, that pay thee tribute fish' (ll. 31–2). Here the element of water, which the opening lines of the poem endorse, along with soil, air and wood, as one of the estate's 'better marks', is figured as ideally contained and static. While the 'high-swoll'n' river proves itself unreliable, even mildly threatening, the ponds turn water into property, and fish into the tangible realization of that relationship. In line with the poem's strategy of wilfully confusing natural processes and economic relationships, the fish 'leap' forward to 'pay' their 'tribute', as though the water itself owes the lord its right to exist. Those fish, in turn, are brought to the lord's table for distribution in the poem's definitive act of hospitality.

Accordingly, the considerable dynamism of 'To Penshurst' is also carefully constrained, as people and local produce alike converge on the great house. Famously, 'all come in, the farmer and the clown, / And no one empty-handed, to salute / Thy lord, and lady' (ll. 48–50). Ponds bring fish;

[101] 'Microhistory and Cultural Geography', quote at 525.
[102] BL Add. MS 34105, fol. 193v; see also BL Add. MS 34218, fols. 37r–56r. Willan, *River Navigation in England*, pp. 16–17.
[103] *Ben Jonson*, ed. C. H. Herford, Percy and Evelyn Simpson (11 vols., Oxford, 1954–70), vol. VIII.

farmers bring capons; young women bring 'An emblem of themselves, in plum, or pear' (l. 56). The centripetal movement is critical, suggesting clear social and economic horizons to the lives of those bound to the estate. Even local patterns of marketing are magically subsumed into the economy of gift-giving, self-sufficiency and hospitality. The only exceptions to this model, also drawn towards the estate but from outside its boundaries, are the uniquely licensed figures of poet and king, and in each case their routes of travel are either obscured or mystified. Jonson is simply there, absorbed into the fabric of the estate through the conjoined mysteries of poetry and patronage. James, meanwhile, the poem's only real traveller, is described as happening upon the house by chance, 'when hunting late, this way, / With his brave son' (ll. 76–7). This is a deft Jonsonian touch. On the one hand, James's own unfettered travel signifies his proprietorial status in relation to the nation. His movement performs in part the functions of an Elizabethan progress, although the decisively haphazard nature of his itinerary accords with this monarch's preference for informality and social exclusion. He hunts with his son, evading the gaze of the populace. On the other hand, and equally importantly, the lack of any evident pathway preserves the poem's controlling image of insulation. Penshurst is bound to a wider political unit, but without overtly admitting connections which might disturb the poem's social fantasy of community and placement.

Yet this poem, like so many of those that would follow its model, nevertheless admits an appreciation of pressures impinging upon its fantasy of enclosure. As the opening lines insist, Penshurst is standing out against wider trends of consumption and display among the aristocracy. (Unlike the new Elizabethan prodigy houses, Jonson insists, Penshurst is '*not* ... built to envious show' (l. 1; my italics).) Such landowners, Jonson recognizes, are driven more by a sense of competition with their peers than a commitment to local communities. But positioning Penshurst as exceptional in resisting such trends carries a degree of risk, establishing a binary that the poem struggles to maintain. Furthermore, the enclosure at the Sidney estate is manifestly not complete, since there is one mysterious absence when James visits. The poem states that Sidney's wife, Barbara Gamage, reaps 'The just reward of her high huswifery' despite herself being 'far' from the estate (ll. 85, 87). Fantasy is here, albeit obliquely, exposed as such; the Sidneys, as much as other aristocrats, were bound perforce into wider familial, social, economic and political networks, which often drew both husband and wife away from their home.[104]

---

[104] See esp. J. C. A. Rathmell, 'Jonson, Lord Lisle, and Penshurst', *English Literary Renaissance*, 1 (1971), 250–60.

Therefore, as much as the final lines endorse the values of a settled family –
insisting that whereas the builders of 'proud, ambitious heaps' may have
'built', the lord of Penshurst more properly 'dwells' – the underlying
impression is of a precious ideal being defended against almost unassailable pressures (ll. 101–2). And within its local context, the Medway, as
much as any other object in the poem, signals those pressures, as it links
the estate, however tenuously and contentiously, to places beyond its
borders.

   In the hands of the generation of poets following Jonson, the model of
isolation was reworked under the weight of changing social and political
forces. For Carew, the careful exercise of Jonsonian imitation in the much-
anthologized 'To Saxham' is complemented by a more personally and
politically charged piece, 'To my friend G. N. from Wrest'.[105] This poem,
which deserves more critical attention than it has received, looks unnervingly outward, from 'the temperate ayre' of Wrest Park, Bedfordshire, to
'the cold nights out by the bankes of Tweed', where Carew had served in
1639 with the King's forces in the Scots Wars. Significantly, at this
moment of acute stress between England and Scotland the Tweed resumes
its ancient status as a border, and it is this as much as the weather that has
left the poet feeling unsettled and exposed. Although the poem's closing
lines seek the distance of metaphor by translating the addressee's activity
into 'the pursuit / Of Bucks, and Stags' – the mere 'embleme of warre'
(ll. 108–9) – the accent on human conflict is irrepressible. At Wrest Park,
by studied contrast, the local stream, guided at once by nature and 'her
Hand-maid', art, seems to conspire in the house's seclusion. Carew
ponders the function of the great house's moat, following it as it traces
'spacious channells' which

> slowly creepe
> In snakie windings, as the shelving ground
> Leades them in circles, till they twice surround
> This Island Mansion, which i' th' center plac'd,
> Is with a double Crystall heaven embrac'd,
> In which our watery constellations floate,
> Our Fishes, Swans, our Water-man and Boate
> Envy'd by those above, which wish to slake
> Their starre-burnt limbes, in our refreshing lake,
> But they stick fast nayl'd to the barren Spheare,
> Whilst our encrease in fertile waters here

[105] *The Poems of Thomas Carew*, ed. Rhodes Dunlap (Oxford, 1949).

Disport, and wander freely where they please
Within the circuit of our narrow Seas.   (ll. 71, 76–88)[106]

The closing three lines of this passage are curiously opaque. The final
phrase, 'the circuit of our narrow Seas', might be taken to suggest a conven-
tionally pastoralized image of nationhood, like John of Gaunt's 'precious
stone set in the silver sea'.[107] This inkling of a broader vision, however, is
constrained in context by the representation of the 'Island Mansion' as an
abundant world unto itself, enclosed as though by its own 'Seas', and envied
even by the constellations above. To 'wander freely' is to wander within the
'snakie windings' of water within the estate. Even the 'Water-man' is thus
constrained: a figure so suggestive of placelessness in contemporary discourse
translated at a stroke into an emblem of property. Against the gathering
forces of history – and, equally, against the very laws of hydrology – the poem
struggles to assert an essential principle, for poet and estate alike, of isolation.

By comparison, Andrew Marvell's *Upon Appleton House*, written roughly
a decade later than Carew's poem, wrestles more openly and dynamically
with the issue of retirement, as a result twisting conceits of native pastoral into
peculiar new shapes.[108] This distended country-house poem, occasioned by
the retreat from public life of Marvell's patron, the parliamentarian
commander Sir Thomas Fairfax, eschews the political and social wisdom
inherited from Jonson. Appleton House, in comparison with the likes of
Penshurst and Wrest, is acknowledged as altogether more exposed to the
forces of history.[109] Notably, in his attention to the present Marvell revises
conventional images of contented tenants and servants, replacing them with
specialized labourers, not necessarily bound to the land by any more than
bonds of temporary employment.[110] Indeed the mowers notoriously bring
to the estate connotations of warfare and violence, as they 'massacre the
grass', while one accidentally 'carves the rail' (ll. 394–5). Moreover, although
the poet, towards the end, situates himself comfortably by the bank of the

---

[106] Information about the estate design before the extensive and well-documented improvements of the
late seventeenth and early eighteenth centuries is sparse; however, it is clear that these changes
involved the removal of a preexistent moat, and the development instead of canals (Linda Cabe
Halpern, 'Wrest Park 1686–1730s: Exploring Dutch Influences', *Garden History*, 30 (2002), 136).

[107] Shakespeare, *Richard II*, 2.1.46.

[108] *The Poems of Andrew Marvell*, ed. Nigel Smith (London, 2003), pp. 210–41.

[109] Although my reading of the poem will focus on forces of social change, the poem has equally, and
valuably, been situated within the pressing political circumstances of its historical moment. See esp.
Derek Hirst and Steven Zwicker, 'High Summer at Nun Appleton, 1651: Andrew Marvell and Lord
Fairfax's Occasions', *Historical Journal*, 36 (1993), 247–69.

[110] Rosemary Kegl, '"Joyning my Labour to my Pain": The Politics of Labor in Marvell's Mower
Poems', in *Soliciting Interpretation: Literary Theory and Seventeenth-Century English Poetry*, ed.
Elizabeth D. Harvey and Katharine Eisaman Maus (Chicago and London, 1990), pp. 89–118.

River Wharfe, contemplating its 'wanton harmless folds' as he waits for fish to 'twang' his 'lines' (ll. 633, 648), the central image of this river is more equivocal. After reviewing the 'landskip' of the estate's pastures, the scene suddenly changes:

> Then, to conclude these pleasant acts,
> Denton sets ope its cataracts;
> And makes the meadow truly be
> (What it but seemed before) a sea.
> For, jealous of its Lord's long stay,
> It tries t'invite him thus away.
> The river in itself is drowned,
> And isles th'astonished cattle round.   (ll. 465–72)

The image is almost certainly topical, based on a controlled action at the estate of Denton, thirty miles upstream, of opening fish-pond sluice gates. In practice, this would have had benefits both for the Denton ponds and the Appleton meadows, on which the inundation had an acknowledged fertilizing effect.[111] The fact that Fairfax owned both estates prompts, yet also defuses any political barb within, the grumble at his 'long stay'. But there is also something more profoundly unsettling about this passage, as it imagines, under whatever circumstances, the collapse of all distinction between land and water. For a moment, at least, the river fails to perform as a river; it 'in itself is drowned'. While the tone throughout is comic – 'Let others tell the paradox,' the poem continues, 'How eels now bellow in the ox' (ll. 473–4) – it takes a controlled event as occasion to ponder the exposure of the estate to overwhelming external forces. Though technically owned and manipulated by Fairfax, for this stretch of its existence, the pressing waters of the Wharfe bring with them suggestions at once of the nation beyond and of a wider disorder that impinges alike upon the estate and its lord. The speaker's immediate response, like Fairfax's reaction to the nation's situation, is notably self-absorbed: 'But I, retiring from the flood, / Take sanctuary in the wood' (ll. 481–2). As a whole, however, this poem persistently questions the country-house poem's governing fantasy of isolation. Fairfax's estate – like Fairfax, Marvell and even the mowers – is subject to greater forces, variously shaping the nation beyond in political, social and economic terms.

Written around the same time as Marvell's country-house poem, Denham's *Cooper's Hill* represents a distinct shift of vision. For Samuel Johnson,

---

[111] John Barnard, 'Marvell and Denton's "Cataracts"', *Review of English Studies*, 31 (1980), 310–15.

Cooper's Hill marked the origin of 'local poetry', a 'species of composition' in which description of 'some particular landscape' is blended with 'historical retrospection or incidental meditation'.[112] In the present context, its concern with the view (or 'prospect') from a hill, rather than with a landscape demarcated by bounds of property, marks a turn towards a more public and forthright reflection on relations between the land and wider issues of social and political order.[113] Moreover, the poem demands attention here for the centrality of rivers and water in its makeshift discourse of national identity, framed and reframed (in successive versions) within the changing political circumstances of the 1640s and 1650s. In the course of the poem the flow of water accrues multiple levels of significance, relating variously, and interconnectedly, to poetry, economics and politics. As numerous critics have commented, *Cooper's Hill* articulates a doctrine of *concordia discors*, which held that harmony may be derived out of conflict between opposing forces.[114] Here I want to suggest, more specifically, that attending to the functions of rivers in *Cooper's Hill* may help to elucidate some of the political and spatial implications of *concordia discors* in Denham's poem. For all its essential conservatism, its attention to the Thames admits qualities of dynamism, aligned with contemporary economic discourse on river improvement, which remould the models of national identity apparent in previous poetry of place.

More than any previous topographical poem, *Cooper's Hill* is concerned with the engagement between the poet and the scene before him. The speaker is at once specifically located and capable of transcending this location: 'Through untrac't ways, and aery paths I fly', he claims, 'More boundless in my Fancy than my eie' (ll. 11–12). Yet the 'wandering' nature of eye and fancy alike is tempered by the poem's concentration on the Thames:

> My eye descending from the Hill, surveys
> Where *Thames* amongst the wanton vallies strays.
> *Thames*, the most lov'd of all the Oceans sons,
> By his old Sire to his embraces runs,
> Hasting to pay his tribute to the Sea,
> Like mortal life to meet Eternity.　　　　　　　　　(ll. 159–64)

---

[112] Quoted in *Expans'd Hieroglyphicks: A Critical Edition of Sir John Denham's Coopers Hill*, ed. Brendan O Hehir (Berkeley and Los Angeles, 1969), p. 3.
[113] References are to *Expans'd Hieroglyphicks*. Unless stated otherwise, I use the B text.
[114] See esp. Earl R. Wasserman (*The Subtler Language: Critical Readings of Neoclassic and Romantic Poems* (Baltimore, 1959), pp. 45–88).

The Thames, as seen throughout this chapter, had long provided a subject for river poetry. Geographically and economically, it was the nation's most prominent river. Politically, its status was amenably hazy: its high tidal flow marked it as freely available to the people, while the placement of key royal residences on its banks signalled the proprietorial gaze of the monarch. It stood, one might say, as a ready, yet malleable, symbol of the English constitution. In *Cooper's Hill*, attention to the Thames, at the centre of the poem, indicates a desire to identify principles of order and direction in the national landscape. Hence the early representation of the river 'stray[ing]' 'amongst the wanton vallies', gives way to a purposeful progression downstream, which Denham inflects politically as well as morally. Rivers move to seas; lives move to eternity; tributes are paid to superior forces.

As this passage continues, it develops a definitive georgic strain, attending in turn to agricultural and mercantile rewards:

> No unexpected inundations spoyl
> The mowers hopes, nor mock the plowmans toyl:
> But God-like his unwearied Bounty flows;
> First loves to do, then loves the Good he does.
> Nor are his Blessings to his banks confin'd,
> But free, and common, as the Sea or Wind;
> When he to boast, or to disperse his stores
> Full of the tributes of his grateful shores,
> Visits the world, and in his flying towers
> Brings home to us, and makes both *Indies* ours;
> Finds wealth where 'tis, bestows it where it wants
> Cities in deserts, woods in Cities plants.
> So that to us no thing, no place is strange,
> While his fair bosom is the worlds exchange.   (ll. 175–88)

The slide from agriculture to international trade is a pivotal, though not unproblematic, moment in the poem. By envisaging the Thames as the 'God-like' agent, at once fertilizing the land and venturing out to claim 'both Indies' for England, Denham endorses the dynamism of economic exchange. Trade – or, to be more specific here, the associated neocolonial flows of power outward and goods inward – is encoded as another natural function of the land. The socio-spatial foundations of this prosperity are at once suggestive and opaque. Landowners, perhaps appropriately given the poem's effort to remove itself from a realm of political and military contest-ation, into which such men and women were inevitably drawn in the mid-seventeenth century, are invisible. Moreover, in a further point of contrast to the country-house poem, the poet's position on Cooper's Hill is figured as merely occasional, like that of a casual tourist, while the focus on a mower (like Marvell) and ploughman identifies specialist labourers, with no necessary bond to a given piece of land other than that of a daily wage. Connections between subjects and spaces are thus loosened, as the poem gestures towards the displacements and alienations of nascent agrarian capitalism. Indeed the fundamental ambivalence of the text in the face of these shifts is epitomized by the attention to the anthropomorphized river. It is the river, rather than human subjects, that assumes the principal burden of economic agency, its flows distributing 'his Blessings' and 'his stores'. Indeed, following the poem's syntax, it is even the river's 'flying towers' which enact the miracle of international trade, just as it is the river's 'bosom' that offers itself as 'the worlds exchange'.

This pattern is clarified in Denham's metaphorical invocations of rivers. Early in the poem, the idea of the water cycle provides a metaphor for the financial ebbs and flows that characterize the lives of people working in the city:

> Where, with like hast, though several ways, they run
> Some to undo, and some to be undone;
> While luxury, and wealth, like war and peace,
> Are each the others ruine, and increase;
> As Rivers lost in Seas some secret vein
> Thence reconveighs, there to be lost again.   (ll. 31–6)

Whereas the circulation of water, for many contemporary commentators, signified fundamentally positive forces of change, Denham instead couches the image in a conservative economic morality. The water cycle is here figured in terms of dissipation and loss, which underpin the poem's attack on the pursuit of 'luxury' and 'wealth'. The crux, for Denham as for contemporary commentators on river improvement, is the relation between national advancement and economic competition between individual subjects. Crucially, *Cooper's Hill*, for all its endorsement of social and economic dynamism, ultimately seeks to contain the potentially transformative connotations of the figure of circulation. The poem represents corporate prosperity as a natural product of the land, but eventual 'ruine' as the inevitable result of any pursuit of individual interests, whether economic or political. And it invokes rivers to support each argument.

The poem's climactic image of fluvial circulation assumes the form of political metaphor. The actions of political insurgents, 'forcing Kings to give / More than was fit for Subjects to receive' (ll. 345–6), is likened to the efforts of husbandmen to control the flow of a swollen river. The river 'can endure' the 'high-rais'd banks' erected to prevent flooding of crops:

> But if with Bays and Dams they strive to force
> His channel to a new, or narrow course;
> No longer then within his banks he dwells,
> First to a Torrent, then a Deluge swells:
> Stronger, and fiercer by restraint he roars,
> And knows no bound, but makes his power his shores.   (ll. 353–8)

In its earlier version, of 1642, the final lines clinch a point about the relation between the respective powers of princes and people:

> Therefore their boundlesse power let Princes draw
> Within the Channell, and the shores of Law,
> And may that Law, which teaches Kings to sway
> Their Scepters, teach their Subjects to obey.   (A Text; ll. 351–4)

In both versions, the image naturalizes and reifies England's monarchical constitution, echoing the earlier endorsements of orderly and linear flows. In the later version, albeit more subtly, the poem's overt argument for the primacy of the royal prerogative also works implicitly to inscribe royal authority on the land. The river *is* monarchical authority: and such essentially natural forces, Denham suggests, will violently resist efforts to prevent or redirect their courses.

It is a curious fact, in a poem so thoroughly engaged with processes of social and political interaction, that Denham's metaphor should echo contemporary proponents of river improvement. Like the arguments raised by such writers, the underlying vision of nationhood in *Cooper's Hill* is founded on principles of circulation. While the country-house poem had focused its gaze on isolated units of property, Denham's poem is far more engaged with the relation between place and the wider, encompassing space of the nation. Hence the centrality of the Thames. The ideological game Denham plays, however, with considerable if not complete success, is to subordinate these principles to the interests of conservative social and political values. Indeed, while Denham doubtless appreciated that the Jacobean, and Jonsonian, myth of placement had been ruthlessly exposed, by the 1640s, as the stuff of nostalgic fantasy, his poem nonetheless seeks to contain the more radical connotations of contemporary discourse on the circulation of water. It is therefore hardly surprising that Denham's poem should have been so influential on eighteenth-century poetry of place and landscape: poetry which refashioned preexistent ideas of tradition and place, as it embraced colonialism, endorsed the extraordinary fortunes being embedded in the landscape by men successful in the marketplace, and made little effort to sentimentalize bonds between landlords and their tenants and labourers. It was a model amenable to an age of parliamentary enclosure, landscape gardening, and the canal.

The narrative of literary history traced in this final section has been selective, constructed in an effort to centre attention on one particular dynamic in the poetry of place and prospect. It has been concerned with the tension between place and mobility, and it has argued that attention to images of rivers may help to elucidate certain poems, and in turn their cultural contexts, in this regard. As Denham's poem indicates, this is not an obviously linear narrative, but one characterized throughout by ambivalence in the face of change. Other strains, in fact, were more forthrightly reactionary. For instance, just as Taylor was envisaging rivers as malleable lines of connection on the face of the country, Charles Cotton was aligning himself with the pastoral mode in his celebration of the river on his estate which he fished in seclusion: 'my beloved Nymph fair *Dove*'.[115] This tradition, arguably, would be just as influential as that of Denham for writers of succeeding generations; indeed the eighteenth century would inevitably bring its own distinct pressures to bear upon both rivers and poetry. But the seventeenth-century trajectory from Jonson to Denham is nonetheless illuminating in the present context, offering a sequence of struggles to reconcile values of place and enclosure with emergent forces of mobility and economic improvement. Despite the overwhelming social conservatism of the tradition, individual poems are drawn inevitably into an engagement with the debates and transformations that shaped the wider period.

Indeed the fact that Denham wrote in the age of Taylor underscores the point – fundamental to the argument and structure of this chapter as a whole – that changes in spatial relationships and meanings were neither linear nor uncontested. For all the confidence of Sir Edward Turner in the Parliament of 1665, rivers remained uncertain sites, prompting reassessments of relations between subjects and spaces. I have argued, however, that across the period there were undeniable shifts in the terms and premises of debate. Increasingly, poets and social commentators reconceived the relation between real and imagined journeys along England's waterways, focusing attention on the labours of watermen and processes of economic exchange. Increasingly, also, it becomes possible to trace the emergence of a model of nationhood which is in part founded upon, and sustained by,

---

[115] Walton and Cotton, *Compleat Angler*, p. 320.

myriad acts of human mobility. Hence the central position within the chapter of the waterman: a figure routinely stigmatized as a mere vagrant, but one who becomes a focal point for the period's debates over the meanings of rivers. As will become apparent in the following chapter, these debates over mobility – with their definitive concern with the mobility of commoners – are pursued even more intensely in discourse on roads.

CHAPTER 2

Roads

While rivers are natural systems, exploited in the early modern period as signs of potential human circulation, roads are physical products of mobility worn onto the landscape, forged by need and defined by custom. Indeed in most cases 'a road was hardly regarded as a structure at all', but rather as 'an abstract right of way'.[1] Hence, when a particular path was unclear or unpassable, travellers had a legal right to take an alternative route, even if this involved passing through enclosed fields or crops.[2] Indeed in parts of the country bridges were the only physical structures that truly gave shape to a traveller's route.[3] These practical considerations are encoded in the contemporary terms, 'way' and 'highway', most commonly used to designate overland routes. But 'road', though uncommon in the period, is not an anachronistic term, and in the present context it may helpfully underscore my concern in this chapter with the long and uncertain project to define the nation's highways in more concrete terms.[4] 'Ways', that is, had to be translated into 'roads'. Moreover, they had to become objects of knowledge, marked on maps and communicated by word of mouth. In practical terms, this project was effectively stalled for much of the early modern period, as the maintenance of roads failed to keep pace with increases in usage. Yet preexistent meanings of roads, and appreciations of those who used them, came under intense pressure in the sixteenth and seventeenth centuries. Above all, reflections on roads become inextricably intertwined with perceptions of that most problematic of all types of traveller: the

---

[1] J. Crofts, *Packhorse, Waggon and Post: Land Carriage and Communications under the Tudors and Stuarts* (London, 1967), pp. 14–16; F. G. Emmison, '1555 and All That: A Milestone in the History of the English Road', *Essex Review*, 64 (1955), 16. For a contemporary legal definition of a way, broken down into particular types, see Michael Dalton, *The Country Justice* (1630), p. 66.

[2] W. T. Jackman, *The Development of Transportation in Modern England*, 3rd edn (London, 1966), p. 5; Sidney and Beatrice Webb, *English Local Government: The Story of the King's Highway* (London, 1913), p. 6.

[3] See David Harrison, *The Bridges of Medieval England: Transport and Society, 400–1800* (Oxford, 2004).

[4] Emmison, '1555 and All That', 16.

mobile commoner, unmoored from traditional coordinates of place and identity.

My central concern in this chapter is with ideas of road networks. If discourse on rivers is shaped by myths of circulation, that on roads, I would suggest, is shaped equally by the idea of the network. The network emerges in the period as a critical way of representing and understanding the relation between specific places within the nation, separated by any number of miles. Ideas of networks were not new to the early modern period; indeed, as I will demonstrate below, they can be traced back to the Roman era, and underpin the production of road-books and itineraries from early in the age of print. But networks can take many different forms, and changing approaches to road networks evidence efforts to renegotiate relations between the local and the national, and between the individual subject and English space. Once local roads are accommodated into national systems, nationhood may be defined by networks, each village and town deriving meaning from its connections with all other places. For Henri Lefebvre, the transition to a regime of abstract space, from the Middle Ages onward, is typified by the establishment of networks.[5] Yet an analysis of networks, I want to argue, must attend not merely to physical roads and road-makers, but also to the organization of knowledge. While physical 'ways' existed throughout the period – etched onto the landscape by the feet of horses and people, and the occasional wheels of carts, wagons and coaches – their positioning within networks is a product of myriad acts of human knowledge.

The organization of knowledge, however, must be appreciated as not merely an elite operation, to be studied through atlases and government discourse, but socially multifarious and contested. A manuscript itinerary for a queen is one thing; a pocket-guide to the country for pedlars is another; and the recurrent myth of rogues' maps, circulating in a criminal under-world, is another again. As this book aims to demonstrate, anxiety about popular mobility informs all early modern discourse on space. Within this context, concerted efforts to legitimize such forms of movement mark a critical development in English spatial history. Once the spatial knowledge of the common traveller is embraced rather than feared, and once that traveller is meaningfully situated in relation to the body politic, then the nature of nationhood is significantly transformed. The English nation can be equated with the sum of the quotidian actions of its citizens, who bring networks into being as they enact myriad lines of social and economic

---

[5] *The Production of Space*, trans. Donald Nicholson-Smith (Oxford, UK, and Cambridge, Mass., 1991), esp. pp. 117–18, 266.

connections. While it would be absurd to claim that this transformation occurs by 1700 – if indeed it has ever fully happened – I want to suggest that an analysis of textual and discursive struggle, centring on efforts to legitimize the voices and perspectives of commoners on the road, may help us to understand more fully the contested meanings of national space.

The chapter is necessarily drawn to a diverse range of texts and sources. Unlike rivers, roads were not considered poetic.[6] Perhaps only Michael Drayton, of all early modern poets, gives them any considered attention, but that is merely further evidence of the unique capaciousness of his *Poly-Olbion*. They have little place on the stage either; although inns and alehouses, I suggest in Chapter 3, provide opportunities for authors to interrogate the emergent economy of mobility. Otherwise, the chapter is drawn particularly to various new genres, which emerge in part as ways of articulating topical concerns. These include itineraries, road-maps, pamphlets of directions for pedlars and chapmen, rogue pamphlets (a term I will use in preference to alternatives, such as 'coney-catching pamphlets'), and spiritual biographies and autobiographies. Roads, on the basis of this evidence, were essentially prosaic. On occasion, the exploration will cover ground that has been traversed by other recent works of literary and cultural history. Roads were important in Garrett A. Sullivan's study, *The Drama of Landscape: Land, Property, and Social Relations on the Early Modern Stage*, underpinning fresh interpretations of Shakespeare's *Cymbeline* and Richard Brome's *The Jovial Crew*.[7] But my approach equally engages with works of social, economic and geographic history. While the great tradition of transport history, which produced a series of valuable books on roads in the early twentieth century, may have faded, various studies of human and commercial mobility as agents of change continue to add substance to our appreciation of the period. Within this context, fresh attention to the meanings of roads promises to extend and clarify a wider, interdisciplinary project.

The chapter has an underlying chronological narrative, which draws it towards the crucial Restoration decades: the time of Ogilby, of Daniel Defoe's first contributions to debates on roads, and of John Bunyan's influential reconception of the mobile commoner. As demonstrated in the preceding chapter, this was a period in which the routes of domestic travel, and the meanings of human mobility, were subjected to critical reassessment. Yet it would be a misrepresentation of the entire early modern period to structure

---

[6] James Turner, *The Politics of Landscape: Rural Scenery and Society in English Poetry 1630–1660* (Cambridge, Mass., 1979), p. 166.
[7] (Stanford, 1998), pp. 127–93.

the present discussion teleologically, as though we can understand discourse on roads throughout the sixteenth and seventeenth centuries as a linear progression towards an age of enlightenment. I believe there are important connections, for instance, between the project of Ogilby and that of Bunyan; however, these may best be considered in a chapter that considers them as part of parallel yet intertwined traditions, engaged with parallel yet intertwined concerns. Hence the chapter is divided as much thematically and generically as chronologically. The first section considers the functions, from the Elizabethan era through to the Restoration, of ideas of road networks. While the mysterious remnants of Roman roads prompted puzzling reflections on preexistent national structures, I suggest, cartographers and proponents of national economic improvement increasingly posited innovative, rival versions of connectedness. And the long second section examines the cultural history of the mobile commoner: from the Elizabethan rogue pamphlets, through shifting appreciations of pedlars, chapmen and chapwomen, to the genre of spiritual autobiography.

NETWORKS: HIGHWAYS AND THE NATION

In this section I want to suggest that a range of writers and cartographers, throughout the sixteenth and seventeenth centuries, contributed to a fundamental reassessment of the ways in which local roads might be appreciated as parts of larger networks of communication. For the majority of early modern men and women, experience and knowledge of roads was without question a matter of local identities. Moreover, tensions between localism and nationalism were inscribed in laws of highway maintenance, which gave responsibility for roads to individual parishes at a time when through-traffic was increasing both in volume and as a percentage of road-use.[8] Efforts to imagine and represent national networks were impelled largely by practical developments in transportation, which placed rapidly increasing demands on the roads. Yet there were also cultural determinants to these shifts: from the reflections of antiquarians and poets on Roman roads, through various efforts to represent a modern English network, to arguments that the system was failing to meet the needs of modern nationhood. The section therefore presents a study in the complex and uneasy emergence of spatial abstraction in the early modern nation, concerned with the ways in which the meanings

---

[8] Cyril Hughes Hartmann, *The Story of the Roads* (London, 1927); Webb and Webb, *Story of the King's Highway*, p. 2.

of places may be transformed by virtue of their positioning within increasingly sophisticated networks.

Even for those most committed to values of locality, the shadowy presence on the landscape of remnants of the Roman road network insistently suggested other ways of appreciating relations between place and space. Generations of antiquarians puzzled over these roads, and reflected on their uses and significance to the contemporary nation. William Harrison, in his 'Description of Britain', apologizes that he has left himself limited space for a description of roads, having devoted 'more time ... than was allotted unto me' on the rivers. Crucially, however, his description looks to a historical pattern, tracing 'the foure high waies sometime made in Britaine by the princes of this Iland'. Although he acknowledges arguments that this network was Roman in origin, he endorses the more common view of the time, that it was surveyed and constructed under the rule of ancient British kings, in order to protect the safety of their subjects. The highways, he writes, were intended to 'leade such as travelled into all parts thereof, from sea to sea'.[9] For other writers, this explanation was laced with elements of supernaturalism; in one account, the king Mulmutius, a 'great Sorcerer, perform'd that by the Assistance of his Art, and of Devils, which it was impossible for Men to do; for that in a few Days *England* was furnish'd with Highways of a beautiful and admirable Structure, from one End to the other'.[10] The claims of Rome, however, were unavoidable to committed antiquarians. William Camden presented a decisive case in his Elizabethan *Britannia*, while in the mid-seventeenth century William Burton developed an extensive commentary on a Roman text known as the 'Antonine itinerary', which provided antiquarians with the best available information about the geographical arrangement of Roman Britain.[11] According to Camden, to seek places mentioned in the itinerary without following the traces of roads would be to 'wander out of the way'.[12]

There was something intimidating about the Roman roads. William Dugdale describes, in awed terms, archaeological excavations on one road which discovered 'Gravell and Sand ... ten foot deep in the earth, and eighteen foot in breadth, with great flint stones in the bottom'.[13] The poet

[9] Harrison, 'Description of Britain', in Raphael Holinshed, *Chronicles*, 3 vols. (London, 1587), I.112.
[10] Nicolas Bergier, *The General History of the Highways, In all Parts of the World. More Particularly in Great Britain* (1712), p. 160.
[11] *A Commentary on Antoninus His Itinerary, or Journies of the Romane Empire, so Far as it Concerneth Britain* (1658).
[12] *Britannia*, trans. Abraham Holland (1610), p. 65.
[13] *The Antiquities of Warwickshire* (1656), p. 6.

Richard James, meanwhile, compared Roman civilization with his own, on the basis of the roads:

> Austins voice is true,
> Empire condignly was to Romans due.
> Our wayes are gulphs of durte and mire, which none
> Scarce ever passe in summer without moane;
> Whilst theirs through all the world were no lesse free
> Of passadge then the race of Wallisee.[14]

Such responses suggest a significant degree of discomfort in the face of Roman achievements. Not all early modern men and women would agree with Burton that 'what ever of Magnificence or Elegancy our *Britain* could boast' is owed directly to the Romans.[15] Significantly, Camden is more judicious, reflecting on the roads as indices of political repression. They owe their origin, he suggests, to the fact that 'the Romanes were wont to exercise their souldiers, and the common multitude, lest being idle, they should grow factious'. Their sheer physical weight and determined straightness, as well as the appreciation of their design for military usage, might therefore suggest colonial tyranny as much as Burton's 'Magnificence or Elegancy'. By comparison, Camden's contemporary countrymen assert a greater degree of freedom as they 'dis-member' the Roman roads, mining them for gravel.[16] For all the antiquarian fervour underpinning the *Britannia*, it is striking that this is one act of historical wastage that Camden mentions in surprisingly dispassionate terms.

Perhaps the most resonant record of debates about the meanings of Roman roads is provided by the sixteenth song of Drayton's *Poly-Olbion*, along with John Selden's appended antiquarian notes, or 'illustrations'. The issue of the highways' origin sets Drayton and Selden, not for the first time, at loggerheads. In response to Drayton's privileging of the British history narrative, Selden dutifully recounts the purported achievements of Mulmutius, before noting that, 'by more polit conceit and judicious authority these our waies have bin thought a worke of the *Romans*'.[17] Drayton's decision to prioritize the British narrative, made against the 'judicious authority' of his principal source, Camden's *Britannia*, is indicative of his desire to associate these most concrete signs of national cohesion with indigenous tradition rather than colonial repression. Hence Watling

---

[14] *Iter Lancastrense*, ed. Thomas Corser, Chetham Society Old Series 7 (1845), p. 2. 'Austin' is identified in a marginal note as St Augustine, while 'the race of Wallisee' is identified by the poem's editor as a reference to Wallesey Race Course. On James, see further below, pp. 191–2.

[15] *Commentary*, sig. A3r.   [16] *Britannia*, p. 64.

[17] *The Works of Michael Drayton*, ed. J. William Hebel, 5 vols. (Oxford, 1931–41), IV.326. Quotes from the poem itself are referenced by song and line, rather than (as here) volume and page.

Street, which stands in the long poem as one of the few artificial features in the landscape to assume the power of speech, begins:

> My Song is of my selfe, and my three sister Streets,
> Which way each of us runne, where each his fellow meets,
> Since us, his Kingly Waies, *Mulmutius* first began,
> From Sea, againe to Sea, that through the Iland ran.
> Which that in mind to keep posterity might have,
> Appointing first our course, this priviledge he gave,
> That no man might arrest, or debtors goods might seize
> In any of us fowre his militarie Waies. (16.95–102)

The emphasis on the 'priviledge' of legal freedoms enjoyed on the highways implicitly connects the benign reign of Mulmutius with the highway law of Drayton's own time, which defined 'the king's highway' in terms of freedom of movement. In the words of one legal text, 'It is called the Kings High-way, for that the King at all times hath therein passage for himselfe and all his People; and may punish all Nusance therein.'[18] Selden concurs, tracing to Mulmutius the principle that 'none should distraine in the Kings High-way, or the common Street, but the King and his Ministers' (IV.325). Roads, crucially, are non-property, and their centuries of usage document a continuity of nationhood, shaped by commoners as much as monarchs, that straddles the Roman era. Indeed 'The Sixteenth Song', perhaps more than any other, is determined to situate contemporary practices in relation to ancient traditions, and to assess the present in relation to the past. The burden of Watling Street's speech is not the roads but the 'ancient folk' – specifically, the Saxon tribes – that have peopled the countries that they span (16.138).

While Drayton does not enter into debates about whether the Roman system included subsidiary networks, it is important to him that the four principal roads may be described with a degree of certainty. Hence Fosse Way 'holds from shore to shore the length of all the Ile, / From where rich *Cornwall* points, to the *Iberian* Seas, / Till colder *Cathnes* tells the scattered *Orcades*'; Icning Way 'set out from *Yarmouth* in the East' and bore south until it 'Upon the *Solent* Sea stopt on the *Ile*-of-*Wight*'; and Rickneld Way spanned from the 'farther shore' of south Wales to meet the Tyne in the north-east, where it 'dissolv'd' in 'the *German* Sea' (16.104–6; 16.113, 118; 16.119, 123–4). Selden is more sceptical; 'To endevor certainty' in the roads, he comments, 'were but to obtrude unwarrantable conjecture, and abuse time & you' (IV.326). But for Drayton the image of roads dissolving into water at the coasts typifies his governing conception in the song of a model

---

[18] Dalton, *Country Justice*, p. 69.

of spatial and cultural cohesion that is at once rooted in time and physically traceable on the landscape. It provides a grid which Watling Street's description of the 'ancient folk' subsequently fills with civilization. The account is not entirely free of tensions, particularly when it touches on the north of Wales, where he narrates the efforts of 'the English *Offa* ... / To shut the *Britans* up, within a little nooke' (16.199–200). Yet the aim throughout, to suggest a continuity of national identity founded in the people of the land, remains clear.

Drayton is less assured, however, when history collides with contemporary practice. Around Hampstead Hill, on the outskirts of London, the voice of Watling Street gives way, and in its place '*Hie-gate* boasts his Way; which men do most frequent' (16.255). This shift to the present leads to a predictable rant, concluding the song, directed against the activities of merchants in London, selling English staples such as 'our Tinne, our Leather, Corne, and Wooll' in exchange for the 'trash' demanded by the 'idle Gentry' of the capital (16.356, 358, 342). Within this context, the significance of the Roman roads dissolving into the seas must be appreciated as twofold: they unite a geographically distinct space, but also mark unquestionable limits to that space. In Drayton's mind, the roads do not indicate trajectories across the seas, either to Rome or anywhere else. But before the song reaches this negative climax, it is more ambivalent about the kinds of traffic passing through the countryside towards Highgate. Peryvale, for instance, boasts:

> Besides; my sure abode next goodly *London* is,
> To vent my fruitfull store, that me doth never misse.
> And those poore baser things, they cannot put away,
> How ere I set my price, nere on my chap-men stay.   (16.239–42)

While Peryvale's voice betrays in the first couplet traces of the sort of pride that corrupts London itself, this description of production and consumption is otherwise conventional enough. The subsequent lines, however, are more quizzical, suggesting that the chapmen will find, somewhere, a market even for the 'baser' produce that may be scorned by Londoners. This is a telling gesture towards other kinds of networks, and other kinds of spatial knowledge, superimposed upon the landscape and its ancient structures. These are the multiple, everyday, unchartable movements of traffic, and they suggest kinds of spatial connections very different to those of the Roman roads.

Though undeniably idiosyncratic in so many ways, Drayton's struggle to reconcile abiding structures with quotidian actions typifies his social and cultural context. Tensions between the local and the national – individual motivations and public structures – were in fact inscribed in the laws of highway maintenance enacted in 1555. This act, which provided the basis for road law throughout the early modern period, introduced a requirement that all resident male inhabitants of a parish commit four (a figure increased to six in the revised act of 1563) days of labour per annum to road maintenance.[19] Each parish was required to appoint a surveyor to coordinate the work, and the parish as a whole was liable to be presented to Quarter Sessions for any shortcomings in its work. The underlying principle of the legislation was to preserve existing structures for existing purposes. The 1555 act is quite particular about these purposes, stating its concern only with 'Highewais ... leading to any Market Towne'. Though subsequent acts are inconsistent on this matter of definition, the 1555 stipulation can nonetheless be traced through the following century, entwined with the abstract notion of the 'king's highway'. One representative guide for surveyors of highways, for instance, states that the parish workers are responsible for roads 'leading to some market town, which is *via Regia*, the Kings highway, free for all men to passe with cart and carriage'.[20] The networks that matter, according to this model, are not those linking one end of the country and another, but those that centre on local market towns. The law thus encodes a spatiality of localism, endorsing the position that the 'economic horizon' for most people should remain, as one modern historian writes, 'bounded by the market town'.[21] As William Harrison describes them, at weekly markets 'all manner of provision is to be bought and sold for ease and benefit of the country round about'.[22]

The parochial system of highway maintenance also prioritized systems of local knowledge. Surveyors were local officers, of a similar stature to constables. They did not bring to their task any special expertise; on the contrary, their role was to endorse an existing body of knowledge about relevant roads. Like the Rogationtide ceremonies intended to reinforce memories of parish boundaries through the ritual of 'beating the bounds', work on the roads rehearsed local custom, affirming by acts of cleansing and repairing crucial distinctions between property and highways. Notwithstanding the threat of punishment from above, the quality and location of roads was thus

[19] 2&3 Philip and Mary, c.8. On early modern highway law and its implementation, see especially Jackman, *Development of Transportation in Modern England*, pp. 29–69; Webb and Webb, *Story of the King's Highway*, pp. 14–61. For evidence on the system of parochial roadworking in practice, see F. G. Emmison, 'Was the Highways Act of 1555 a Success?', *Essex Review*, 64 (1955), 221–34.
[20] John Layer, *The Office and Duty of Constables* (1641), p. 162.
[21] Alan Everitt, 'The Marketing of Agricultural Produce', in *The Agrarian History of England and Wales*, Vol. IV: 1500–1640, ed. Joan Thirsk (Cambridge, 1967), p. 501.
[22] *The Description of England*, ed. Georges Edelen (Ithaca, 1968), p. 246.

understood as the business of the parish. Hence the legislation underscored an inevitable degree of antagonism towards travellers passing through parishes, especially those using heavy carts, wagons or coaches. Legislators hardly helped matters in this regard, devising largely unworkable restrictions on the sizes and weights of vehicles, which remained in place for much of the seventeenth century.[23] For the traveller, meanwhile, accessing local knowledge was critical to the act of travel. As Catherine Delano-Smith argues, wayfinding, for those without local knowledge, was a matter of constant engagement with locals themselves, gathering information about distances, landmarks, quality of roads, turns to be avoided, and so forth.[24] Without access to such information, in an age before maps were used for identifying routes, and even before road-signs became more than a rarity, space remained obstinately mysterious to the traveller.

The textual form that characterizes this mode of travel, and that bridges the pre-modern and modern eras, is the itinerary.[25] Whereas extant medieval itineraries had characteristically been individualized, assuming the form of records of particular journeys, in the age of print itineraries served to regularize appreciations of journeys along arterial roads. These itineraries, many of which were plagiarized from a handful of key sources, break journeys down into lists of stages. Harrison, for instance, taking his English itineraries from John Stow's *Summarie of English Chronicles*, lists twelve journeys in the following form:

> The way from Walsingham to London
> From Walsingham to Pickenham   12 miles
> From Pickenham to Brandon Ferry   10 miles
> From Brandon Ferry to Newmarket   10 miles[26]

Such itineraries do not overtly challenge assumptions of local knowledge, since they do not give any information about directions, alternative routes, links to sites off the main roads, or quality of roads. For these matters, oral consultation remained vital. But the principle of the stage, which the itinerary, more than any other kind of text, inscribed as a model for travel, was fundamental to the development of road-travel. Stages do not necessarily equate

[23] See, e.g., 14 Charles II, c.6; and *Stuart Royal Proclamations*, ed. James F. Larkin and Paul L. Hughes, 2 vols. (Oxford, 1973–83), I.231. On these efforts, see H. J. Dyos and D. H. Aldcroft, *British Transport: An Economic Survey from the Seventeenth Century to the Twentieth* (Leicester, 1971), pp. 31–2.

[24] 'Milieus of Mobility: Itineraries, Route Maps and Road Maps', in *Cartographies of Travel and Navigation*, ed. James R. Akerman (Chicago and London, 2006), p. 45.

[25] On the itinerary, see Catherine Delano-Smith and Roger Kain, *English Maps: A History* (London, 1999), pp. 148–52; and Delano-Smith, 'Milieus of Mobility', pp. 34–45.

[26] *Description of England*, p. 399; *The Summarie of English Chronicles* (1566), fols. 198r–200r.

to a day's journey, nor are they necessarily regular in distances. The sheer repetition of particular itineraries in printed texts, however, serves to encode standardized models of significant journeys, and identifies certain places as nodal-points within spatial networks. Pickenham, for instance, assumes significance in its relation to Walsingham in one direction and London in the other. The meanings of place are subordinated to those of space.[27]

In the seventeenth century, developments in the representation of networks were intertwined with two epochal practical advances. Firstly, a national postal system emerged for private and commercial users in the middle decades of the century, founded on the structures used by the state. In the words of a 1642 tract, this system ensured that 'any man may with safetie and securitie send letters into any part of this Kingdome, and receive an answer within five days'.[28] Secondly, stage-coach routes multiplied rapidly in the latter decades of the century: and while the total volume of coach traffic may have remained small in relation to other forms of travel, its impact on ideas of mobility is hard to overestimate. The coach made travel possible for new types of travellers, including women and the infirm, and reduced the times and costs of journeys.[29] Some commentators worried about the way in which stage-coaches concentrated on some towns at the expense of others, and about how passengers would no longer pause to 'understand the Trade of the place they are in'.[30] Place, this writer feared, simply did not mean what it once did. Yet these developments relentlessly extended preexistent notions of networks, prompting a new wave of efforts to represent these structures. The post roads now provided the standard model for itineraries. While this model is arguably misleading in the way that it situates London at the centre of all networks and implicitly understates the significance of inter-provincial routes, it nonetheless asserts a powerful indigenous national transport structure that finally supersedes that of the Roman grid.[31] The contemporary nation was creating its own networks, in its own social and political image.

Ogilby, unquestionably the pivotal figure in the Restoration project to understand and represent this consolidating network, was notably sanguine

---

[27] Cf. Howard Marchitello, 'Political Maps: The Production of Cartography and Chorography in Early Modern England', in *Cultural Artifacts and the Production of Meaning: The Page, the Image, and the Body*, ed. Margaret J. M. Ezell and Katherine O'Brien O'Keefe (Ann Arbor, 1994), p. 32.

[28] *A Full and Cleare Answer to a False and Scandalous Paper, Entituled; The Humble Remonstrance of the Grievances of all his Majesties Posts of England* (1642), p. 1. See further Crofts, *Packhorse, Waggon and Post*, pp. 102–8.

[29] Crofts, *Packhorse, Waggon and Post*, pp. 125–32; Stella Margetson, *Journey by Stages: Some Account of the People who Travelled by Stage-Coach and Mail in the Years between 1660 and 1840* (London, 1967).

[30] *The Grand Concern of England Explained* (1673), p. 37.

[31] John Chartres, 'The Eighteenth-Century Inn: A Transient "Golden Age"?', in *The World of the Tavern: Public Houses in Early Modern Europe*, ed. Beat Kumin and Ann Tlusty (Aldershot, 2002), p. 208.

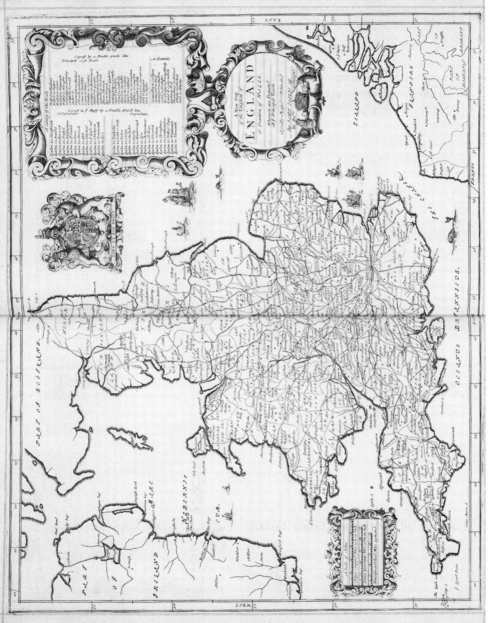

Fig. 3.1 Map of the post-road network of England and Wales from John Ogilby, *Britannia* (1675)

about the comparison between ancient and modern roads. He dismisses efforts to trace the roads to the reign of Mulmutius, accepts that the system was devised by the Romans for military purposes, then states that 'with *New Towns, New Ways* have gradually succeeded'.[32] The social and economic structures of seventeenth-century England and Wales, that is, have produced their own appropriate networks of inland communication.[33] Ogilby originally intended his *Britannia* to be a much more ambitious, 'encyclopaedic volume'. In 1673, in fact, he published a broadside sheet appealing for information under a list of nineteen headings, ranging from 'Cities, Towns Corporate, Market-Towns and Fair-Towns', through 'Improvements in Husbandry, Housewifery', to 'Places of Birth, Education or Habitation of Eminent Persons, in all Ages'.[34] Although his project might therefore have looked somewhat different had he lived beyond 1676, the cultural signifi-cance of his single volume is hard to overstate. Here Ogilby 'illustrates' his nation by presenting 'a Geographical and Historical Description of the Principal Roads thereof' (t.p.). In his dedication to Charles II he is more expansive about the economic function of this work, comparing inland trade to international trade, and stating that he has 'Attempted to *Improve Our* Commerce *and* Correspondency *at Home, by* Registring *and* Illustrating *Your Majesty's* High-Ways, Directly *and* Transversly, *as from* Shore *to* Shore' (sig. A1r–v). Knowledge thus translates into economic advancement: or, in the signal cry of Ogilby's age, 'improvement'.

While Ogilby is best known for his strip-maps of the nation's roads, it is important to set these in the context of his volume as a whole. The *Britannia* is organized around a sense of the nation's post-roads as a logical and hierarchical system. He categorizes the roads as 'independants' ('such as Commencing actually at LONDON'), 'dependants' ('such as being com-puted from LONDON, Commence not actually there, but branch out of the foresaid Independants'), 'principal cross roads' ('leading directly from *Town* to *Town*'), and 'accidental' cross-roads ('consisting of several shorter Branches, some *Independant* some *Dependant*') (sig. B1v). This system offers to make sense of the magnificent initial map of England and Wales, on which roads claim primacy in relation to the more familiar cartographical markings of rivers and county borders (Fig. 2.1). More importantly, it provides structure for the individual descriptions of routes, which form

---

[32] *Britannia* (1675), sig. B1v. Unless stated otherwise, all references are to this edition.
[33] Despite the title of his book, Ogilby is only concerned with 'the Kingdom of England and Dominion of Wales', and does not touch upon Scotland or Ireland.
[34] *Queries in Order to the Description of Britannia* (1673).

Fig. 2.2 Road-map from John Ogilby, *Britannia* (1675).

the bulk of the work. Each strip-map is accompanied by two pages of additional information. The maps trace individual roads, using innovative techniques to provide a fresh degree of information about the nature and quality of particular routes, as well as indicating crossroads and landmarks (Fig. 2.2). The accompanying pages give: details about direction and distance of travel; notes about counties passed through, rivers crossed, road-quality and location of inns; lists of 'turnings to be avoided'; and a discursive itinerary. These pages consistently address the reader as a figure progressing along the road; setting out from Monmouth to Lampeter, for instance, 'you leave the Town at 4 furlongs, then crossing the *Monnow*, you at 2' 3. pass through *Rockfield* a discontinued Village', and so forth (p. 153).

There has been some dispute about the extent to which Ogilby's *Britannia* was ever used by those on the road (i.e. for wayfinding), or even by those planning journeys. Although it has long and widely been assumed that the book served just these purposes, recent scholarship has pointed to some obvious complicating factors, such as the weight and cost of the volume, and its unfamiliar techniques of representation.[35] In the final section of this chapter, below, I will return to this issue, considering the publication of a rash of cheap versions of maps and itineraries in the years immediately after the *Britannia* was first printed, targeted particularly at mobile commoners.[36] Here, though, it is worth dwelling on the fact that, even in the cumbersome and expensive original volume, Ogilby approaches the representation of space through the subjectivity of the traveller. To know the nation is to experience it in motion, unfolding like the scrolled strip-maps which lead the eye down one column after another. This is a very different experience to that of reading the chorographies published earlier in the century. Indeed, while Ogilby's volume explicitly invokes Camden, inviting readers to situate it in this generic frame, its spatial economy is perhaps equally influenced by Ogilby's extensive work as a translator and author of texts on foreign countries and continents. Like so many of his contemporaries, he was coming to perceive the riches to be garnered from international trade, appreciating the globe as a mesh of existing and potential networks.[37] Like

---

[35] See esp. Delano-Smith, 'Milieus of Mobility', pp. 53–4; Delano-Smith and Kain, *English Maps*, pp. 169–70. I am also grateful to Garrett A. Sullivan for providing me with a copy of his unpublished paper, 'The Atlas as Literary Genre: Reading the Inutility of John Ogilby's *Britannia*', a piece which influenced the work of Dr Delano-Smith. These arguments respond to assumptions made by, among others, Katherine S. Van Eerde (*John Ogilby and the Taste of His Times* (Folkestone, 1976), pp. 137–9).

[36] See pp. 106–11.

[37] On this issue, see esp. Jerry Brotton, *Trading Territories: Mapping the Early Modern World* (London, 1997); and Robert Markley, *The Far East and the English Imagination, 1600–1730* (Cambridge, 2006), pp. 30–69.

somewhat fewer of them, I would suggest, he was prepared to approach the description of his own nation in a similar spirit. Therefore, whether one experiences these roads by actually travelling them or by reading the *Britannia* in one's study is to some extent immaterial. Regardless of how it was actually used, the book prioritizes and legitimizes the experience of the traveller, figuring movement along the nation's roads as an orderly, economically important business. It turns 'ways' into 'roads', which can be known, charted and catalogued. It imposes the statute mile as a measure across the nation, erasing the inconsistent customary standards employed in different places in favour of a knowable universal standard. And it reinforces the experience of space in terms of stages, attributing value to each place according to its relation to other places within the network.

Ogilby's traveller, however, had limited options. The *Britannia*'s focus on post-roads made sense of the nation's roads at the expense of limiting individual choices. Localized networks – the kind of ways that legislators had in mind when framing the 1555 highways act – have no place in this system. Moreover, despite Ogilby's original goal of comprehensive description, many villages and towns are either omitted from his grid or are listed only in passing, as 'Turnings to be avoided'. Indeed, in the absence of more comprehensive road maps, one way of moving beyond the generic strictures of the itinerary was, somewhat paradoxically, to prioritize abstract distances, as the crow flies, over particular routes. This was the strategy that John Norden introduced to English readers, in his *England: An Intended Guyde For English Travailers* (1625). In the 1590s, Norden had pioneered the charting of roads on county maps; by comparison, the *Intended Guyde* was a much simpler project. There is in fact something opportunistic about the work, since it merely exploits what was still a relatively specialized skill: the ability to determine distances from maps. The *Intended Guyde* simply gives tables for each county, in each case enabling the user to determine distances between twenty or so settlements, in any combination (Fig. 2.3). A national table allows readers to make rough connections from one county table to another, thereby multiplying the number of potential itineraries that the book facilitates. Subsequent editions, published after Norden's death, added miniature county maps in the bottom right corner of each table.[38] Despite its obvious limitations, the book was highly successful, and was without doubt used by travellers who were willing to combine its imperfect information with oral advice from stage to stage. There is some evidence that it even became associated in the public imagination with the highways it so obviously does

---

[38]   *A Direction for the English Traviller* (1635, 1643).

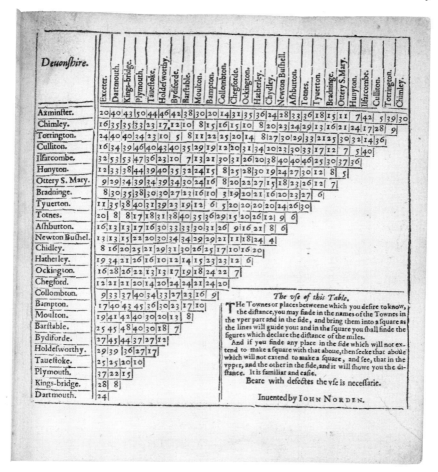

Deuonſhire.	Exceter.	Dartmouth.	Kings-bridge.	Plymouth.	Taueſtoke.	Holdeſworthy.	Bydiforde.	Barſtable.	Moulton.	Bampton.	Collombton.	Chegforde.	Ockington.	Hatherley.	Chydley.	Newton Buſhell.	Aſhburton.	Totnes.	Tyuerton.	Bradninge.	Ottery S.Mary.	Hunyton.	Ilfarcombe.	Culliton.	Torrington.	Chimley.
Axminſter.	20	40	43	50	44	46	42	38	30	20	14	31	35	36	24	28	32	36	18	15	11	7	42	5	39	30
Chimley.	16	35	35	33	23	17	12	10	8	15	16	15	10	8	20	23	24	29	13	16	21	24	17	28	9	
Torrington.	24	40	40	34	23	10	5	8	11	22	25	20	14	8	27	30	29	33	21	25	30	32	14	36		
Culliton.	16	34	39	46	40	35	29	19	12	20	31	34	20	23	30	33	17	12	7	5	40					
Ilfarcombe.	32	53	53	47	36	23	10	7	13	21	30	31	26	20	38	40	40	46	25	30	37	36				
Hunyton.	12	33	38	44	39	40	35	32	24	15	8	25	28	30	19	24	27	30	12	8	5					
Ottery S.Mary.	9	29	24	39	34	39	34	30	24	16	8	20	22	27	15	18	23	26	12	7						
Bradninge.	8	30	35	38	30	30	27	23	16	10	3	19	20	21	16	20	23	27	6							
Tyuerton.	11	35	38	40	31	39	23	19	12	6	5	20	20	20	20	24	26	30								
Totnes.	20	8	8	17	18	31	38	40	35	36	29	15	20	26	12	9	6									
Aſhburton.	16	13	13	17	16	30	33	33	30	31	26	9	16	21	8	6										
Newton Buſhel.	13	13	15	22	20	30	34	34	29	29	21	11	18	24	4											
Chidley.	8	16	20	25	21	29	31	30	26	25	17	10	16	20												
Hatherley.	19	34	21	26	16	10	12	14	15	23	23	12	6													
Ockington.	16	28	26	22	13	13	17	19	18	24	22	7														
Chegford.	12	21	21	20	14	20	24	24	21	24	20															
Collombton.	9	33	37	40	34	33	27	23	16	9																
Bampton.	17	40	43	45	36	30	23	17	10																	
Moulton.	19	41	42	40	30	20	13	8																		
Barſtable.	25	45	48	40	30	18	7																			
Bydiforde.	27	45	44	37	27	12																				
Holdeſworthy.	29	39	36	27	17																					
Taueſtoke.	25	25	20	10																						
Plymouth.	37	22	15																							
Kings-bridge.	28	8																								
Dartmouth.	24																									

The vſe of this Table.

THe Townes or places betweene which you deſire to know, the diſtance, you may finde in the names of the Townes in the vper part and in the ſide, and bring them into a ſquare as the lines will guide you: and in the ſquare you ſhall finde the figures which declare the diſtance of the miles.

And if you finde any place in the ſide which will not extend to make a ſquare with that aboue, then ſeeke that aboue which will not extend to make a ſquare, and ſee, that in the vpper, and the other in the ſide, and it will ſhowe you the diſtance. It is familiar and eaſie.

Beare with defeᵈts the vſe is neceſſarie.

Inuented by IOHN NORDEN.

Fig. 2.3 Distance table for Devonshire, from John Norden, *England: An Intended Guyde For English Travailers* (1625).

not list; in 1646, three years after the second edition was published, Richard Pollard, estate steward to Henry, Earl of Bath, recorded spending one shilling and sixpence in Exeter for 'a book of the highways in England'.[39]

While Norden's *Guyde* was ultimately superseded by tables derived from Ogilby, the model was adapted to that later era by John Adams, who

[39] *Devon Household Accounts, 1627–59: Part Two. Henry, Fifth Earl of Bath, and Rachel, Countess of Bath, of Tawstock and London, 1637–1655*, ed. Todd Gray (Exeter, 1996), p. 50.

Fig. 2.4 Detail from John Adams, *Angliae totius tabula cum distantiis notioribus in itinerantium usum accommodata* (1677).

published a map of the nation criss-crossed by hundreds of ruled lines showing the distance between one place and another (Fig. 2.4).[40] Adams appreciated the limitations of his work, especially when he was persuaded to add rivers but had no way of indicating the extent to which his ruled lines correlated with viable river-crossings. The model, however, proved extremely successful.[41] Three years later he published a weighty companion volume, *Index Villaris: Or, an Alphabetical Table of all the Cities, Market-Towns, Parishes, Villages, and Private Seats, in England and Wales.* This work lists places, categorizing them by country, hundred, latitude, longitude, 'Deanery, Rates, &c.', and has symbols denoting types of landowners, market-town status, and various other matters. It transforms the map, with its 780 listed places, into a container for new information, according with a contemporary drive, also witnessed by Ogilby, to catalogue and quantify the nation. Moreover, his acknowledgement of the fact that '*the face of the* Kingdom' has '*altered*' over time suggests a dynamic model of spatial organization (sig. π4v). Cartography, he therefore acknowledges, can only offer one intervention in the necessarily multifarious project of documenting spatial knowledge.

The fact that roads are not marked on Adams's map makes it an equivocal achievement. Despite the myriad lines of potential connection, the map in fact effaces actual routes and the knowledge of those who used and maintained them. Yet, unlike Ogilby's *Britannia*, the work is not constrained by hierarchized networks, nor by the paths followed by established postal services. The viewer is invited to imagine potential routes, within a spatial model which suggests that every place, however small or remote, is connected to every other place. No particular routes are prioritized; instead, it envisages a virtually limitless number of journeys, for an equally limitless number of reasons. This represents a conception of national space utterly at odds with that of Drayton, and those searching for meaning in the remnants of those solid and straight roads built by the Romans. Those roads suggested order, control, surveillance; to realists, such as Camden, they suggested also slave labour and the imposition of colonial authority. Adams smashes those structures, acknowledging instead an emergent regime of liberal humanism. However impractical, his map represents the era's boldest exercise in imagining an abstract space of quantifiable and documentable knowledge, and unfettered and unregulated movement. This will be the space, as Lefebvre demonstrates, of capitalism.[42]

---

[40] *Angliae totius tabula cum distantiis notioribus itinerantium usum accommodata* (1677). It was issued in a twelve-sheet and also a more manageable two-sheet format.
[41] Adams discusses his cartographical techniques in *Index Villaris* (1680), sig. π4r.
[42] *Production of Space*, esp. pp. 49, 266.

Adams peddled fantasies. Like contemporary commentators on rivers who followed lines on maps and imagined limitless acts of circulation, his spatial conceit is founded on a suppression of the more problematic local knowledges of roads and road networks. Indeed, at the same time that his maps were selling so well, other commentators were becoming increasingly aware of the fact that the existing road networks, and also the sixteenth-century regime of road-maintenance, was insufficient for the demand of the late seventeenth century. At the very time that knowledge of roads was being brought into circulation in a variety of ways, their condition in many parts of the country was deteriorating. In the age of Ogilby and Adams, however, we can trace the emergence of genuine debate about current and potential uses of the roads. While some commentators fulminated against the growth of inland transportation, mixing old prejudices with more topical complaints, an increasing number of writers reassessed the roads under the influence of the period's cultural preoccupation with the cause of economic improvement.[43] Like those who wrote on rivers at this time – and the lists overlap, since many people clearly saw the two issues as interrelated – these commentators wanted to bend the road system to contemporary needs.

Some impetus for change was coming from above. Gradually, commentators and legislators were grasping the fundamental point that a regime of parish-based labour, with its assumptions of local networks and communal obligations, was incompatible with the goal of improvement.[44] Moreover, there was an increasing acceptance of the fact that the existing system placed greatly uneven burdens on parishes, depending on their proximity to major national roads. There had been an effort in the Interregnum to alter the basis on which the roads were maintained, moving from a system of statute labour to one of taxation.[45] In the Restoration, while this act was repealed along with all other Cromwellian legislation, the tenor of highway law nonetheless shifted. Although as late as 1670 highway acts continued to rehearse the premise that the law existed to 'preserve' the roads from misuse and overuse, by 1691 the cause of 'the advancement of Trade' and 'increase of Wealth' was given equal weight.[46] Further, the first English turnpike act, passed in 1663, though quite limited in extent, experimented with a radical

---

[43] For an example, see *The Grand Concern of England Explained*.

[44] Cf. Greg Laguero, 'Infrastructures of Enlightenment: Road-Making, the Public Sphere, and the Emergence of Literature', *Eighteenth-Century Studies*, 29 (1995), 50.

[45] *An Ordinance For Better Amending and Keeping in Repair the Common High-Waies Within this Nation* (1654). On the implementation of this ordinance, see Webb and Webb, *Story of the King's Highway*, pp. 19–20; and Jackman, *Development of Transportation*, pp. 52–3.

[46] 22 Charles II, c.12; 3 William and Mary, c.12.

new model for funding roadworks, placing the financial demands on road users rather than local communities. Although by no means widespread until well into the eighteenth century, turnpikes acknowledged and legitimized through-traffic in a way that the sixteenth-century legislation, with its model of local networks centred on market-towns, did not. Other writers proposed still more radical schemes to fund road improvement. William Mather, 'a Late Surveyor of the Highways in Bedford', suggested a tax on the basis of the poor rate; others perceived a need to move more decisively away from parish-based models, imposing a uniform system of taxation and placing control of local structures under the hands of a 'Surveyor General'.[47]

The physical construction of roads also come under scrutiny. The 1555 model, based as it was on the maintenance of customary ways – the endless scouring of local networks assumed to be rooted in custom and history – could not accommodate, either in theory or practice, the changing patterns of road-use. The first known proponent of actually 'making' highways was Thomas Procter, a professedly 'simple man' who published a pamphlet in 1607 which contains an equally prescient argument for the creation of canals.[48] His text is even accompanied by designs for new roads, showing possible arrangements of timber frames, 'stones, gravel, or such like matter' (Fig. 2.5). But the suggestion that this could be accomplished within the existing model of parochial labour was hopelessly unrealistic. His proposal was that each parish could build half a furlong of road each year, which would stand unused until such time as they could be joined together, thus creating a network that would render any future work unnecessary. After Procter, the cause lay dormant until the latter decades of the century, when a number of writers argued more purposefully that abstract highways should be translated into reliable and identifiable roads. For Thomas Mace, it was a matter at once of regularization and civilization. To be 'put out of [one's] way', to be 'confound[ed]' by sprawling and indistinct roads, or to be forced into 'contesting for the way' with others, are for Mace symptoms of profound disorder.[49] His proposals, though less concrete than Procter's, are designed to give definition to roads and road users. Roads, therefore, should as much as possible 'be brought into *straight-lines*', just as a new law of travel should bring '*irregular* and *troublesome persons*' into 'an orderly way of *Civility* in their Travel' (p. 2).

---

[47] *Of Repairing and Mending the Highways* (1696), t.p.; E. Littleton, *A Proposal for Maintaining and Repairing the Highways* (1692), p. 3. Cf. Edward Chamberlayne, *Englands Wants* (1685), pp. 3–5.
[48] *A Worthy Worke Profitable to this Whole Kingdome* (1607), sigs. A3r, A2v.
[49] *Profit, Conveniency, and Pleasure, to the whole Nation* (1675), t.p., pp. 2–3.

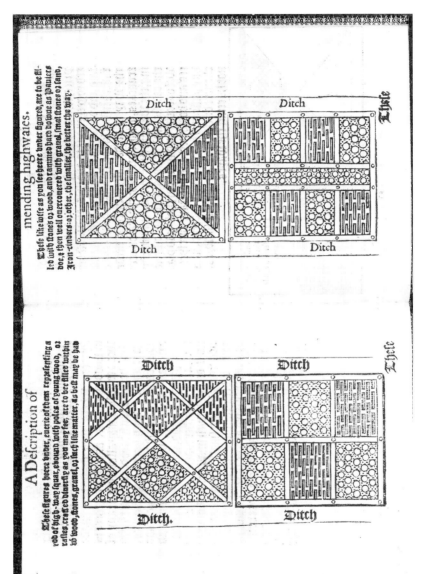

Fig. 2.5 Proposed road-building designs, from Thomas Procter, *A Worthy Worke Profitable to this Whole Kingdome* (1607).

Arguably the most thorough and cogent proposals of the period, however, were produced at the tail-end of the seventeenth century by a man who would, in the following decades, transform the literature of mobility. I will return to Defoe's *Tour thro' the Whole Island of Great Britain* in the Epilogue, as a way of reviewing the central developments traced throughout this book. Earlier in his career, however, Defoe addressed the matter of improving the highways in his *Essay Upon Projects* (1697). For him, meditation on the remains of Roman roads prompts a reflection on nationhood. Taken as 'a Civil Government', he declares, 'we must allow' that the Romans 'were the Pattern of the whole World for Improvement and Increase of Arts and Learning, Civilizing and Methodizing Nations and Countries Conquer'd by their Valour' (p. 72). Those roads, therefore, the remnants of which stand as 'tokens of their Grandeur and Magnificence', should inspire a spirit of emulation and industry. For Defoe, as for Mace before him, the goal of improvement was underpinned by a commitment to regularization. For a start, the hierarchy of roads should be clarified, so that the main post-roads are thoroughly improved, while decisions are made about which 'Cross-Roads, By-Roads, and Lanes' should be 'look'd after' and which 'may be wholly slighted and shut up, or made *Drift-ways, Bridle-ways*, or *Foot-ways*' (p. 96). Then it is necessary to clarify the distinction between roads and property. Defoe sets correct breadths for different categories of roads, and argues that the imposition of these standards will not only ensure sufficient room for traffic passing in each direction, but will also solve the problem of waste ground adjoining highways. For, while the concept of a highway remains abstract, and travellers have the right to stray from what there is of an established path when conditions are poor, 'a great deal of waste-Land [is] thrown in as it were for an Overplus to the High-way' (p. 79). Neither properly common nor usefully ownable, such land exists 'to no purpose' (p. 80). Consequently, a key element of Defoe's solution is to erect cottages 'At the end of every Two Miles, or such like convenient distances', and to grant tenancy of them to poor men who would become responsible for the quality and security of 'their' stretch of road. These tenants would be paid one shilling per week, and given the use of half an acre of land, reclaimed from the waste associated with the old highways (p. 99).

Defoe's vision involves the imposition of civility on space and populace alike. As a result of his central innovation, he claims, 'a Man might Travel over all *England* as through a Street, where he cou'd never want, either Rescue from Thieves, or Directions for his way' (p. 84). As in Mace's text, and as in so many of the texts to be considered in the next section, knowledge of one's way becomes a key index of spatial and civil order. Critically, that knowledge is figured as the property of the nation, rather than of individual communities; hence Defoe joins other critics of the time in suggesting the erection of signposts 'at every turning … for the Direction of Strangers' and to inform them of the distance to their destination (p. 101).[50] But Defoe's vision of civilized circulation comes at a price. The cottagers may facilitate mobility but are themselves effectively barred from it: transformed at the stroke of a pen from unsettled threats to the nation into agents of order, fixed in place for life. Moreover, Defoe borrows from Roman absolutism the idea of slave labour.[51] The heavy labour involved in building the roads, he suggests, should be assigned to criminals, as an alternative to hanging, transportation or whipping (pp. 91, 103). Indeed it would be 'a proper Work for Highwaymen': a suggestion that turns those who had become, by the late seventeenth century, key indices of disorder on the highways into agents of reform (p. 91). Not content with this, he proposes further 'an Agreement with the *Guinea*-Company to furnish 200 *Negroes*, who are generally Persons that do a great deal of Work' (p. 104).

Defoe's essay represents a curious blend of economic dynamism and social repression, fixing the problem of disorderly roads in part by fixing in place key categories of disorderly subjects. As a result, national space is civilized not just because roads open before the traveller like streets, but because travellers are implicitly defined by their status and purpose. His argument therefore typifies the fraught status of roads in economic and political discourse, right through to the end of the seventeenth century. For roads had always coupled a promise of connection with a threat of disorder. The legislative regime of the 1555 act, endorsed by subsequent legislators and underscored by social commentators such as Harrison, had sought to manage the anxiety of unruly mobility by privileging local networks and local knowledge. Yet this model was set in tension with ideas of national networks, from the fragmentary Roman roads with their suggestions of ancient cohesion, through to the codification of the post-road system in the seventeenth century. In this context, it is surely no coincidence that the most radical vision of connectedness is that of Adams's line-map, which effaces actual roads and their users. As I will demonstrate further in the following section, other kinds of texts confront more rigorously the cultural questions invoked by the figure of the common human subject on the road.

---

[50] Cf. Chamberlayne, *Englands Wants*, p. 36.
[51] The idea of employing vagrants as slave labourers on the roads also had a history in English law, proposed in 1547 by one of the most punitive of all vagrancy statutes, 1 Edward VI, c.3.

NEVER OUT OF THEIR WAY: COMMONERS ON THE ROAD

According to a proverb that may well have originated in the sixteenth century, a beggar is never out of his way.[52] This proverb, rehearsed in the pamphlet literature of the early modern period, situates the beggar as fundamentally placeless, moving through the country in a random and indiscriminate manner.[53] But, like so many proverbs, there is something altogether too comfortable about this model, situating the beggar as a person with no directions, and by implication no knowledge of the space through which he or she moves. At a time when many contemporaries were troubled by intensifying patterns of human and mercantile traffic on the roads, this stereotype represents an easy stigmatization of popular mobility. To be mobile and poor, it implies, is to be pointless. It also holds at bay an alternative representation, that I suggest is considerably more threatening to traditional models of social and spatial order, and that becomes increasingly apparent throughout the period. This is the commoner who knows his or her way all too well, and whose spatial knowledge as a result frustrates, undermines, or challenges dominant models of social surveillance and control.

The mobility of common men and women was perceived as one of the most urgent social problems of the late sixteenth and early seventeenth centuries. Although rural and urban communities had always been porous, accepting a degree of change related to the land-market, as well as the movement of certain categories of workers, such as apprentices and servants, the nature and volume of mobility increased markedly in the Elizabethan era. While this might once have been described as a phenomenon characteristic of those on the fringes of society, or even of an 'underworld' of beggars and vagabonds, it is now understood to have been socially endemic. Social historians have examined various different kinds of mobility, from the activities of professional traders, through those migrating from one place to another, to that of the genuinely displaced and homeless.[54] In particular,

---

[52] Morris Palmer Tilley, *A Dictionary of the Proverbs in England in the Sixteenth and Seventeenth Centuries* (Ann Arbor, 1950), B228.

[53] See, e.g., Greene, *The Second and Last Part of Conny-catching* (1592); reprinted in *The Elizabethan Underworld*, ed. A. V. Judges (London, 1930), p. 177.

[54] On professional traders (in contemporary terminology, 'pedlars', 'chapmen' and 'chapwomen'), see esp. Laurence Fontaine, *A History of Pedlars in Europe*, trans. Vicki Whittaker (Durham, N.C., 1996); David Rollison, *The Local Origins of Modern Society: Gloucestershire 1500–1800* (London and New York, 1993), pp. 45–63; Margaret Spufford, *The Great Reclothing of England: Petty Chapmen and their Wares in the Seventeenth Century* (London, 1984). On migration, see esp. *Migration and Society in Early Modern England*, ed. Peter Clark and David Souden (London, 1987); Malcolm Kitch, 'Population Movement and Migration in Pre-Industrial Rural England', in *The English Rural Community: Image and Analysis*, ed. Brian Short (Cambridge, 1992), pp. 62–84; *The Self-Contained*

researchers have shown how the Elizabethan discovery of the category of the 'labouring poor' challenged existing models of social order, which did not admit a place for people who were physically able yet still incapable of sustaining themselves within their 'home' environments.[55] Such people were forced into itinerant or semi-itinerant lives, and learned through experience to adopt attitudes towards labour that were more occasional and opportunistic than those of orthodox social discourses. Agricultural day-labouring at peak periods of demand, for instance, or unskilled work in rural and urban industries, could help an individual piece together a living. In contemporary terms, such a person was living by 'shift'.[56]

In this section I want to follow the gaze of contemporary legislators and commentators, focusing on forms of popular mobility that were considered morally dangerous and socially subversive. The law categorized such kinds of travel as vagrancy, while Elizabethan literature fashioned the related category of the rogue. Such categories offer valuable parameters for the present approach, since they represent efforts by a dominant culture to make sense of phenomena that were in fact more complex than these stereotypes allow.[57] While relatively few people were entirely and permanently uprooted from all coordinates of place, and while the identities of mobile commoners were generally more fluid and makeshift than categories such as 'vagrant' or 'rogue' allow, it is important to consider contemporary efforts to analyze and categorize. Crucially, vagrants and rogues were by definition homeless, characterized rather by their relationship to the road – the opposite of home – than to any location.[58] Hence the significance of their spatial knowledge. The extent to which a mobile commoner may know his or her 'way', I want to suggest, becomes a key focus of debate. The nightmare vision, in opposition to that of the proverbially placeless beggar, is glimpsed in a pamphlet by Thomas Dekker, which describes a type of rogue who knows very well the identities and locations, across the country, of gentlemen he can cheat. Dekker writes that he 'seems to have good skill

Village? The Social History of Rural Communities 1250–1900, ed. Christopher Dyer (Hatfield, 2006). On vagrants and the labouring poor, see esp. A. L. Beier, *Masterless Men: The Vagrancy Problem in England 1560–1640* (London, 1985); Steve Hindle, *On the Parish? The Micro-Politics of Poor Relief in Rural England c.1550–1750* (Oxford, 2004); Paul Slack, *Poverty and Policy in Tudor and Early Stuart England* (London, 1988).

55 Slack, *Poverty and Policy*, pp. 27–31.   56 Hindle, *On the Parish?*, pp. 15–95.
57 Cf. the approach in a number of recent works of cultural and literary analysis. See esp. William C. Carroll, *Fat King, Lean Beggar: Representations of Poverty in the Age of Shakespeare* (Ithaca, 1996); Patricia Fumerton, *Unsettled: The Culture of Mobility and the Working Poor in Early Modern England* (Chicago and London, 2006); *Rogues and Early Modern English Culture*, ed. Craig Dionne and Steve Mentz (Ann Arbor, 2004); Linda Woodbridge, *Vagrancy, Homelessness, and English Renaissance Literature* (Urbana and Chicago, 2001).
58 Turner, *Politics of Landscape*, p. 166.

in Cosmography, for he holds in his Hand a Map, wherein he hath laid down a number of Shires in England, and with small pricks hath beaten out a path, teaching how a man may easily ... travel from Country to Country, and have his Charges borne'.[59]

While the idea of a rogue's map is undoubtedly a product of an overly active authorial imagination, it highlights a concern that would shape debates about mobile commoners through to the end of the seventeenth century. I want to argue that, as these debates develop, it is possible to trace subtle yet substantial shifts in perceptions of popular mobility. These are evident even in the rogue pamphlets, which famously betray a degree of fascination with the facility and ingenuity of the placeless trickster. They become more evident still in the seventeenth century, as new kinds of texts reassess the functions of petty traders, such as pedlars and chapmen, and seek to bring their forms of spatial knowledge into alignment with that produced by cartographers. And, from the middle decades of the seventeenth century onwards, representations of religious nonconformity consistently focus on spatial mobility. Spiritual autobiographies, in fact, provide some of the period's most sophisticated images of purposefully itinerant commoners. These are not the only texts involved in rethinking the meanings of popular mobility – Patricia Fumerton, for instance, rests a compelling argument on a fundamentally secular autobiography, of a late-seventeenth-century sailor – but seem to me to be the most cogent and consistent in their attention to commoners on the nation's roads.[60] John Bunyan's allegorical representation of commoners navigating paths through a hostile landscape in *The Pilgrim's Progress*, which will demand attention at the end of this section, is perhaps the most striking of such efforts. However his peers view Bunyan's Christian, he maintains to the end a knowledge of, and commitment to, a true 'way'.

Rogue literature flourished at a historical moment at which the state was working to define the boundaries between licit and illicit mobility. Indeed, as others have demonstrated, there was undoubtedly a degree of reciprocal influence between literature and the law, as pamphleteers at once responded to the lead given by legislators and in turn helped to give shape to the image of the vagrant encoded in the law.[61] Though 'rooted in fact', therefore, these pamphlets lend substance to shadowy cultural anxieties; in A. L. Beier's

---

[59] *Lantern and Candle-light* (1608); reprinted in *Rogues, Vagabonds and Sturdy Beggars: A New Gallery of Tudor and Early Stuart Rogue Literature*, ed. Arthur F. Kinney (Amherst, 1990), p. 256.
[60] *Unsettled.*   [61] See Woodbridge, *Vagrancy*, p. 4.

words, rogue literature 'crystallized and reflected the discourses of official and learned opinion'.[62] Here, I want to focus on the ways in which rogue pamphlets represent mobility. The discussion begins with matters of definition, setting legal statements alongside satiric strategies of stigmatization, then considers the construction of key myths of spatial organization and knowledge among displaced commoners. While the rogue pamphlet became, over time, increasingly preoccupied with an urban landscape, and as a result somewhat detached from debates over vagrancy, its dominant image of the cannily peripatetic commoner challenged, and in certain respects subverted, orthodox cultural appreciations of popular mobility.

The Elizabethan state's efforts to distinguish between licit and illicit forms of mobility is evident in two related legislative projects. Firstly, the Elizabethan poor laws replaced traditional practices of giving to beggars and the indigent, which had been in decay since the Reformation, with a parish-based system of support. To be accepted as a member of a parish henceforth became critical, since it was this degree of placement that qualified an individual for relief. In extreme cases, parish officers moved poor men and women across parish boundaries, thereby reinforcing the stigma of place-lessness.[63] Those attempting to find work, and even to settle, in new places were subject to restrictions at once on 'inmates' lodging in established houses, and on the erection of new cottages.[64] Poor men and women on the road, whether temporarily or semi-permanently, were thus figured as potential drains on the resources of a town or village, who must as a result be defined clearly as outsiders. Secondly, a series of vagrancy statutes codified popular prejudices and fears. The 1598 act, which was perhaps the most influential of all, is remarkable for the effort it devotes to definition:

And be it also further enacted … That all persons calling themselves Schollers going about begging, all Seafaring-men pretending losses of their Shippes or Goodes on the Sea going about the Country begging, all idle persons going about in any Cuntry eyther begging or using any subtile Crafte or unlawfull Games or Playes … all persons that be or utter themselves to be Proctors, Procurors Patent Gatherers or Collectors for Gaoles Prisons or Hospitalles; All Fencers Bearewardes common Players of Enterludes and Minstrelles wandring abroade … all Juglers Tynkers Peddlers and Petty Chapmen wandring abroade; all wandering persons and common Labourers being persons able in bodye using loytering and refusing to worcke for suche reasonable Wages as is taxed or commonly gyven in suche Partes where

---

[62] Slack, *Poverty and Policy*, p. 104; A. L. Beier, 'New Historicism, Historical Context, and the Literature of Roguery: The Case of Thomas Harman Reopened', in *Rogues and Early Modern English Culture*, p. 99; Beier, *Masterless Men*, pp. 7–8.

[63] Hindle, *On the Parish?*, p. 319.   [64] *Ibid.*, p. 302.

such persons do or shall happen to dwell or abide ... shalbe taken adjudged and deemed Rogues Vagabondes and Sturdy Beggers.[65]

The language here, though often vague, repeatedly invokes images of wilful placelessness; vagrants are defined by 'wandering' and 'loytering', or 'refusing to work for ... reasonable wages'.[66] Yet the motivation to categorize is fundamental, as the act constructs a rough taxonomy of those who *'shalbe taken adjudged and deemed* Rogues Vagabondes and Sturdy Beggers'. Significantly, some of these categories are, by definition, not necessarily purposeless and indigent; paradoxically, in fact, this brief list, including pedlars, tinkers and players, generally categorizes people according to types of work being undertaken. Yet they all accord with the act's project to distinguish between the placed and the placeless: those who belong within local communities, and therefore fit into wider models of regional and national order, and those who are 'removed from the social networks that generate identity'.[67] While it would be futile to argue that none of those categorized as vagrants was actually involved in activities that we would recognize as criminal, such as theft or fraud, the point of the acts was to create a new category of criminality. Henceforth, as Paul Slack argues, 'vagrants and idle paupers' were widely represented 'as the complete obverse of all that was acceptable'.[68] To be placeless was a crime.

The authors of early rogue pamphlets saw themselves as contributing to this project of social distinction. Texts such as Thomas Harman's *A Caveat for Common Cursitors Vulgarly Called Vagabonds* (1566), insist on their documentary status, and frame for this purpose a kind of journalistic discourse heavy with narratives of personal experiences. Harman, who did more than anyone else to shape the genre of rogue literature, also did his best to introduce a new term to define illicit mobility. In place of 'vagabond' or 'vagrant' he proposes the word 'cursitors', which he defines as 'runners or rangers about the country, derived of this Latin word *curro*'.[69] Although this may in part be understood as simply a pedantic effort to Latinize common speech, it also serves to underscore the fundamental concern with forms of mobility that are perceived to be random or untraceable. Cursitors, the text repeatedly reminds its reader, 'wander', and they do so 'wilily', 'wretchedly' and 'wickedly' (pp. 109, 115, 121). They 'range about all the coasts' (p. 110).

[65] 'An acte for the punyshment of rogues, vagabondes and sturdy beggars' (39 Elizabeth c.4), in *Tudor Economic Documents*, ed. R. H. Tawney and Eileen Power, 3 vols. (London, 1951), II.355.
[66] Hindle, *On the Parish?*, p. 308.　　[67] Sullivan, *Drama of Landscape*, p. 175.
[68] *Poverty and Policy*, p. 25.
[69] *A Caveat for Common Cursitors*; reprinted in *Rogues, Vagabonds and Sturdy Beggars*, p. 113.

These forms of popular mobility are carefully contrasted to legitimate labour; Harman writes that cursitors, 'not minding to get their living with the sweat of their face, but casting off all pain, will wander, after their wicked manner, through the most shires of this realm' (p. 116). To be a vagrant, therefore, is to be avoiding labour. Here is surely one source of the image that becomes popular in seventeenth-century drama, of the vagrant or beggar whose life takes the form of extended holiday.

Harman also highlights the threat of cursitors by juxtaposing their criminal wandering with legitimate forms of localized mobility. Underpinning the book, as Elizabeth Hanson argues, is 'an ethic of neighborliness', evident especially in its consistent idealization of settled rural communities. Significantly, then, it is the business of these communities that Harman's cursitors commonly target.[70] At 'fairs and great markets' they 'lie and linger in highways' and 'bylanes', and assault those who are purposefully travelling those roads (p. 117). 'Yea, if they meet with a woman alone riding to market, either old man or boy, that [they] well knoweth will not resist, such they filch and spoil' (p. 115). As demonstrated above, in the spatial vision of the 1555 Highways Act, endorsed by conservative commentators throughout the period, roads were fundamentally local resources. Hence travel by local people along local roads for the purposes of localized economic exchange was always accepted as a way of strengthening, rather than undermining, traditional social structures. Harman's text is therefore conventional in its valorization of these practices, and canny in its contrasting of them with the uncharted paths of unplaced outsiders. Suitably, his image of a nation cleansed of cursitors also centres attention on legitimate traffic: 'then shall we surely pass by the highways leading to markets and fairs unharmed' (p. 110).

In a number of pamphlets, the threat posed by mobile commoners is accentuated by suggestions that they may be structured into elaborate networks. Random wandering is one thing, but an organized society with its own occult knowledge of the nation represents another degree of threat entirely. Harman's *Caveat* is merely suggestive in this regard, noting the existence of 'certain houses in every shire' which welcome rogues rather than 'honester men' (p. 117). Subsequent writers elaborated upon such suggestions. Greene, for instance, describes the transportation of stolen horses along established routes across the country.[71] Dekker claims that the 'fraternities' of rogues have a network of 'lodgings' across the country, which stand

---

[70] Elizabeth Hanson, *Discovering the Subject in Renaissance England* (Cambridge, 1998), pp. 100–1.
[71] *The Second and Last Part of Conny-catching*; reprinted in *Elizabethan Underworld*, p. 154.

'for the most part an equal distance one from another'. When any of their number commits a robbery, they immediately travel 'twelve miles at the least' to a safe house, thus avoiding detection within the space of a legitimate rural community. He concludes: 'So that what way soever these night-spirits do take after they have done their deeds of darkness, they know what pace to keep, because, what storms soever fall, they are sure of harbour, all their journeys being but of one length.'[72] Other studies of rogue pamphlets have noted the way in which they create 'shadow structure[s]' which mimic the authorized organizations and hierarchies of contemporary society.[73] Yet it has not hitherto been recognized that these structures have a spatial dimension, which shadows contemporary efforts to chart national networks for authorized forms of transportation. Dekker's nefarious houses, positioned roughly twelve miles apart, are thus darkly akin to inns marking stages along the nation's principal highways. Crucially, though, knowledge of these networks is unavailable to those who use the roads legitimately.

In Dekker's *O Per Se O*, the perception of occult networks is epitomized by an extended description of a rogues' fair, held at Deerhurst in Gloucestershire. Although the account of 'Durrest Fair' is presumably a complete fabrication, Dekker creates a seductive illusion of fact. At this fair, none of the traders is honest and none of the transactions is legitimate:

> None here stands crying, 'What do you lack?' for you can ask for nothing that is good, but here it is lacking. The buyers and sellers are both alike, tawny and sun-burned rascals, and they flock in such troops, that it shows as if Hell were broke loose. The shopkeepers are thieves, and the chapmen rogues, beggars and whores; so that to bring a purse-full of money hither were madness, for it is sure to be cut.[74]

Comedy serves here as a strategy of containment. While most fairs attracted fringe elements of beggars and petty criminals, Dekker imagines Deerhurst as a simple inversion of an authorized culture of exchange. At this fair, therefore, there is no need to worry over the distinction between an honest shopkeeper and a thief, a chapman and a rogue. Yet the text registers, nonetheless, profound anxieties about the movements of commoners. The rogues share money, discuss 'how the world goes abroad', 'enact … orders for fresh stealing of clothes', and arrange future meetings.[75] Above all,

---

[72] *O Per Se O* (1612); reprinted in *Elizabethan Underworld*, pp. 177, 379.
[73] See esp. Woodbridge, *Vagrancy*, p. 6; and Karen Helfand Bix, '"Masters of Their Occupation": Labor and Fellowship in the Cony-Catching Pamphlets', in *Rogues and Early Modern English Culture*, pp. 171–92.
[74] *Elizabethan Underworld*, pp. 368–9.   [75] *Ibid.*, p. 369.

therefore, the invention of the rogues' fair admits a fear of unchecked and unknowable circulation: of goods, money, information and individuals.

As evidenced by Dekker's text, rogue literature is founded on a desire to expose occult forms of knowledge, thereby asserting control over the threatening and unknown. The pamphlets are preoccupied with forms of verbal and physical disguise. The dictionaries of 'beggars' cant' which become characteristic of the genre, all of which derive as much from the Elizabethan work of John Awdeley and Harman as from any actual engagement with rogues, purport to translate a language which defines their unplaced community. Similarly, authors are drawn repeatedly to scenes in which fraudulent beggars, and others guilty in various ways of counterfeiting identities, are disrobed.[76] In spatial terms, the project of the rogue pamphlet is to distinguish between licit and illicit mobility. This parallels various state initiatives, such as the use of badges to distinguish legitimate and properly settled paupers, the issuing of passports to those with good cause to be on the road, and the foundation of Bridewell.[77] In the arena of discipline and punishment, it also parallels the use of stocks for vagrants. Not surprisingly, Harman endorses such efforts to arrest illicit mobility:

> A Stock's to stay sure, and safely detain,
> Lazy lewd Loiterers, that laws do offend,
> Impudent persons, thus punished with pain,
> Hardly for all this, do mean to amend.[78]

Harman's concentration on the stocks relishes the capacity of this particular instrument to 'safely detain' the wanderer, fixing the problem of the mobile poor by literally fixing them in place. As Woodbridge argues, the stocks signify that 'the crime of vagrants was mobility'.[79]

But rogue pamphlets are informed equally by an appreciation of limitations on the project of revelation and placement, due in part to the material conditions of print culture itself. The stocks were a temporary punishment, merely retarding an individual's mobility for a matter of hours or days. Likewise, the pamphleteers repeatedly express concern at the ways in which rogues might resist or evade the state's project of stigmatization, using arts of performance and deceit. They even had a word, supposedly taken from the rogues' cant, for a man who forged passports, thereby

---

[76] The classic instance is Harman's narrative of the exposure, through physical stripping, of Nicholas Jennings (*Caveat*, pp. 130–2). On this case, see Beier, 'New Historicism'.

[77] Hindle, *On the Parish?*, pp. 433–45; Beier, *Masterless Men*, pp. 146–70; Robert Jütte, *Poverty and Deviance in Early Modern Europe* (Cambridge, 1994), pp. 158–65.

[78] *Caveat*, p. 153.   [79] *Vagrancy*, p. 55.

turning vagrants into legitimate travellers; 'A Jarkman', according to
Awdeley, 'is he that can write and read, and sometimes speak Latin. He
useth to make counterfeit licenses which they call "Gibes," and sets to Seals,
in their language called "Jarks".'[80] Language and learning, therefore, are
exposed as manipulable and potentially unreliable. In turn, this realization
transformed the business of writing about rogues, especially by the 1590s
when most of the significant pamphlets were produced by professional
authors in London. As a number of important studies of rogue pamphlets
have demonstrated, such writers increasingly came to appreciate the extent
to which they were themselves complicit in an economy of performance and
mobility.[81] This obviously helps to explain the curious shifts of focus and
tone in the rogue pamphlets, from the objective detachment and moral
outrage of classic social complaint literature, to a mode of description that
positively revels in the facility of the coney-catcher. The 'official sobriety of
taxonomy', as Lawrence Manley argues, is supplanted by 'the gay deceptions
of fiction'.[82]

Given these emergent qualities of moral ambivalence and authorial
performativity, the rogue pamphleteers' representations of relations between
subjects and spaces become increasingly fraught and unstable. While Harman
may confidently identify popular mobility as a crime, in subsequent texts it
may equally signify a form of success within a freshly fluid economy. Hence
Thomas Nashe, whose stylistic innovations did so much to galvanize a
generation of pamphleteers, creates a protagonist, in *The Unfortunate Traveller*,
who at the end of the text cheerfully listens to a moralized exhortation
against (foreign) travel, then blithely continues with his journeys.[83]
Moreover, in many of the later rogue pamphlets, physical mobility is
subordinated to qualities of performativity and trickery, demonstrated
within the mercantile environment of London. Greene, for example, who
virtually ignores 'the more visible half of the tradition, vagabondage',
constructs narrative after narrative in which countrymen are cheated out
of their money by urbane coney-catchers, whose performative identities are
shaped in the image of their environment.[84] Their ability to remain
unidentifiable indicates a quality of placelessness that inheres even within

---

[80] *The Fraternity of Vagabonds* (1561); reprinted in *Rogues, Vagabonds and Sturdy Beggars*, p. 93. Cf.
Harman, *Caveat*, p. 134.

[81] See esp. Jean-Christophe Agnew, *Worlds Apart: The Market and the Theater in Anglo-American
Thought, 1550–1750* (Cambridge, 1986), pp. 63–9; Lawrence Manley, *Literature and Culture in Early
Modern London* (Cambridge, 1995), pp. 341–55.

[82] Manley, *Literature and Culture in Early Modern London*, p. 343.

[83] Nashe, *'The Unfortunate Traveller' and Other Works*, ed. J. B. Steane (Harmondsworth, 1972).

[84] Manley, *Literature and Culture in Early Modern London*, p. 348.

the geographically delimited space of the city. In *The Black Book's Messenger*, Greene centres attention on the highwayman – who would emerge in time as a heroic heir to the rogue – framing an entire pamphlet as a supposed criminal biography.[85] Often represented as a man of relatively high social status with a base in the city, the highwayman exploits a superior knowledge of the roads, overpowering naive countrymen. Suitably, when Richard Head revived the rogue tradition in the Restoration, marrying it with a continental picaresque tradition, his hero moves from a life as a vagrant and fraudulent beggar through to that of a highwayman.[86]

Dekker followed the trend towards city-based rogue literature, in pamphlets such as *The Belman of London* and *The Gull's Horn-Book*. In his pamphlet *1603. The Wonderfull Yeare*, however, he translates the Elizabethan image of the rogue into a new context, which allows him to concentrate afresh on issues of popular spatial knowledge. Indeed here he represents the figure of the unsettled commoner in ways that I believe may help, by way of a conclusion to my discussion of the rogue pamphlet, to clarify its treatment of popular mobility. Although *The Wonderfull Yeare* is actually several different things at once, in part it is the first of Dekker's plague-pamphlets.[87] As such it reflects consistently upon the meanings of place and community. *The Wonderfull Yeare* consistently rails at those who choose to flee the city – particularly those who are wealthy enough to be able to do so – rather than staying to support their neighbours. Though he does not understand the cause of plague, Dekker, like many of his contemporaries, perceives clearly enough that the poor suffer more acutely from it than the rich. Narrative after narrative within the text's journalistic framework demonstrates at once the folly of the 'runaways' and the residual bonds of place. In one instance, a man is refused a bed in a rural inn when he contracts the plague, and dies on the road, comforted only by another Londoner he encounters who is himself 'returning (like Æneas out of hell) to the heaven of his owne home'.[88] Their encounter provides an emblem of civic community, reminding the reader of what the dying man has chosen to abandon. In due course the returning Londoner buries the plague-victim, then returns to the city in order to resituate the dead man in a social context, as he brings his clothes and the news of his death to his family.

---

[85] Reprinted in *Rogues, Vagabonds and Sturdy Beggars*, pp. 187–205.
[86] *The English Rogue* (1665). This popular book expanded in subsequent volumes; however, the degree of Head's own involvement in this process is unclear.
[87] Dekker, *The Plague Pamphlets*, ed. F. P. Wilson (Oxford, 1925).
[88] *1603. The Wonderfull Yeare* (1603), sig. E1v.

But this idealized model of community does not hold. Notably, the worthy traveller himself dies the next day, having contracted the plague in the course of his act of charity. Moreover, the text's overt argument is undermined by other narratives, such as that which centres on another citizen who dies in an alehouse in a 'Countrey Towne'. While none of the locals is prepared to take the forty shillings offered to bury the man's corpse, an 'excellent egregious Tinker' passing through the town accepts the task for a quarter of that sum. If the narrative initially suggests a man being duped, however, it soon turns in the tinker's favour:

But the Tinker knowing that wormes needed no apparell, saving onely sheetes, stript him starke naked, but first div'de nimbly into his pockets, to see what livings they had, assuring himselfe, that a Londoner would not wander so farre without silver: his hopes were of the right stampe, for from out of his pockets he drew a leatherne bagge with seven poundes in it: this musicke made the Tinkers heart dance: he quickely tumbled his man into the grave, hid him over head and eares in dust, bound up his cloathes in a bundle, & carying that at the end of his staffe on his shoulder, with the purse of seven pounds in his hand, backe againe comes he through the towne, crying aloud, Have yee any more Londoners to bury, hey downe a downe dery, have ye any more Londoners to bury.[89]

The tinker's engagement with the unnamed country town is opportunistic and speculative. Against the weight of a text which otherwise extols values of placement, he represents a counter-discourse that posits communities as socially closed and economically stagnant. Fear of the plague is figured, in this discourse, as fear of risk. By contrast, he who accepts the brute fact of death, with all its potential to erase identity and render meaningless attachments to people and places, profits and continues on his way. While he may not express any obvious direction, his travel is by no means purposeless. Instead, it bespeaks a speculative engagement with space, founded on profoundly unsettling popular forms of knowledge.

The tinker was one of a number of occupations in early modern England defined by mobility. In Chapter 1 I discussed the figure of the waterman, a type routinely stigmatized as placeless. Now I want to consider those whose work involved travelling the roads of the nation, people such as tinkers, pedlars, chapmen and chapwomen. Harman was equivocal about pedlars, concluding only that since they 'seek gain unlawfully against the laws and statutes of this noble realm, they are well worthy to be registered among the number of vagabonds' (p. 134). In his judgement he was merely echoing the

---

[89] *1603. The Wonderfull Yeare*, sigs. F1r–F3r.

vagrancy act of 1572, the position of which was reiterated (as noted above) in 1598. And even when these categories of workers were omitted from vagrancy legislation, in 1604, they continued to suffer from legal harassment and popular suspicion. They were included in a list of 'rogues and vaga-bonds' published in a manual for constables as late as 1692, Gregory King classified them as 'vagrants' when calculating the nation's population in 1696, and social historians have demonstrated the daily risks they faced from officious authorities.[90] Despite this shadow of distrust, however, representations of these mobile workers, and particularly those involved in the transporta-tion and marketing of consumer goods, were gradually transformed. I want to suggest, in particular, that a cluster of Restoration texts designed for the use of chapmen and chapwomen seeks to align popular and elite forms of knowledge, situating the mobile trader in a landscape which was in the process of being reconceived by cartographers and economic theorists.

As the most visible manifestations of nascent forms of mercantile exchange, pedlars, chapmen and chapwomen inevitably attracted suspicion and hostility. At a time when transportation of goods on rivers was, for all its potential value economically, relatively uncommon, and the sight of wheeled vehicles on the roads was rare, most mercantile traffic was organ-ized on a very small scale. These petty traders generally worked independ-ently, and while some kept a horse or two many more simply carried packs on their backs. Crucially, their activities cut across what conservative commentators, such as Harrison and Harman, accepted as legitimate prac-tices of exchange.[91] Such writers, as demonstrated above, perceived the exchange of goods as a fundamentally localized process, centred on the market-town and supplemented by specialized fairs. Hence the valorization, in both social commentary and Tudor legislation, of travel to and from markets. But processes of marketing were becoming infinitely more com-plex than that; indeed, as against the Tudor ideal, marketing was being loosened from constraints of place. Notably, agricultural produce was increasingly being traded privately, beyond the open marketplace, and subsequently transported out of local regions. Meanwhile, consumer goods, including such items as 'laces and ribbons, buttons and thread',

---

[90] Robert Gardiner, *The Compleat Constable* (1692), p. 32 (see also Edmund Wingate, *The Exact Constable* (1680), p. 69); King, *Two Tracts*, ed. George E. Barnett (Baltimore, 1936), p. 18; Beier, *Masterless Men*, pp. 89–90; Spufford, *Great Reclothing*, pp. 9–10.

[91] Cf. Linda Woodbridge, who argues that pedlars were suppressed because they represented a threat to 'competing commercial interests: fairs, weekly markets, trade guilds, shops, and ultimately Goldsmith's Row and the Pawn' ('The Peddler and the Pawn: Why did Tudor England Consider Peddlers to be Rogues?', in *Rogues and Early Modern English Culture*, p. 151).

and also cheap books and broadsheet ballads, were being circulated across the country in ever-increasing volume.[92] Together, the labours of England's vast array of petty traders transformed their nation, underpinning the development of what economic historians have identified as a consumer society.[93]

In this context it is hardly surprising that, at least in the sixteenth and early seventeenth centuries, pedlars, chapmen and chapwomen were regularly figured, at once in literature and popular discourse, as unnervingly mysterious. Though it is clear from historical research that most pedlars actually maintained homes and families, they were, for the duration of their journeys, displaced outsiders.[94] In England, the fear of difference was underscored by the fact that many of the petty traders travelling the roads were Scottish, and thus marked as cultural and even political outsiders.[95] Attacks on them seized on their apparent placelessness. For Sir Thomas Overbury, in the satiric succinctness of Jacobean character literature, a tinker 'Is a mooveable: for he hath no abiding place'.[96] He is reduced, in other words, to the status of a piece of personal property, or a marketable item; to have 'no abiding place' is to have no legitimate, identifiable position in society.[97] Inevitably, connections were also made between such mobile individuals and petty crime, particularly crimes of property. While there was unquestionably some foundation for such charges, since the loose body of pedlars always included some individuals living on the fringes of destitution, the association stood as a generalized strategy of stigmatization. As a result, and driven by an uncanny cultural logic, those involved in mysterious new forms of mercantile circulation become perceived as thieves, illicitly spiriting away items that belong in local places. Accordingly, representations of them commonly focus on the mysterious contents of their packs. One Tudor Justice of the Peace, for example, alleged that, 'beinge abroad they all in generall are receavers of all stolen things that are portable, as namely the Tynker in his Budgett, the pedler in his hamper, the glasseman in his baskett'.[98] In extreme circumstances, such lingering anxieties could breed paranoia. For instance, John Reynolds, one of the leaders of the Midlands Revolt of 1607, was 'a pedlar or tinker by trade, who became known as "Captain Pouch" because of the leather satchel which, he claimed, contained "sufficient matter to defend them against all comers"'. Not surprisingly, the reality proved

---

[92] Spufford, *Great Reclothing*, pp. 5–6.
[93] *Ibid.*, esp. pp. 18–20; Neil McKendrick, *et al.*, *The Birth of a Consumer Society: The Commercialization of Eighteenth-Century England* (London, 1983), esp. pp. 86–8.
[94] Cf. Fontaine, *History of Pedlars in Europe*, p. 164.   [95] Spufford, *Great Reclothing*, pp. 27–8.
[96] *The Overburian Characters*, ed. W. J. Paylor (Oxford, 1936), p. 34.
[97] *OED*, sub 'movable', B 2–3.   [98] *Tudor Economic Documents*, II.343.

somewhat more mundane. 'On his apprehension', however, Reynolds' pouch 'was allegedly found to contain only a piece of mouldy cheese.'[99]

Literary representations lend shape to these anxieties. Woodbridge analyzes the remarkable early Jacobean play by Thomas Heywood, *If You Know Not Me, You Know Nobody*, in which the poor pedlar, Tawnycoat, confounds expectations of unreliability and criminality. Indeed Tawnycoat's honesty is implicitly contrasted with the dubious individualism of international merchants. The play, Woodbridge argues, 'confirms the peddler's function as a scapegoat whose criminalization drew public scrutiny away from his high-caste double, the high-flying international trader'.[100] Other instances, however, are less critical of the popular stereotype. Sir John Harington, for instance, wrote an epigram in which a pedlar accepts payment from a married woman in the form of sexual favours, and subsequently engages in a battle of wits in an effort to recoup his financial losses. Throughout the struggle, the husband, who has lost both materially and sexually, remains ignorant of the subtext of their negotiations. The poem suggests, therefore, that pedlars, like women, represent threats in need of containment.[101] Similarly, Shakespeare's Autolycus, the best-known of all literary pedlars, poses a range of associated threats to the rural community created in Act 4 of *The Winter's Tale*. Margaret Spufford, the foremost authority on seventeenth-century chapmen and chapwomen in England, praises the realism of Shakespeare's representation.[102] Yet Autolycus is indebted equally to cultural traditions, such as the rogue pamphlet, as he takes shape as not merely a petty trader but an opportunistic criminal: 'a snapper-up of unconsidered trifles', and a deft con-man in the company of rural simplicity (4.3.25–6). When he claims that he is 'proof against [the] title' of 'rogue', along with 'what shame else belongs to't', he delineates a subjectivity hardened to social and legal judgements (4.4.832–4). The fact that he unwittingly aids the comic resolution does not in any way redeem him, nor place him at the end within the play's reconstituted community. For all the play's undeniable festivity, he remains to the close an agent of individualism and transgression.[103]

Like the pedlars and rogues of Elizabethan literature and legislation, Autolycus wanders. Indeed when he sings the lines, 'And when I wander

---

[99] Steve Hindle, 'Imagining Insurrection in Seventeenth-Century England: Representations of the Midland Rising of 1607', *History Workshop Journal*, 66 (2008), 26.

[100] 'Peddler and the Pawn', pp. 158–66 (quote at p. 163).

[101] Harington, *The Most Elegant and Witty Epigrams* (1618), sig. I7r–v (book 3, no. 38).

[102] *Great Reclothing*, pp. 88, 145.   [103] Cf. Carroll, *Fat King, Lean Beggar*, pp. 170–1.

here and there, / I then do most go right' (4.3.17–18), he evokes at once the proverbial beggar, never out of his way, and the language of the Elizabethan vagrancy acts, which represent 'Tynkers Peddlers and Petty Chapmen wandring abroade'.[104] In reality, the majority of pedlars on the English roads were relatively well organized, both financially and spatially. They were bound into complex webs of credit with both their suppliers and their customers, and they followed regular routes.[105] It was not until the middle of the seventeenth century, however, that the negative stereotype of the wanderer was challenged by new images of a pedlar's movement, which acknowledge and reinforce this degree of organization. A pivotal figure in this respect is John Taylor, who in 1637 published *The Carriers Cosmographie*, a guide to the movements of 'carriers, waggons, foote-posts and higglers'. While this text implicitly distinguishes carriers – those who make a living from the transportation of goods and letters – from pedlars and others on the road in order to sell goods, Taylor's text typifies an emergent desire to make sense of the period's rapid increases in the circulation of goods and information. Moreover, as opposed to the more public developments in transportation, such as the emergence of the stage-coach and the foundation of a postal system, *The Carriers Cosmographie* concerns itself specifically with some of the smallest of operators. Indeed Taylor draws attention to one such type by making the *Oxford English Dictionary*'s first recorded use of the word 'higgler': an 'itinerant dealer; esp. a carrier or a huckster who buys up poultry and dairy produce, and supplies in exchange petty commodities from the shops in town'. He might equally have mentioned hawkers, badgers, broggers, woolmen, corn-carriers, or a host of other specialized traders.[106] Taylor's fundamental point is that the movements of such men and women, far from being random, follow patterns that can be traced and tabulated. To use the conceit of his text's title – which invokes cosmography, the most comprehensive of all forms of cartographic and written description, founded on assumptions that the entire universe can be brought within the realm of human knowledge – their movements have meaning. They are mappable.

---

[104] *Tudor Economic Documents*, II.355
[105] Fontaine, *History of Pedlars in Europe*, esp. pp. 73–93.
[106] A hawker was 'A man who goes from place to place selling his goods'; a badger was 'One who buys corn and other commodities and carries them elsewhere to sell; an itinerant dealer who acts as a middleman between producer (farmer, fisherman, etc.) and consumer'; a brogger was 'An agent; a jobber'; a huckster was 'A retailer of small goods, in a petty shop or booth, or at a stall' (*OED*). On the definition and activities of such types, see esp. Ray B. Westerfield, *Middlemen in English Business Particularly Between 1660 and 1760* (New Haven, 1915; repr. New York, 1968).

In the latter decades of the seventeenth century, the cultural project to reposition the peripatetic trader within the landscape gathered pace. This was underpinned by a range of practical developments, particularly in the distribution of consumer items. For instance, some producers of such goods were now employing travelling traders directly, so as to ensure methodical lines of distribution. These workers became known as 'Manchester men'.[107] Moreover, the national postal system was extended, and from 1689 included a number of 'cross-posts' that did not involve passage of an item through London.[108] Such innovations at once accustomed contemporaries to the idea of regular and methodical systems of transport, and imprinted newly refined networks of trade and communication onto the land. A wider cultural effort to bring the hitherto occult knowledge of the pedlar into alignment with the elite knowledge of Ogilby and his peers, meanwhile, may be traced through a range of cheap descriptive and cartographical works. As noted above, recent scholarship on Ogilby has stressed the elitism of his weighty *Britannia*, and has sought to rebut assumptions that it was used with any regularity by travellers.[109] But such arguments fail to consider various efforts, in the years immediately after the publication of the *Britannia*, to translate it into smaller and cheaper formats. Ogilby drew attention to this himself, bemoaning in one publication the 'careless' plagiarism of his work.[110] Yet he also contributed to it: either willingly or, as he claimed, in a grudging effort to forestall the pirates. His *Itinerarium Angliae* (1675) publishes the *Britannia's* maps without its prose itineraries, although this remains a relatively weighty volume. *Mr. Ogilby's Tables of his Measur'd Roads* (1676) and *Mr. Ogilby's Pocket Book of Roads* (1679), by comparison, tabulate journeys along major roads, but do not include maps. The latter specifically draws attention to the question of cost, as the man who revised Ogilby's work, William Morgan, states in a preface that, in order 'To make it more Useful and less Chargeable', the printer has 'added Several Roads and Reduced the price to 8d. a sheet'. A companion sheet-map of England was sold separately, at ten pence (sig. π2r-v), while Ogilby's *English Travellers Companion* (1676) represented the major networks in more abstract form, as lists of place-names arranged like the branches of a tree (Fig. 2.6). The intended use of these twinned texts was underscored by

---

[107] Fontaine, *History of Pedlars in Europe*, pp. 92–3; Westerfield, *Middlemen in English Business*, pp. 313–14.
[108] Westerfield, *Middlemen in English Business*, p. 365.   [109] See above, pp. 81–2.
[110] *Mr. Ogilby's Tables of his Measur'd Roads* (1676), sig. a1v. For an example of a work heavily indebted to Ogilby – presumably the kind of text he had in mind when complaining about imitators – see W. H., *Infallible Guide to Travellers* (1682).

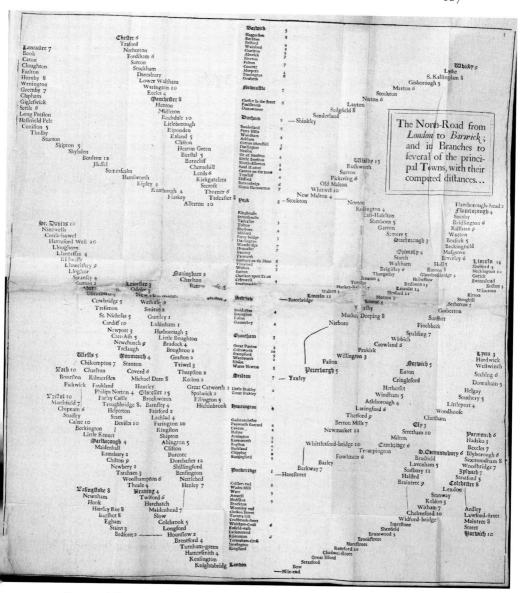

Fig. 2.6 'The North Road from London to Barwick', from John Ogilby, *English Travellers Companion* (1676).

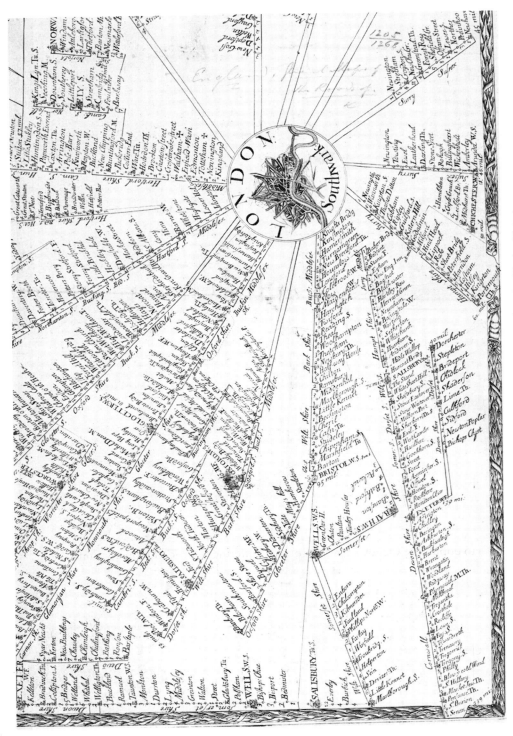

Fig. 2.7 Detail from William Berry, *The Grand Roads of England* (1679).

Morgan in the preface to a fresh edition of the *Pocket Book of Roads* later in the century:

For it being next to impossible in a small Volume to lay down all the Roads that every man may have occasion to travel, because from one and the same place a thousand men may have a thousand several ways to go; therefore we have added the Map, that if you do not find in the Book the Road you would go, by finding in the Map the place where you are and whither you would go, you will easily see what Road will bring you thither.[111]

The very point of the book, he insists, is to facilitate the needs of individual purchasers. When he observes that 'a thousand men may have a thousand several ways to go', he calmly accepts the validity of each one of those 'ways', within a nation held together by human mobility.

   This translation of Ogilby's model into cheaper and more functional forms was furthered by a number of other contemporary cartographers. John Adams's *Angliae totius tabula* (1688), for example, is a national map that charts different categories of roads, and provides in the margins a list of towns and larger villages. Richard Carr's *A Description of all the Postroads in England* (1668) is roughly half the size of *Angliae totius tabula*, and claims to represent 'A perfect direction to travel all England by Post seven miles par houre, and five in the Winter, as you will find an order for it in all Post-houses'. In William Berry's similarly compact *The Grand Roads of England* (1679), meanwhile, the niceties of cartographical accuracy are subordinated more ruthlessly still to the imperatives of the cheap and simple format. Here the Exeter to Wells route runs from north to south along the lower left-hand margin of the page, in an effort to represent a common journey in an otherwise unused patch of the page (Fig. 2.7). As this strategy suggests, the niceties of latitude and longitude, and perhaps even the points of a compass, are of little significance to a traveller on the road. Ultimately, the extent to which these works, and others like them, were actually used by commercial travellers must remain unknown. Doubtless most such men and women continued to rely for directions on a combination of personal experience and advice from locals. Their achievement, however, is to popularize Ogilby's spatial economy, offering to the commoner visions of national networks that might be combined with their own, more specific, knowledge.

   These texts converge in turn with a range of cheap pamphlets that were specifically marketed to the mobile trader. Printed lists of English markets

---

[111] *Mr. Ogilby's and William Morgan's Pocket Book of the Roads* (1691), sig. A1v.

and fairs, by time and place, had been common enough from the time of Harrison, and therefore seem relatively conventional in a publication such as *Mr. Ogilby's Tables of his Measur'd Roads*.[112] Others perceived a value in more ambitious catalogues of spatial information. *A Book of the Names of all Parishes, Market Towns, Villages, Hamlets, and Smallest Places, in England and Wales* (1657), for example, though based on the reproduced distance-tables from Norden's *England an Intended Guide*, includes lists of places and gives their distances from London and shire towns. It is a work, it proclaims on the title-page, 'very necessary For Travoilers, Quartermasters, Gatherers of Breefs, Strangers, Carriers, and Messengers with Letters'.[113] Later in the century, the project of Taylor's *Carriers Cosmographie* was revived by *An Account of the Days of the Going out of all the Carriers, Waggoners, and Stage-coaches, that come to London, Westminster and Southwark, from all Parts of England and Wales also of Fairs and Roads* (1690). And in the Restoration, if not before, almanacs were marketed directly at petty traders. Probably the most successful, *The City and Country Chapmans Almanac*, was published in an annual run that lasted, at least, from 1684 to 1694.[114] It contains information about markets and fairs, as well as descriptions of post-roads, 'A Table of Interest for Several Sums of Money', another table for calculating prices according to quantities of an item, and a list of miscellaneous 'Things necessary for Chapmen to know'. The latter is composed mainly of information about quantities: of a barrel of ale, a ream of paper, a butt of wine, and so forth.[115]

It is possible to relate a text such as this to the contemporaneous projects of both the Royal Society and political arithmeticians such as Gregory King and William Petty. These projects were informed by developments in the collection, organization and storage of knowledge, across Europe, that helped to shape and define the early modern period.[116] As a result, England was by the beginning of the eighteenth century 'participating in a general "culture of fact"'.[117] It is also worth recalling that Ogilby himself set out – influenced by his own connections with the Royal Society – with ambitions to produce

[112] For Harrison's list, see *Description of England*, pp. 391–7.
[113] Norden's tables also remained in circulation in *A Direction for the English Traveller*, which was published in a series of editions between 1635 and 1677.
[114] Wing A1403A–A1411.
[115] This list summarizes the content of the almanac for 1685, published in 1684 (Wing A1403A). Cf. *The Chapmans and Travellers Almanack* (1693–5; Wing A1393–5); *The English Chapmans and Travellers Almanack* (1696–9; Wing A1651–5).
[116] See esp. Justin Stagl, *A History of Curiosity: The Theory of Travel 1550–1800* (Chur, Switzerland, 1995), pp. 95–153.
[117] Barbara J. Shapiro, *A Culture of Fact: England, 1550–1720* (Ithaca and London, 2000), quote at p. 5.

an encyclopaedic description of his nation, underpinned by an equally ambitious design for the collection of data, and that the *Britannia* represents only a fraction of this vision. In the present context, one might therefore argue that certain cultural imperatives concerning the organization of knowledge were reverberating downwards from the elite to the populace. Yet this would be an incomplete interpretation, for what was driving this movement with equal force was a desire to consolidate and document existing popular forms of knowledge. Not every pedlar in the country would have known every fact contained in *The City and Country Chapmans Almanac*; knowledge on the ground is inevitably more piecemeal than that. The text's function, however, is to gather localized strains of popular knowledge and place them in a coherent, national framework. By implication, this situates individual petty traders within national networks, positing their movements and actions as purposeful and economically logical. Though such people continued to suffer from a degree of popular suspicion and resentment in the course of their business, texts such as these contributed to a transformation of their significance. The organized trader of *The City and Country Chapmans Almanac* is far removed from the wandering pedlar of Elizabethan social and legal discourse.

Pedlars left few records of their experiences. There were no models to follow and no genres moulded to the task, even if an individual happened to have the ability and time to attempt it. Yet the documentation and justification of popular mobility emerges as an important, albeit not central, goal of another kind of text which also flourished in the second half of the seventeenth century. The wave of religious life-writing – spiritual biographies and, more importantly, autobiographies produced by and about dissenting commoners – consistently positions its subjects as purposefully and legitimately mobile. These texts transform, sometimes quite pointedly, existing stigmatized representations of itinerancy, and endorse popular and potentially transgressive forms of spatial knowledge. If patterns of early modern popular mobility typically produced, as Fumerton argues, a 'radically unsettled' and 'perpetually speculative subject', one critical achievement of spiritual autobiographies is to attribute meanings to these patterns.[118] Mobility may in fact be translated into a sign of a capacity to question orthodoxies and hierarchies, and to achieve a more fundamental settledness.

The history of religious dissent in England is in part shaped by challenges to the spatial discipline of the authorized Church. This issue could

---

[118] *Unsettled*, p. 51.

undoubtedly be traced back into Catholic times; here, however, it is worth acknowledging the extent to which the Protestant Church situated its subjects within a regime that had spatial, as well as theological and moral, determinants. Parish churches, at which attendance on Sundays was compulsory, and in which seating was arranged to encode local hierarchies, represented the intertwined religious and political authority of the national Church. Dissent, or merely degrees of dissatisfaction, might thus be registered by refusal to acknowledge the authority of these buildings. The simple act of 'gadding' to hear a sermon outside one's parish, for example, provided an important form of collective activity for the Elizabethan Puritan movement.[119] Itinerancy, meanwhile, was associated with non-conformity throughout the period. The Family of Love was initially propagated by an itinerant artisan, while Catholic priests sustained their religion by travelling in disguise between country houses.[120] Suitably, Martin Marprelate, in whose fictional name some of the most damaging Elizabethan pamphlets of religious critique were launched, was fashioned by his creators as a placeless observer of the nation's clergy.[121] In the following century, the massive social upheavals of the Civil War underpinned a fresh spread of radicalism, especially within the ranks of commoners in the parliamentary armies.[122] Significantly, subsequent efforts by Church and state to reassert order focused, among other things, on spatial discipline. The Five Mile Act of 1665 banned identifiable non-conformist preachers from residing within a comfortable gadding distance of settlements.[123] It branded them as outcasts from the space of religious community, thereby reaffirming the traditional association of settledness and conformity.

Religious life-writing, from the 1640s onward, consistently subverted these orthodoxies. Increasingly, dissenters translated geographical mobility into a sign of spiritual enlightenment and reformist fervour. This pattern is suggested, for example, in *Anna Trapnel's Report and Plea* (1654), which narrates the author's journey from London into Cornwall. As well as including one of the first ever descriptions of travel in England by stage-coach, the text

---

[119] Patrick Collinson, *The Religion of Protestants: The Church in English Society 1559–1625* (Oxford, 1982), pp. 258–60.

[120] On Christopher Vittels, who probably worked as a joiner before taking to the road for the Familist cause, see Christopher Marsh, 'Christopher Vittels', *ODNB*; and on the wider movement, Marsh, *The Family of Love in English Society, 1550–1630* (Cambridge, 1994). A. G. Dickens, *The English Reformation* (Batsford, 1989), p. 425.

[121] See *The Martin Marprelate Tracts*, ed. Joseph L. Black (Cambridge, 2008).

[122] Christopher Hill, *The World Turned Upside Down: Radical Ideas during the English Revolution* (London, 1975), pp. 57–72.

[123] 17 Chas. II, c.2.

presents a remarkable record of Trapnel's prevarication before deciding upon the journey. In the period before her departure she prays, considers the implications of biblical texts, and receives divine visions of her path. Ultimately, she concludes, it is only 'Satan and my fearful nature' that combine to hold her back, and these she manages to overcome (p. 3). It is also evident, in a somewhat more exuberant register, in Abiezer Coppe's endorsements of itinerancy. In one anecdote, Coppe recalls giving all his money to a beggar, despite having 'between 8. or 9. miles more to ride ere I came to my journeys end: my horse being lame, the waies dirty, it raining all the way'.[124] The story, which gains power from its geographical specificity, imaginatively transposes the beggar and the itinerant radical, suggesting an inherent virtue in being propertyless. It is as though the beggar shares the spiritual purity of Coppe himself, just as Coppe embraces the social integrity that he perceives in poverty. Later in the same text he describes 'falling down flat upon the ground before rogues, beggars, cripples, halt, maimed; blind, &c kissing the feet of many, rising up againe, and giving them money'.[125]

Laurence Clarkson's autobiography, *The Lost Sheep Found*, pursues more rigorously the equation of physical and spiritual mobility.[126] In justification of his book, Clarkson states his aim 'to consider what variety of By-paths, and multiplicity of seeming realities, yet absolute notions, the souls of the Elect may wander and travel through, seeking rest, and yet find none till the day unexpected' (p. 3). The idea of travel, as indicated by this early usage, serves different purposes for Clarkson. As a youth, he recalls, he would walk up to ten miles from his home in search of a worthy sermon, while in his later years, as an itinerant preacher, he travelled across the country, though particularly in East Anglia and Kent. Yet travel was also spiritual and sectarian, as Clarkson describes his associations with different religious groups in the complex terrain of the 1640s. Hence he 'travelled into the Church of the Presbyterians', and later 'took my journey into the society of those people called *Seekers*' (pp. 7, 19). Along the way he invokes the Old Testament model of Jewish captivity; dissatisfied with the Baptists, he states that he 'was but still in *Egypt* burning Brick' and 'was minded to travel into the Wilderness' (p. 19).[127] Throughout the text, a strain of self-disgust for

---

[124] *A Second Fiery Flying Roule* (1649), p. 6. [125] *Ibid.*, p. 8.
[126] *The Lost Sheep Found* (1660) was published, like Clarkson's other works, under the name Laurence Claxton.
[127] Clarkson perhaps has in mind Exodus 1.14: 'And they made their lives bitter with hard bondage, in morter, and in brick, and in all manner of service in the field: all their service, wherein they made them serve, was with rigour.'

the mistakes of his past is underscored by the way in which he invokes existing models for the representation of itinerancy, such as the Elizabethan rogue pamphlets. Like these rogues, Clarkson is sexually promiscuous, sleeps rough in a 'Church-porch', and admits a governing desire to '[get] monies' through 'my subtilty of reason' (pp. 21, 24). Like the quintessential vagrant, he moves almost at random (p. 21). At one point, he writes, 'I set my Cane upright upon the ground, and which way it fell, that way would I go' (p. 21). For all the text's evident self-mockery, however, it retains throughout an underlying sense of Clarkson's life as a 'progress'; his experiences have provided him with a process of discovering the true path by the experience of repeatedly being 'out of the way' (e.g. p. 51). The point is underscored in the second half of the book, which shifts from narrative to theological discourse, constructed from a position of spiritual assuredness.

Clarkson's experiences of spatial and spiritual instability were shaped by the unprecedented upheavals of the 1640s and 1650s. There is in fact an undertone of detached bewilderment in his mapping of 'my travels through the seven Churches' of his nation, akin to that found in contemporary accounts of the New World (p. 34). By comparison, the rash of Quaker life-writing that emerges in the final few decades of the century is fundamentally concerned with the foundation, across the space of the English nation and beyond, of an institution. In these texts the moment of revelation, which is beyond question to the author, typically marks the prelude to a methodical, and often relentless, programme of travel in the interests of the Quaker movement. While this model may be observed in numerous works, it is worth concentrating at this point on the most influential of them all, George Fox's *Journal*. Fox's work, which was compiled from his notes after his death, has been criticized as shapeless.[128] It lacks the spiritual drama and self-scrutiny of other spiritual autobiographies, such as Bunyan's *Grace Abounding*, and seems incapable of prioritizing between the minutiae of journeys and more urgent matters of the spirit.[129] But such criticism misses the point that structure in the *Journal* is more spatial than spiritual. Although he makes a few trips outside of England, the book is shaped by the author's strong sense of nationhood, and his indefatigable efforts to construct a network connecting places and people throughout the land. While Fox makes clear at numerous points that this effort was paralleled by

[128] On the composition and publication history of Fox's *Journal*, see *The Journal of George Fox*, ed. John L. Nickalls (Cambridge, 1952), pp. vii–xii. Unless otherwise stated, references are to this edition.

[129] The book's formlessness is routinely noted by readers, with varying degrees of frustration. See, for instance, Paul Delany, *British Autobiography in the Seventeenth Century* (London, 1969), p. 107; Dean Ebner, *Autobiography in Seventeenth-Century England* (The Hague and Paris, 1971), pp. 134–5.

a similarly demanding programme of writing and publishing, the text's valorization of physical travels remains paramount throughout.[130]

Fox's representation of his travels balances a commitment to the 'impulsive journey', inspired by God, with an underlying method of geographical coverage. His *Journal* is consistent with other Quaker autobiographies in its description of scenes in which the subject claims to be unable to tell the secular authorities about his or her future movements. The Quaker, Fox's associate Edward Pyott asserts in a letter transcribed into the *Journal*, is 'guided to do the *Will* of *God* ... and we, in the *freedom* of his *Will* walk by the *Power*, either as it *Commands* or *Permits*, without any *Condition* or *Enforcement* thereunto by Men'.[131] Yet Fox's own journeys were concerned above all with the organization of the Quaker movement, which grew rapidly through most of his adult life, and depended upon a careful maintenance of records and correspondence.[132] Hence travel, however it was represented in texts, was in practical terms an indispensable vehicle of proselytization and administration. It was a way, in effect, of enacting the 'state within a state' which the Quakers created.[133] Fox, who unquestionably perceived himself as a central figure within the movement, felt compelled to demonstrate these structures and connections in the course of his travels. A comment in 1656, for example, sets into perspective his more than usually frenetic mobility of the preceding months: 'And after this time, when I was at liberty [out of Launceston gaol], I was moved to go over most parts of the nation, the Truth being spread up and down over the nation' (p. 280). Inspiration is fused with method here; the divine directive is essentially to find a way of achieving maximum geographical and social coverage of England. The methodical nature of such journeys is typified by his visits to 'the Land's End' in Cornwall, where 'an honest fisherman was convinced' (p. 363; cf. p. 445). As it has for countless travellers and tourists over the centuries, Land's End signifies for Fox the natural limit to a journey through England. His own presence there asserts the existence of a network linking the fisherman at the western edge of the land with thousands of other Quakers in towns and villages across the country.

If the *Journal* seems overly methodical, therefore, this is because method was fundamental to Fox. It records an itinerary of his travels, from one place to another, as though inviting a reader to map his extensive coverage of the

---

[130] On the use of print by Fox and the Quaker movement, see further Kate Peters, *Print Culture and the Early Quakers* (Cambridge, 2005).

[131] This letter is not quoted in full in Nickalls's edition. See Fox, *Journal* (1694), p. 215.

[132] Craig W. Horle, *The Quakers and the English Legal System 1660–1688* (Philadelphia, 1988), pp. 1–18.

[133] Horle, *Quakers and the English Legal System*, p. 15.

land. When he reaches a settlement, his most common actions are either to disrupt a service in the 'steeple-house', thereby confronting the authority of the established Church in its own base, or to arrange a meeting in his inn or alehouse. Buildings held no special significance for Fox; therefore inns, in which he purchases the use of space and defines himself unashamedly as one passing through, marginal to the physical community of the particular town or village, offered entirely appropriate spaces in which to evangelize and lend some definition to the Quaker movement.[134] Fox is keenly aware of popular connections made between Quakers and rogues. If the period's legislation did not necessarily encourage this equation, nor did it discount it, and Quakers were commonly imprisoned, stocked or whipped on a range of pretexts.[135] Hence he attacks those who 'have numbred them, who are *honest Men, Godly Men, holy Men,* Men that *fear God,* among *Beggars, Rogues,* and *Vagabonds'.*[136] It is the corrupt authorities, he asserts, that 'give them the Names of *Vagabonds* and *Wanderers'.*[137] As the *Journal* demonstrates, in all its relentless detail, his own methodical journeys are in fact the antithesis of a vagrant's wandering. He has a purpose, at once spiritual and managerial, and a heavenly guide. On occasion he also mentions long distances covered in a day, either on foot or on horseback, as though he is concerned to underline the text's equation of travel with gruelling and legitimate labour.

Moreover, while Fox's text is fundamentally egocentric, positing travel as a matter of personal vocation, he is repeatedly drawn to defend the wider principle of a commoner's right to traverse the country. He carefully records instances when he was illegally refused service at inns, and demonstrates a pugnacious appreciation of his rights within them (e.g. pp. 77, 91). When asked by an innkeeper on one occasion to report to the village constable, according to the 'custom', Fox 'told them I should not go, for I was an innocent man, and that custom was for suspicious persons' (p. 94). Several years later he confronted a drunken innkeeper who insisted on drinking in Fox's chamber. When the man proved unresponsive to advice 'concerning his eternal good', Fox resorted instead to the law of inns, asserting that 'the chamber was mine for the time whilst I lodged in it', and calling for a key (p. 286).[138] Highways, meanwhile, are repeatedly declared as open and

---

[134] According to the customary practice of the time, Fox's meetings would have taken place, most often, in private dining rooms, over which he quite reasonably asserted a proprietary right, rather than the common dining-rooms which became standard only in the nineteenth century. (See Thomas Burke, *English Inns* (London, 1943), p. 14.)

[135] Horle, *Quakers and the English Legal System,* pp. 47, 142–3.   [136] *Journal* (1694), p. 203.

[137] *Ibid.,* p. 208.   [138] On the laws governing inns, see below, pp. 127–8.

public spaces, in accordance with the laws governing their use. He declares at one point, to a man trying to stop his passage along a road, that 'he ought not to stop us in the King's highway for it was as free for us as for them' (p. 522). For Fox and his fellow Quakers, in fact, freedom of conscience was inseparable from freedom of movement. As Edward Pyott wrote to Major-General Desborough in 1656, at a time when he and Fox were imprisoned: 'Much might be said as to the liberty of Englishmen to travel in any part of the nation, England being as the Englishman's house by the law, and he is to be protected in any part of it' (p. 265). This statement provocatively aligns laws of property with laws of the road, confronting in the process deep and longstanding prejudices against the peripatetic commoner. While religion is of course implicit in the statement, Pyott explicitly defines only a category defined by national identity: 'Englishmen'.

Bunyan, though his own life was altogether more settled than that of his Quaker contemporary, did more than any other person in the seventeenth century to popularize Fox's vision of unfettered mobility. His own auto-biography, *Grace Abounding*, is somewhat surprising in its locatedness. Indeed it demonstrates rather that what he coyly refers to as 'my calling', his work as a tinker, bore little relation to the aimless wandering of Elizabethan paranoia. While his occupation inevitably drew him into 'the country', as though following familiar territorial circuits, the narrative depicts a life firmly centred within Bedford.[139] His experiments in allegorical fiction, however, fused images of spiritual aspiration and social exclusion, realizing the biblical metaphor of 'the way' within the landscape of seventeenth-century England.[140] Hence his *Heavenly Foot-man*, which is now recognized as an early work, constructs a figure who is at once a Christian everyman and a commoner drawn from everyday life on the highways. Moreover, for Bunyan his placelessness and poverty are critical; 'I am apt to think sometimes', he concludes the text, 'that *more Servants than Masters, that more Tenants than Land-lords will inherit the Kingdom of Heaven*'.[141] In *The Pilgrim's Progress*, Bunyan famously expands upon this model, constructing a landscape that is more coherently allegorical but without allowing a reader to forget its alignment with contemporary England.

One small index to the relationship between topicality and allegory in *The Pilgrim's Progress* lies in the imperfect correlation between 'way' and

---

[139] *'Grace Abounding' with other Spiritual Autobiographies*, ed. John Stachniewski (Oxford, 1998), p. 16.

[140] The key biblical text for Bunyan in this respect was John 14.6: 'Jesus saith unto him, I am the way, the truth, and the life: no man cometh unto the Father, but by me.'

[141] *The Miscellaneous Works of John Bunyan*. Vol. V: '*The Barren Fig-Tree*', '*The Strait Gate*', '*The Heavenly Footman*', ed. Graham Midgley (Oxford, 1986), p. 177.

'king's highway'. While the former term is derived solely from the Bible, the latter draws in part upon resonances from contemporary legal discourse. Early in the second part of the book, when Christian's wife, Christiana, travelling with their children and her servant, Mercy, reaches the Slough of Despond, she despairs at its unrepaired condition: 'She perceived also, that notwithstanding the command of the King to make this place for pilgrims good; yet it was rather worse than formerly.' The narrator asks his informant if this could possibly be true. '"Yes," said the old gentleman, "too true. For that many there be that pretend to be the King's labourers; and that say they are for mending the King's highway, that bring dirt and dung instead of stones, and so mar, instead of mending."'[142] This allusion to the Tudor highway laws in *The Pilgrim's Progress*, which amplifies a reference in the first part of the book, is quite possibly a unique moment in English literature.[143] Indeed, as F. G. Emmison has commented, reflecting upon the definitive requirements of statutory road-maintenance in these laws, 'it is astonishing that this perennial and ubiquitous duty has left so little mark in contemporary literature'.[144] Here Bunyan turns the poor reputation of statute labourers on the roads to allegorical effect. Just as those working on the English roads – and the requirement to do so, in theory at least, covered all men – had done little more than simulate the part of true labourers, for over 100 years, to the manifest detriment of the roads, so those who merely observe the outward forms of Christianity are responsible for the erosion of the true Church from within.

Way and highway alike are figured as spaces of mobility. Of course, the way is not rendered with geographical consistency, and therefore frustrates readers who 'assume a Newtonian universe in which objects can be placed in a continuous grid of space and time'.[145] Though typically figured as 'straight and narrow', it must also be felt by the reader, if the book is to succeed, as a manifestation of the pilgrim's spiritual experience, rather than a linear route (p. 59). Yet the familiar terminology consistently, and creatively, invites the reader to draw connections with contemporary life. In particular, characters are sensitive to rights of movement on the king's highway. Christian, for example, warns Apollyon: 'beware what you do, for I am in the King's highway, the way of holiness' (p. 93). Later, Great-heart insists on the distinction between Grim's property and the 'King's

---

[142] *The Pilgrim's Progress*, ed. Roger Sharrock (Harmondsworth, 1965), pp. 233–4.
[143] Cf. pp. 46–7.
[144] '1555 and All That', 22. Emmison, however, discerns no references at all in imaginative literature.
[145] James Turner, 'Bunyan's Sense of Place', in '*The Pilgrim's Progress': Critical and Historical Views*, ed. Vincent Newey (Liverpool, 1980), p. 96.

highway', berating the giant for placing his lions in the way of the pilgrims (p. 269). On the basis of such instances, James Turner perceives the 'king's highway' as 'an idealized private estate in which the ragged and down-trodden pilgrim has "a privileged place"'.[146] His resort to a language of property, however, seems unnecessary given the legal status of the king's highway in Bunyan's England. The key point is that the highway may be claimed as a common space of authorized mobility, defined by its otherness to the exclusiveness and exclusions of property. The pilgrims are privileged as long as they continue their laborious and purposeful journeys; Grim's crime, meanwhile, is simply that he seeks to block their passage.

The highway also offers a vehicle for imagining an elect community in the process of defining itself. Mobility, figured as pilgrimage, is a condition of godly existence. As Philip Edwards suggests, 'Bunyan's use of the image of the pilgrim is deeply affected by the biblical phrase "pilgrims and strangers"'. In Hebrews 11.13, Paul refers to those who 'died in faith' as recognizing themselves as 'strangers and pilgrims on the earth', in search to the end of 'a country'.[147] To be a 'stranger', then, is to be displaced from the coordinates of home. In the terms of centuries of orthodox morality, as I have attempted to demonstrate throughout this section, a stranger is some-one without place and purpose, and therefore represents a fundamental threat to social and political order. Against the weight of this discourse, *The Pilgrim's Progress* provocatively associates placement and neighbourhood with hypocritical outward conformity and spiritual torpor.[148] To be settled is to be complacently inactive. By extension, property and temporal author-ity are hindrances to the true pilgrim; as Bunyan's famous marginal note reminds the reader, 'Sins are all lords and great ones' (p. 131). By contrast, estrangement and mobility are signs of godliness. Hence to be accused in Vanity Fair as 'a rogue', and consequently to be stocked, is translated into a sign of rectitude. The hypocrites perceive that true pilgrims must be stigmatized as rogues, and immobilized, in order to neutralize the threat that they pose to the practices and values of the Fair. The pilgrims' existence, and their knowledge, is correctly perceived as dangerous in its otherness.

It would of course be possible to exaggerate the social radicalism of this book; it is religious allegory, after all, and also a book in which only a

[146] 'Bunyan's Sense of Place', p. 103 (quoting from *Pilgrim's Progress*, p. 245).
[147] 'The Journey in *The Pilgrim's Progress*', in '*The Pilgrim's Progress': Critical and Historical Views*, p. 113.
[148] Cf. Adam Sills, 'Mr. Bunyan's Neighborhood and the Geography of Dissent', *ELH*, 70 (2003), 67–87.

minority of those encountered on the king's highway are at the same time in the true way of Christ. In any history of human mobility in England, however, *The Pilgrim's Progress* demands attention, on account of its representation of journeys undertaken by commoners as purposeful, and its associated valorization of a popular knowledge of space. Towards the end of the second part, the reader is told that the pilgrims' guide, Mr Greatheart, 'had in his pocket a map of all ways leading to or from the Celestial City' (p. 357). In the context of the book's allegorical model, in which an individual's navigation of 'the way' is an exercise in realizing, or enacting, his or her election, this image seems doubly incongruous: at once subordinating individual enlightenment to an external chart, and positing a model of multiple paths rather than a single 'way'. Yet the unmistakable evocation of Restoration road maps, with their networks converging on London, is pointedly topical. It is possible that Bunyan encountered these maps in the years between his publication of the first part of *Pilgrim's Progress* in 1678, in which there are no references to maps, and the second part in 1684.[149] By comparison with these new kinds of texts, his image appears to suggest, there are other forms of spatial knowledge, and other ways of imagining nationhood. In the context of Bunyan's book, the uncanny geography of the guide's map embraces and encodes the knowledge of the elect commoner, connecting a community of the godly on the earth and beyond.

There are manifold differences between the various authors and texts considered in the course of this chapter. Drayton, Ogilby, Defoe, Harman and Bunyan – some of the key figures discussed above – are in most respects an incongruous combination. Yet each was concerned, in different ways and from different perspectives, with the relation between individual subjects and the space of the English nation. Moreover, each was concerned, in the texts upon which I have focused, with roads as potential keys to understanding these relations. Roads form networks for the circulation of people, goods and information. The nature and quality of these networks, as numerous commentators agreed, reflects upon the social and economic constitution of the nation. Ogilby appreciated this well enough when he set out to document a coherent and functional network, and so did Defoe when he swelled a chorus of complaint about the inadequacies of the roads.

---

[149] The temporal distance between the two parts is in fact greater than the publication dates suggest, since the first part was probably finished by 1671, while Bunyan was imprisoned and before the publication of Ogilby's work. By the time that the second part was published, Bunyan had been free for seven years, and was in demand as a travelling preacher, especially in London (Richard L. Greaves, 'John Bunyan', *ODNB*).

Yet roads also provide spaces for myriad quotidian acts of travel, founded upon the spatial knowledge of commoners. Hence they raise the issue, which is so central within this book, of popular mobility. As I have attempted to demonstrate, efforts to justify the movements of commoners, forged in the face of orthodox discourses of settlement and locality, are instrumental to the wider reconception of English society.

The fact that I have concluded the chapter with a consideration of a religious allegory demonstrates clearly enough that this is not a straightforward narrative of transformation. The history of space – like the related histories of capitalism and liberal humanism – is more conflictual and multifarious than that. Cultural debates and discursive shifts need to be unpicked from disparate kinds of texts, written for different audiences and purposes, across the period. The mix of genres considered above typifies this degree of multiplicity. As I have attempted to show, various different genres gave shape to, and were in turn informed by, anxieties and arguments about the uses and users of roads. In some cases – as, for example, road-maps or rogue pamphlets – the connection is fundamental; in others – such as spiritual autobiography – it is rather more peripheral. All the texts analyzed in the course of the chapter, however, contributed to vital debates about the meanings of mobility, which I believe are critical to any appreciation of the spatial history of early modern period England.

CHAPTER 3

Inns and alehouses

The preceding chapters have considered England's principal routes of travel. But to appreciate the literature of domestic travel in this period requires attention also to sites which lent shape to the human uses of these systems. Indeed the growing numbers of inns and alehouses provided contemporaries with perhaps the clearest of all indices of human mobility. To the extent that rivers and roads were fashioned into networks, inns and alehouses were positioned as nodal points on those networks. Significantly, they are places of encounter, which bring myths of local community into collision with the exigencies of circulation and occasion. They are sites, therefore, which invite reflection at once on the social consequences of the period's changing patterns of mobility, and the relation of domestic travel to wider patterns in the production of space. For, in Henri Lefebvre's analysis, the 'form of social space is encounter'.[1]

Here I want to attend to some of the ways in which literary texts, by staging encounters within inns and alehouses, make sense of the period's changing practices of mobility. In particular, I suggest that representations of such encounters in many respects epitomize wider struggles to negotiate between preexistent assumptions of forms of hospitality founded on inter-personal connections, and freshly mercantile structures of movement and interaction. While an innkeeper or alehouse-keeper may assume the title of 'host' and his or her client that of 'guest', their respective roles in fact stretch and transform codes of private hospitality. These tensions were hardly new to the early modern period; however, as domestic travel became more common, the contractual relation between host and guest, and their temporary and often uneasy interactions, assumed new prominence. Within this context, literary representations provide some of the period's most subtle reflections upon the encounters which inns and alehouses facilitated. While these encounters are not, by any means, rendered purely commercial

---

[1] *The Production of Space*, trans. Donald Nicholson-Smith (Oxford, 1991), p. 101.

and contractual, they are nonetheless formed into puzzling new shapes by the spaces in which they occur. As a result, such representations reflect, in turn, on a culture within which travel itself was in the process of being commodified.

Inns and alehouses find places in forms of literature that seek to situate human mobility in relation to wider discourses of social order. Others have demonstrated the ways in which traditional genres, such as ballads, help to define alehouses as sites of sociability within local communities.[2] By comparison, my approach is of necessity focused on the provision of accommodation: which was a major function of inns but a relatively minor function of alehouses. Debates over inns and alehouses as sites facilitating mobility, I suggest, are articulated with unprecedented clarity in certain emergent genres, such as character books and jest-books. Such genres, products themselves of a nascent market culture, consistently seize upon the contestations and contradictions of their world, teasing away at the gaps between traditional values and emergent realities. And they are developed still more thoroughly in the most vital, and thoroughly mercantile, literary genre of the age: drama. Indeed, as fixed places which are nonetheless defined by human mobility, inns and alehouses invite dramatic representation in a way that rivers and roads could not. As a result, while Chapter 1 centred attention on poetry and Chapter 2 on prose, the present chapter provides an opportunity to consider the engagement of certain Renaissance dramatists with the wider issues of concern in the book.

The chapter works its way towards an analysis of Ben Jonson's Caroline play, *The New Inn*. Overall, it does not pretend to provide an exhaustive survey of inns and alehouses in early modern literature; instead, it aims to elucidate some of the key cultural anxieties elicited by these sites, through close attention to particular texts. The first section introduces the investigation by outlining the economic functions and legal status of inns and alehouses, and within this context considering their significance in genres such as jestbooks and character literature. The subsequent section discusses the functions of inns and alehouses in early Renaissance drama, considering especially the threats they pose to structures of social order. And the final

---

[2] See, e.g., Patricia Fumerton, 'Not Home: Alehouse, Ballads, and the Vagrant Husband in Early Modern England', *Journal of Medieval and Early Modern Studies*, 32 (2002), 493–518; Theodore B. Leinwand, 'Spongy Plebs, Mighty Lords, and the Dynamics of the Alehouse', *Journal of Medieval and Renaissance Studies*, 19 (1989), 159–84; and Keith Wrightson, 'Alehouses, Order and Reformation in Rural England, 1590–1660', in *Popular Culture and Class Conflict 1590–1914: Explorations in the History of Labour and Leisure*, ed. Eileen Yeo and Stephen Yeo (Brighton, 1981), pp. 1–27.

section attends to *The New Inn*, which I suggest offers one of the most sophisticated early modern literary engagements with debates about commercial hospitality and geographical mobility.

ECONOMIES OF MOBILITY

A marked expansion of commercialized hospitality can be dated roughly from the Reformation. The dissolution of the monasteries removed from the landscape the most common providers of non-commercial hospitality for travellers in England, while the growing quantity of travel and changing attitudes towards charity and poverty meant that individuals were increasingly less likely to offer beds to strangers.[3] As a result, for commoners travelling the nation's roads and rivers the purchase of accommodation became in many cases the only option. In this regard inns and alehouses performed similar functions, distinguished rather by size and status. Inns 'were usually large, fashionable establishments offering wine, ale and beer, together with quite elaborate food and lodging to well-heeled travellers', whereas alehouses were 'normally smaller premises serving ale and beer … and providing rather basic food and accommodation for the lower orders'.[4] Despite these differences, inns and alehouses were alike shaped, and to a considerable extent defined, by economies of mobility. Contemporary efforts to make sense of these practices, I suggest in this section, may be traced from forms of official discourse through to pieces of popular literature. The latter, in particular, instructively tease away at the cultural implications of increased geographical mobility.

The history of the inn is bound to that of the stage. Inns define stages, breaking networks down into manageable and roughly regularized units. For William Harrison, therefore, it made sense to discuss 'Inns and Thoroughfares' in the same chapter of his Elizabethan *Description of England*, since the former lent structure, and a degree of civility, to a person's passage along the latter.[5] This structure was still more pronounced 100 years later, as it was now possible to locate 'significant clusters of inn accommodation occurring, on average, at [intervals of] ten to fifteen miles'.[6]

---

[3] See esp. Felicity Heal, *Hospitality in Early Modern England* (Oxford, 1990). On monastic hospitality, see J. J. Jusserand, *English Wayfaring Life in the Middle Ages*, trans. Lucy Toulmin Smith (London, 1889), pp. 56–61.

[4] Peter Clark, *The English Alehouse: A Social History 1200–1830* (London, 1983), p. 5.

[5] *The Description of England*, ed. Georges Edelen (Ithaca, 1968), pp. 397–406.

[6] John Chartres, 'The Eighteenth-Century Inn: A Transient "Golden Age"?', in *The World of the Tavern: Public Houses in Early Modern Europe*, ed. Beat Kumin and Ann Tlusty (Aldershot, 2002), p. 208.

Alehouses facilitated more casual, yet equally important, forms of circulation. Moreover, both inns and alehouses were not only places to sleep and eat, but also assumed other important roles within emergent mercantile and communication networks. While Harrison endorsed an orthodox position that marketing was something conducted on set days in geographically distinct places, practices of internal trade in England were in fact becoming much more complex.[7] In particular, trading between individuals, either on the fringes of actual markets or completely independent of them, grew in volume and importance.[8] Such transactions, commonly enacted within the rooms of inns and alehouses, avoided the regulations of open markets and allowed for greater flexibility in the timing and nature of transactions. They gave rise to 'a kind of society of wayfarers, partially separate from the settled society of the manor house, village, and market town', and dependent on inns and alehouses.[9]

In all these ways, inns and alehouses were not merely indices of changing practices of mobility, but were themselves lending shape to those changes. Not surprisingly, therefore, legislators and commentators alike turned their attention to them. The state tried various schemes to regulate their uses, worried especially by the growing numbers of alehouses and by fears of 'the great disorders daylie used' within them.[10] Such efforts were underpinned, in part, by the period's widespread fear of unchecked and apparently untraceable popular mobility. At the same time, however, a range of satirists and popular writers teased away at these anxieties, exploring in the process emergent forms of circulation. Hence, while moralists perceived alehouses as a cause of vagrancy, one satirist figured them as 'the onely guesthouse[s]' in a 'Pedlers pilgrimage', suggesting in the process mysterious and unmappable forms of popular mobility.[11] Moreover, as sites linked into wider spatial networks, inns and alehouses inevitably became important for the transmission of news, ranging from information about markets and routes through to matters of national significance. In one text, then, it is stated that an ostler, from 'his long acquaintance with people of all conditions and Countries … ha's the *Geographicall Mappe* of the whole Continent (so farre as this Iland extends) in

---

[7] *Description of England*, p. 246; see above, pp. 102–3.

[8] See esp. Alan Everitt, 'The Marketing of Agricultural Produce', in *The Agrarian History of England and Wales*, Vol. IV: *1500–1640*, ed. Joan Thirsk (Cambridge, 1967), pp. 510–63.

[9] Everitt, 'Marketing', p. 559.

[10] *Stuart Royal Proclamations*, ed. James F. Larkin and Paul L. Hughes (2 vols., Oxford, 1973–83), I.180; see esp. Judith Hunter, 'English Inns, Taverns and Brandy Shops: The Legislative Framework, 1495–1797', in *The World of the Tavern: Public Houses in Early Modern Europe*, ed. Beat Kumin and Ann Tlusty (Aldershot, 2002), pp. 65–82.

[11] Wye Saltonstall, *Picturae Loquentes, or Pictures Drawne Forth in Characters* (1635), sig. E11v.

his illiterate *pericranium*'.[12] In another, it is said that an innkeeper will characteristically launch into 'some strange tale, perhaps collected out of his last nights dreame' as a promotional ploy, part of his aim to minister 'mirth and newes to his weary and welcome Travellers'.[13] Each of these examples, drawn from early seventeenth-century character literature, delineates a commodification of knowledge and communication. Indeed, while the writers do not adopt overtly moralized positions, they register that there is something fundamentally threatening about the illiterate ostler's spatial knowledge, just as there is something at least unsettling about the host's transparent performance of personalized bonds in the interest of commercial gain. In the inn, 'mirth' has a market value. Each piece therefore admits an appreciation of the inn as a space of economic contestation, in which the traveller, or guest, must be careful at every moment to protect his or her own interests.

Such anxieties underpin widespread advice to travellers to be guarded, even secretive, in inns and alehouses. Many worried about the social indecorum of mixing perforce with people of lower degree.[14] The alehouse, one wrote, was a place in which

> every upstart, base-condition'd slave,
> If that hee have but money in his bagge,
> A gentleman unto his teeth will brave,
> And in his pots most malapertly bragge.[15]

Others advised against divulging any information about one's journey to inn employees, who might pass on such details to thieves and highwaymen. Harrison perceived danger throughout the inn: from the ostler, who will be 'very busy to take down [a man's] budget or capcase … to feel the weight thereof', through to the tapster, who 'doth mark [a man's] behavior and what plenty of money he draweth when he payeth the shot'.[16] In the following century, a book purportedly written by a reformed highwayman rehearsed the advice to beware of those who may seem merely hospitable, counselling the traveller to 'be secret, and let little be made known to those that watch to do you wrong'.[17] In this vision, extreme as it undoubtedly is, the inn or alehouse is imagined, by implication, as a place of competition and alienation: a distorted parody of home.

[12] Richard Brathwaite, *Whimzies: Or a New Cast of Characters* (1631), p. 110.
[13] Francis Lenton, *Characterismi: Or, Lentons Leasures* (1631), sig. E1or.
[14] Beat Kumin, 'Public Houses and their Patrons in Early Modern Europe', in *World of the Tavern*, p. 52.
[15] William Hornby, *The Scourge of Drunkennes* (1618), sig. C1v; quoted in Leinwand, 'Spongy Plebs', 162.
[16] *Description of England*, p. 398.
[17] *The Devils Cabinet Broke Open: Or, a New Discovery of the High-way Thieves* (1658), p. 21.

At the centre of this site, the status of the host struck contemporary writers as especially problematic. The host was a propertied man with limited power over his property. 'The true inn', as John Chartres states, 'existed *ad hospitandos homines*, in English law a common calling, which obliged its keepers to receive all who came to seek accommodation.'[18] Hence books of advice for constables and justices of the peace note that an innkeeper or alehouse-keeper may be compelled to lodge a traveller.[19] Character literature, which thrives on paradox, seizes upon the power dynamics between host and guest. Francis Lenton translates the problem into a bawdy register, equating a man's control over the space of his house and the body of his wife as he quips that a host 'cannot subsist without company, tho he be Cuckold for't'.[20] Thomas Overbury's representation is more subtle:

AN HOST

Is the kernell of a signe: or the signe is the shell, and mine Host is the snaile. He consists of double beere and fellowship, and his vices are the bawdes of his thirst. Hee entertaines humbly, and gives his guests power, as well of himselfe as of his house … Hee traffiques for guests by mens friends, friends freind, and is sensible only of his purse. In a word, he is none of his owne: for he neither eats, drinks or thinks but at other mens charges and appointments.[21]

Overbury, like so many of his contemporaries, is fascinated by the translation within the inn of human bonds, such as those of fellowship and friendship, into mercantile terms. As a result, the host's offers of hospitality are predicated, incongruously, upon an abandonment of control over his property. He is a man fixed in place yet without a home: defined, as much as any pedlar, by an economy of mobility. He is, ultimately, 'none of his owne'.

Other forms of popular literature translate the potentially contestatory economic relationship between host and guest into a comic register. In jestbooks, for instance, and particularly those that centre on native jesters, the act of defrauding a host is invariably figured as a laudable demonstration of wit. Hence George Peele is represented as leaving inns with unpaid bills, and even stealing horses and other goods from his host.[22] Similarly, in a tale about Richard Tarlton, Shakespeare's stage-clown exploits the quite legitimate fears of a provincial innkeeper. At 'a time, when Players were put to

---

[18] 'Eighteenth-Century English Inn', p. 207.
[19] See, e.g., Michael Dalton, *The Country Justice* (1630), p. 28.   [20] *Characterismi*, sig. E1ov.
[21] *The Overburian Characters*, ed. W. J. Paylor (Oxford, 1936), p. 20.
[22] *Merrie Conceited Jests: Of George Peele* (1627), pp. 1, 8, 15.

silence, *Tarlton* and his Boy frollickt so long in the Countrey, that all their money was gone', and they could see no way of funding their return to the capital. Since they are unknown at their inn, the boy initiates a rumour that Tarlton is a seminary priest, on the road to spread religious heterodoxy. The innkeeper has him arrested and carried to London: which solves Tarlton's transportation problem. Recognized and discharged by a judge, Tarlton 'stood jesting & pointing at [his captors'] folly, and so taught them by cunning, more wit & thrift against another time'.[23] Innkeepers and alehouse-keepers were expected to report to local magistrates any strangers staying more than one night.[24] While they did not have the right to refuse hospitality to a suspicious traveller, they had a duty to learn what they could about such a person and pass on that information to the authorities. Here, however, the simple honesty of the innkeeper, troubled by the unknown and keen to uphold his duty to the state, is deftly turned into a subject of ridicule. Tarlton's sharper wit, more powerful personal connections, and greater assurance in a spatiality of mobility and encounter, returns the innkeeper to his proper place.

INNS AND ALEHOUSES ON STAGE

Inns and alehouses provide obvious dramatic settings, and occasion as a result some of the period's most sustained literary engagements with issues relating to human mobility. Representations of inns and alehouses in Renaissance drama typically shadow the popular traditions outlined above, exploring the various threats these sites may pose to social order and its myths of hierarchy and difference. Yet their methods are also more complex, since they are not only relatively long by comparison with some of the satiric forms considered above, but also generically dialogic. They thus bring to the stage definitive debates about inns and alehouses, and by extension about mobility more generally. This is not the place for an exhaustive survey of inns and alehouses on the Renaissance stage; however, by way of creating a foundation for the subsequent analysis of Jonson's *New Inn* it will be worth touching upon some of the more important and influential points of comparison from the wider canon. The discussion stretches from Shakespeare to the Caroline stage, and attends particularly to the ways in which a number of key dramatists admit, yet seek to contain, the social threats posed by these sites. Their plays may be seen, as a result, as

---

[23] *Tarltons Jests* (1638), sigs. D4v–E1r.   [24] Hunter, 'English Inns', p. 68

efforts to manage cultural anxieties about mobility, gaining a degree of their dramatic power by virtue of the sheer struggle demanded by this purpose.

Shakespeare's *1 Henry IV* is notable, among not only the history plays but also the wider range of Elizabethan drama set in England, for its social and geographical breadth of vision. Moreover, for all the carnivalesque energy of the London tavern scenes, which commonly absorb critical attention, this play demonstrates equally that taverns and inns are sites shaped by more mundane economic exchanges and desires. Hence it is made clear that the London tavern not only offers a space in which Hal may explore his identity through forms of performance, but also provides a precarious living for its Hostess, Mistress Quickly, and a number of employees. And the play, though essentially focused on other matters, is alert throughout to the edgy social dynamics of this space. While Quickly asserts that the tavern is 'mine own house' (3.3.61), her elite guests casually appropriate it to their uses, exposing her in the process to a torrent of crude taunts. Indeed the scenes might be said to open to question, in accord with the law of inns, the extent to which the house really is her 'own'. These tensions surface most notably when Quickly demands payment of Falstaff's bill, only to be deflected with a combination of elitism and misogyny. While the justice of her demand is undeniable, there is also a logic, within the terms of the play, to the bill remaining unpaid to the end. In the final speech set in the tavern, Falstaff demands yet more service, expressing the cryptic wish that 'this tavern were my drum' (3.3.197–8). However one might choose to interpret this line, the underlying fantasy, which Falstaff effectively enacts at this moment, is of proprietorial authority. The contestation over this space, therefore, remains unresolved.

The play's earlier inn scene, set at Rochester, on the road between London and Canterbury, develops a more conventional narrative of contestation over material resources. Indeed the basic plot for this episode might almost have been adapted from Harrison, centring as it does on a professional criminal, Gadshill, who benefits from collusion with the inn's chamberlain. In the inn-yard, as two carriers rise early and wait for 'gentlemen' who choose to travel in company because they carry 'great charge', the chamberlain assures Gadshill that 'There's a franklin in the Weald of Kent hath brought three hundred marks with him in gold. I heard him tell it to one of his company last night at supper' (2.1.42–4, 51–3). Only later, on the highway itself, is the robbery appropriated into a register of 'jest' (2.2.42): in part through the participation of Falstaff, and in part through a degree of obfuscation about the victims. While one of the travellers cries, 'we are undone, both we and ours forever', an earlier claim that the money to be stolen is 'the King's' and on its way 'to the King's exchequer' posits the conceit of Prince Harry stealing from his father (2.2.46–8). (Later, in fact, he returns the money (4.1.170–1).) Realism can thus give way to symbolism, reflecting outwards to the play's central concern with the relationship between royal father and son. Yet the play's remarkable degree of specificity about places and movements asserts, in the narrative of the Rochester inn as much as that of the London tavern, a counterweight to this dramatic momentum. Geographical mobility, which is a condition of all Shakespeare's histories, remains unsettlingly mired in an economy of commercial hospitality, with all of the petty challenges and material threats that this involves.

The alehouse encounter in the two Induction scenes of *The Taming of the Shrew*, though more obviously marked as liminal in relation to its text than the inn and tavern scenes in *1 Henry IV*, presents an even more acute study in social politics. Here the drunk commoner Christopher Sly is 'practise[d] on' by a passing Lord, who expresses disgust at the discovery of such a 'monstrous beast' (Induction 1.30, 32). The Lord's attendants dress the comatose Sly in 'sweet clothes' and when he wakes they manage – almost – to convince him to 'forget himself', with their assurances that he is a truly 'noble lord' who has suffered a period of 'strange lunacy' (Induction 1.34, 1.37, 2.27–8). Sly, accosted by the hostess as a 'rogue' and assumed by the Lord to be a 'beggar', struggles when he wakes to assert an independent identity:

What, would you make me mad? Am not I Christopher Sly – old Sly's son of Burton Heath, by birth a pedlar, by education a cardmaker, by transmutation a bearherd, and now by present profession a tinker? (Induction 2.16–19)

The comedy here is derived from his self-representation of a trajectory through various categories of geographically unfixed employment. Despite his effort to place himself, as 'old Sly's son of Burton Heath', he appears ultimately to endorse the Lord's assessment. As considered in Chapter 2, even pedlars and tinkers were commonly associated with beggars and vagrants, rather than considered as legitimately employed.[25] The jest, therefore, is founded on an assumption of Sly's fundamental purposelessness and meaninglessness. An identity so essentially rootless, the Lord suggests, is easily enough reshaped.

Yet the sheer fluidity, or adaptability, of Sly's identity might also suggest, as this scene progresses, a canny accommodation to the Lord's fiction. As Theodore Leinwand notes, 'Sly is sufficiently opaque that we cannot be sure whether he has been taken in … or whether he knows full well what has

---

[25] See above, pp. 101–11.

come to pass and so merely tests the limits to which the lord will take his joke.'[26] Moreover, the fact that he is never returned to his own identity (the main action of the play taking over after Sly is installed as the principal spectator) leaves this action suspended as a jest without a punchline. However determined the Lord may be to assert his culture's myths of social distinction, demonstrating that to be mobile is to be without meaning, his control over subject and environment alike is thus never demonstrably established. Indeed Sly himself threatens, albeit confusedly, to unravel the Lord's own structures of social distinction, claiming a pedigree and history for his family: 'Look in the Chronicles', he declares, 'we came in with Richard Conqueror' (Induction 1.3–4). The claim is rendered comic by the muddling of a proverb, confusing William the Conqueror and Richard Coeur-de-Lion.[27] Yet the Lord is no better able to lend meaning to this inscrutable, elusive subject, who emerges as an apt embodiment of the site he so tenuously occupies at the outset of the play.

In Jacobean drama, while social and spatial dislocation remains a common subject, playwrights more consistently centre their attention on London. Admittedly, the city invariably functions synecdochically in such plays, which broadly examine social and cultural shifts across the nation, registering the key upheavals and debates of the era. Nonetheless, their value in the present context – a chapter which is unashamedly concerned more literally with inns and alehouses as sites of commercial hospitality for travellers – is limited. In a handful of plays from the Caroline era, by comparison, a number of important dramatists broaden the vision of Jacobean city comedy, in ways that enable them to attend in a more focused manner to the meanings of mobility across the country. *Beggars Bush*, by John Fletcher and Philip Massinger, and Richard Brome's *The Jovial Crew*, for instance, both centre on groups of beggars, represented as sanitized and romanticized translations from the Elizabethan literature of roguery. In the latter, the act of living with the jovial crew for fixed periods of time becomes a vehicle of self-discovery for elite characters, in accordance with the play's romance structure. The steward who feels compelled to spend part of each year with the beggars is thus revealed in due course as his lord's lost son. The lord's daughters, meanwhile, who are initially unmoved by their socially appropriate suitors, are brought to their senses after a spell of beggary. And

---

[26] 'Spongy Plebs', 173. See also Garrett A. Sullivan, Jr, *Memory and Forgetting in English Renaissance Drama: Shakespeare, Marlowe, Webster* (Cambridge, 2005), pp. 16–18.

[27] Morris Palmer Tilley, *A Dictionary of the Proverbs in England in the Sixteenth and Seventeenth Centuries* (Ann Arbor, 1950), C594.

the beggars themselves are romance creations: fallen poets, soldiers, courtiers, and so on, rather than more realistic representations of the shiftless poor. Their allotted role is to be deserving and grateful recipients of the lord's charity, in a play that presents a fundamentally conservative ideal of landownership as stewardship.[28]

Philip Massinger's *A New Way to Pay Old Debts* is equally concerned to champion traditional models of social relations in the country, yet more searching in its attention to the possibilities of social and geographical dislocation.[29] This play, which it will be worth considering in slightly greater detail in the remainder of the present section, begins in a Nottinghamshire alehouse, with the keeper, Tapwell, and his dissolute client, Welborne, arguing in part about money and service, but above all about a 'name'. Refused a can of ale for his breakfast, Welborne turns on Tapwell:

> Rogue what am I?
>
> TAPWELL. Troth durst I trust you with a looking glasse,
>   To let you see your trimme shape, you would quit me,
>   And take the name your selfe.
> WELBORNE.   How! dogge?
> TAPWELL.   Even so, Sir.
>   And I must tell you if you but advance
>   Your plimworth cloke, you shall be soone instructed
>   There dwells, and within call, if it please your worship,
>   A potent monarch, call'd the Constable,
>   That does command a Citadell, call'd the Stockes;
>   Whose guards are certaine files of rusty Billmen,
>   Such as with great dexterity will hale
>   Your tatter'd, louzie–
> WELBORNE.   Rascal, slave. (1.1.6–17)

Tapwell's logic is simple enough; if Welborne is living in an alehouse and unable to pay his way, reduced to begging money from 'the beggers on high wayes' (1.1.57), he has earned the name of 'rogue' despite the accident of his breeding and the misfortune of his lost inheritance. This debate resonates through the play, invoking the spectre of a gentleman being reduced to beggary only to set him at the end in his proper place. Crucially, his own arguments for the value of 'blood' ultimately win the support of Lady Alworth, who underwrites his revival (1.3.88). As the household cook asks,

---

[28] See Garrett A. Sullivan, Jr, *The Drama of Landscape: Land, Property, and Social Relations on the Early Modern Stage* (Stanford, 1998), pp. 159–93.
[29] *The Plays and Poems of Philip Massinger*, ed. Philip Edwards and Colin Gibson, 5 vols. (Oxford, 1976).

listening to his appeal to her: 'Are not wee base Rogues / That could forget this?' (1.3.109–10).

Tapwell's position, meanwhile, is compromised by his own dependence on the play's acknowledged villain, Sir Giles Overreach. In this respect *A New Way* also demands a topical reading, since Overreach has widely been recognized, from the time of the play's first performance, as 'a fantasia on … Sir Giles Mompesson'.[30] Mompesson obtained a monopoly on the licensing of alehouses and inns, which he proceeded to abuse in various ways, most notably by relicensing establishments that had been closed by local authorities. In *A New Way*, therefore, to be operating under the patronage of Overreach is a sure index of corruption, and Tapwell's alehouse provides the most straightforward instance of his influence. As Albert H. Tricomi has argued, the alehouse is in fact analogous to Overreach's own house, to the extent that it distorts traditional codes of hospitality. Hence, as much as Welborne asserts the rights of a 'guest', Tapwell insists purely on a financial bond, like the upwardly aspiring man that he is.[31] An alehouse is not necessarily corrupt; Welborne, for all his obvious dissipation, appeals to a model of social obligation that is authoritative within the play as a whole. This alehouse, however, epitomizes all the potential for corruption.

In due course, as Welborne rises and Overreach falls, Tapwell appreciates the danger of his own position. He tells his wife, Froth:

> Though he knew all the passages of our house,
> As the receiving of stolne goods, and bawdrie,
> When he was rogue *Welborne*, no man would beleeve him,
> And then his information could not hurt us.
> But now he is right Worshipfull againe,
> Who dares but doubt his testimonie? me thinkes
> I see thee *Froth* already in a cart
> For a close Bawde, thine eyes ev'n pelted out
> With durt, and rotten egges, and my hand hissing
> (If I scape the halter) with the letter *R*,
> Printed upon it.   (4.2.11–20)

---

[30] Martin Butler, '*A New Way to Pay Old Debts*: Massinger's Grim Comedy', in *English Comedy*, ed. Michael Cordner, *et al.* (Cambridge, 1994), p. 132. Cf. Margot Heinemann, 'Drama and Opinion in the 1620s: Middleton and Massinger', in *Theatre and Government under the Early Stuarts*, ed. J. R. Mulryne and Margaret Shewring (Cambridge, 1993), pp. 257–61; and, for a longer, albeit more idiosyncratic, demonstration of the association, see Robert Hamilton Ball, *The Amazing Career of Sir Giles Overreach* (Princeton and London, 1939), pp. 3–20.

[31] '*A New Way to Pay Old Debts* and the Country-House Poetic Tradition', *Medieval and Renaissance Drama in England*, 3 (1986), 182–3.

The play has shifted attention from a temporarily dissolute customer to a dissolute space. The alehouse's position within economies of illicit sexuality and petty crime are revealed, and Tapwell's opening argument about the social politics of roguery is abandoned in his image of his own likely stigmatization 'with the letter R'.[32] The resolution of order is admittedly based on somewhat shaky foundations, as Welborne contrives to con Overreach by fraudulently erasing a name from a property deed. Like so many Renaissance plays, however, *A New Way* entertains the idea that social order may be based on no more than performance and competition, before setting it in its place and affirming instead values of birth and inheritance.

There is undoubtedly a degree of wish-fulfilment to this dramatic model. The alehouse, which is so firmly positioned as representative not only of the power of Overreach but also of more fundamental forces of social and geographical dislocation, is by the close effectively erased from the landscape. Tapwell and Froth also disappear from the play after predicting their own downfall in the fourth act. Indeed one might well argue that the outright fantasy of the resolution actually exposes the very anxieties it is evidently intended to obscure, as the respective demands of social realism and comic closure pull the play in contrary directions. Certainly, as I have attempted to demonstrate throughout this brief survey of Renaissance plays, such tensions are absolutely fundamental to dramatic representations of inns and alehouses. The effort to align plays with conservative doctrine on place is thus repeatedly stretched by attention to the energies of proprietors and clients alike. These sites themselves, in fact, gather about them a vitality that is almost impossible to quell. In the remainder of the chapter I want to develop this suggestion by devoting more detailed attention to another play of the same era as *A New Way*, which seems to me to repay more richly an analysis centred on its representation of inns. For many reasons, it is a play in which the forces that the inn comes to represent cannot so easily be erased by authorial sleight of hand.

ANXIETIES OF MOBILITY: JONSON'S *NEW INN*

By comparison with a play such as Massinger's, Jonson's *New Inn* is not only considerably more improbable in its convoluted romance plot, but also more rigorously sophisticated in its treatment of mobility. Since its unsuccessful premiere in 1629, *The New Inn* has generally received short shrift

---

[32] T. W. Craik's New Mermaids edition of the play (London, 1964) is unquestionably wrong in stating that the 'R' would indicate 'Receiver of Stolen Goods'. The error is corrected in the Edwards and Gibson edition.

from critics. Several recent studies, however, have drawn attention to its subtle interventions in topical debates, particularly those regarding court politics, property and national identities, and dress.[33] I want to extend this process by focusing, as no previous study has done, on the effects of Jonson's decision to set all the action in an inn in Barnet, a town twelve miles out of London on the Great North Road. This decision extends Jonson's concern, late in his career, with an emergent English economy of circulation.[34] Here I suggest that Jonson's evident intent to champion principles of property and placement – in accordance at once with the romance genre and his own ideological predilections – is undermined in part by his interest in the inn itself. Indeed the Light Heart proves rather more resilient than Tapwell's alehouse, asserting to the end irrepressible forces of displacement and exchange at work within the nation.

To a considerable degree, the inn determines the nature of social inter-action and individual transformation in the play. The host of the Light Heart, Goodstock, is in fact Lord Frampul, who disappeared from his home in Oxford at the time of his second daughter's birth. The romance conceit of the play positions Goodstock in an analogous position to that of Prospero in *The Tempest*, as he eventually presides over the reunification of his family and the betrothals of his two daughters.[35] In the opening speeches, he positions himself as a man in control of his house, shaping its values and membership; 'I must ha' jovial guests to drive my ploughs', he declares (1.1.22).[36] The specificity with which Jonson depicts this setting, however, moderates the text's alignment with romance.[37] Crucially, it restricts Goodstock's authority, as his guest, Lord Lovel, is keen to point out:

[33] See esp. Martin Butler, 'Late Jonson', in *The Politics of Tragicomedy: Shakespeare and After*, ed. Gordon McMullan and Jonathan Hope (London, 1992), pp. 172–6; Sheila M. Walsh, '"But yet the Lady, Th'heir, Enjoys the Land": Heraldry, Inheritance, and Nat(ion)al Households in Jonson's *The New Inn*', *Medieval and Renaissance Drama in England*, 11 (1999), 226–63; Rebecca Ann Bach, 'Ben Jonson's "Civil Savages"', *Studies in English Literature, 1500–1900*, 37 (1997), 277–93; Julie Sanders, '"Wardrobe Stuffe": Clothes, Costume and the Politics of Dress in Ben Jonson's *The New Inn*', *Renaissance Forum*, 6 (2002), www.hull.ac.uk/renforum/v6no1/sanders.htm

[34] Cf. Jonson's *The Staple of News*, first performed in 1626.

[35] Critical comparisons between *The New Inn* and Shakespeare's romances are common. See esp. John Lee, 'On Reading *The Tempest* Autobiographically: Ben Jonson's *The New Inn*', *Shakespeare Studies*, 34 (1996), 1–26; Andrew Stewart, 'Some Uses for Romance: Shakespeare's *Cymbeline* and Jonson's *The New Inn*', *Renaissance Forum*, 3 (1998), www.hull.ac.uk/renforum/v3no1/stewart.htm. A trend to read Jonson's play as a parodic rewriting of Shakespearean romance, however, appears to have dissipated, particularly in the wake of Ann Barton's trenchant rebuttal (*Ben Jonson, Dramatist* (Cambridge, 1984), pp. 263–4).

[36] *The New Inn*, ed. Julie Sanders, in *The Cambridge Edition of the Works of Ben Jonson*, gen. eds. David Bevington *et al.*, 8 vols. (Cambridge, forthcoming), Vol. VIII.

[37] Cf. Julie Sanders, *Ben Jonson's Theatrical Republics* (Basingstoke, 1998), p. 145.

> But
> It being i'your free will, as 'twas, to choose
> What parts you would sustain, methinks a man
> Of your sagacity, and clear nostril, should
> Have made another choice than of a place
> So sordid as the keeping of an inn,
> Where every jovial tinker, for his chink,
> May cry, 'Mine Host, to crambe! Give us drink,
> And do not slink, but skink, or else you stink!'
> 'Rogue', 'Bawd', and 'Cheater' call you by the surnames,
> And known synonyma of your profession.
> *Host.* But if I be no such, who then's the rogue,
> In understanding, sir, I mean? Who errs?
> Who tinkleth then, or personates Tom Tinker?
>   ...
> If I be honest, and that all the cheat
> Be of myself in keeping this Light Heart,
> Where I imagine all the world's a play;
> The state and men's affairs, all passages
> Of life, to spring new scenes, come in, go out,
> And shift and vanish; and if I have got
> A seat to sit at ease here i' mine inn
> To see the comedy, and laugh and chuck
> At the variety and throng of humours
> And dispositions that come jostling in
> And out still, as they one drove hence another—
> Why, will you envy me my happiness
> Because you are sad and lumpish?   (1.3.107–38)

Lovel deftly identifies the difference between traditional and commercial hospitality. The inn is not Goodstock's home, however long he may have lived within it; it is rather a space defined by commerce. Indeed its inherently alienating quality is underscored by the revelations – the most bizarre of all those in the final act – that Goodstock has unwittingly been sharing this space for years with his wife and younger daughter. For Michael Hattaway, the inn 'serves as the anti-type of Penshurst, the home of the Sidneys and celebrated in Jonson's famous poem'; it is 'a place where all men may lodge but no man dwells, a thoroughfare for all, and a figure therefore for the social mobility, fashion following and rootlessness of the times'.[38] Yet this interpretation, compelling as it is, overlooks the extent to which Goodstock nevertheless attempts to assert control over it,

---

[38] 'Introduction', to Hattaway's edition of *The New Inn* (Manchester, 1984), p. 22. Cf. my discussion of Jonson's 'To Penshurst', above, pp. 56–8.

transforming it into a version of home and himself into a legitimate romance patriarch. This, I believe, is one of the key tensions in the play.

Goodstock's redemptive project is rendered throughout in spatial terms. He has settled temporarily at the Light Heart, waiting for his opportunity to set his world to rights, after an act of wilful disruption. Revealing himself at the close, he declares:

> I am he
> Have measured all the shires of England over,
> Wales and her mountains, seen those wilder nations
> Of people in the Peak and Lancashire;
> Their pipers, fiddlers, rushers, puppet-masters,
> Jugglers, and gypsies, all the sorts of canters,
> And colonies of beggars, tumblers, ape-carriers,
> For to these savages I was addicted,
> To search their natures and make odd discoveries!   (5.5.92–100)

In all the literature of the early modern period, this stands as a rare instance of acts of travel within the borders of England and Wales being articulated with the same discourse of wonder applied more commonly to foreign exploration. Indeed the very next lines of his speech, albeit referring to Goodstock's wife, invoke a direct comparison with Sir John Mandeville.[39] Yet he concedes that domestic travel is fundamentally aberrant. While Goodstock may 'make odd discoveries', his approach is figured as a personal flaw – an addiction – rather than a legitimate process of enquiry. Moreover, that addiction carries the implicit risk of being oneself tainted by the savagery that characterizes other types of travellers, such as gypsies, beggars and the criminal gangs distinguished by their canting tongue. (An earlier reference to his behaviour, in fact, suggests a greater degree of personal absorption, stating that he would 'lie and live with the gypsies half a year / Together, from his wife' (1.5.63–4).) These preoccupations have directly caused the play's multiple dislocations; as he acknowledges himself, introducing his description of his travels, he is 'the cause of all this trouble' (5.5.92).

The journeys of other central characters in the play offer variations on Goodstock's model of travel as a form of transgression. Lovel, who will eventually win over Goodstock's wilful daughter with his valour, maturity and devotion to love, is defined at the outset as an anomalous guest. Whereas legal discourse on inns insisted that they were 'instituted for

---

[39] 'And here my wife, like a she-Mandeville, / Ventured in disquisition after me' (5.5.101–2). As Sanders notes, *Mandeville's Travels*, which was to the seventeenth century virtually synonymous with outlandish travel narratives, had been republished in 1625, four years before *The New Inn* was first performed (5.5.101n).

Passengers and Wayfaring Men', and therefore assumed that guests would typically stay one night merely to break a journey, Lovel has already stayed a fortnight (1.1.25).[40] Like Goodstock himself, Lovel is obsessive; according to his host, he has spent his time 'poring through a multiplying glass' at fleas and other insects, like a devotee of the new philosophy (1.1.29–40). Moreover, he is throughout curiously unplaced; unusually for a Jonsonian hero, in fact, we never hear about the location or size of his estate. Meanwhile, in the absence of a patriarch, Goodstock's elder daughter, Frances, 'enjoys' the family 'lands' as the assumed heir, not by dwelling upon them but by 'consum[ing]' them in 'clothes and feasting' (1.5.77–9). On this particular journey, made with her chambermaid, Prudence, and a retinue of admirers and retainers, she establishes as a diversion a Parliament of Love, over which Prudence presides. On multiple levels, then, she is evading the responsibilities and duties of her status. Although she defends herself against charges that her journeys are indecorous, the play nonetheless positions her as someone in need of the conjoined disciplines of patriarchy and place. Her commitment to circulation and 'encounter' must give way to family and land (1.6.32).

In the play's thematically central scenes, the Parliament of Love becomes a forum in which Lovel can assert key values of love and honour, and by consequence win the heart of Frances. Importantly, the nature of social encounter in these scenes is rigorously controlled. Within the inn, an upstairs chamber is fashioned as a space of exclusion and civility, in which traditional values may be articulated, and individual transformations effected. Moreover, while Prudence ostensibly presides, the consistent presence of Goodstock, and also the woman who will subsequently be revealed as his wife, suggests a form of domestic authority. While the solemnization of this central romantic union is deferred, the inn has served nonetheless as an agent of miraculous metamorphoses. In one of his final speeches, Lovel thus revises his insistence on the commercial nature of this space:

> Is this a dream now, after my first sleep?
> Or are these fant'sies made i'the Light Heart
> And sold i'the New Inn?   (5.5.120–2)

The point is that his fundamentally pragmatic attitude towards the inn in the opening scenes has been modified, as this particular room within the inn

---

[40] The quote is from the most often quoted authority in the common law of inns, 'Cayle's Case' (Edward Coke, *Reports* (1727), 13 vols., VIII.32).

has been transformed into a space of family. It is almost, though not quite, a space of home.[41]

The insulation of this space, however, is never perfect. While the main characters may be able to leave at the end, in preference to more conventional models of home, the play insists on the inn itself having an independent existence. Scenes set 'below stairs' demonstrate the vitality of the commercial forces that define inns. There is an obvious low comedy to these scenes, which conform to various forms of popular literature in representing shady exchanges and petty corruption. These are, in the words of one character, 'pranks of ale and hostelry' (3.1.125), and it is clear that they are performed beyond Goodstock's authority or awareness. It is also significant that the world downstairs is defined by its relation to networks of mobility. Hence coachmen are greeted as old friends, while the tapster is known colloquially as 'our thoroughfare', on account of his commitment to the circulation of news (3.1.181; 2.5.105). Barnet, after all, served multiple functions at this time, since it marked (according to Ogilby) the end of the first stage on the Great North Road out of London, but was also a destination in its own right for citizens seeking diversion from the city. Hence, while some readers of the play have interpreted the inn as inclusive in nature, providing 'a metaphor for the world', or at least for the English nation, it is important to appreciate how that metaphorical function is constructed out of topical detail.[42] The topical materiality of the setting – as opposed, say, to Prospero's island or the seacoast of Bohemia – renders the project of attending solely to the central characters, as they form into orderly familial groups and prepare to return to their homes, virtually impossible. Other realities intrude.

This tension helps to explain the curiously severe treatment accorded to the London tailor, Nick Stuff, and his wife, Pinnacia. Though associated within the play's spatial logic with the world downstairs, they exploit the power of performance and money in order to straddle, however precariously, social and spatial boundaries. They admit to a habit of appropriating expensive gowns that Stuff has made for customers, and taking day-trips to places on the outskirts of London. For the duration of these trips Pinnacia performs the role of a countess and Nick that of her servant, and at their culmination the couple pursue their role-play in the confines of an inn

---

[41] Cf. Bach, 'Ben Jonson's "Civil Savages"', 287.

[42] Ann Barton, '*The New Inn* and the Problem of Jonson's Late Style', *English Literary Renaissance*, 9 (1979), 399; cf. Bach, 'Ben Jonson's "Civil Savages"', 283; Walsh, '"But yet the Lady, Th'heir, Enjoys the Land"', 234.

bedroom. On this trip, predictably enough, they are exposed when they chance upon the intended recipients of the gown, Frances Frampul and her chambermaid, Prudence. As others have commented, the Stuffs' practice of social transgression curiously parallels that of Prudence herself, who is artificially elevated by her mistress as part of the sports conducted at the Light Heart.[43] Indeed the gown has been ordered for Prudence, rather than her mistress. In due course, Prudence effectively performs her way into the reality of nobility, attracting the eye of Lord Latimer, who declares her 'so all-sufficient in her virtue and her manners / That fortune cannot add to her' (5.5.144–5). In the logic of the play, her essential qualities earn her the right to wear the clothes of the elite, whereas Pinnacia's act is exposed as a morally corrupt sham. Meanwhile, with a degree of violence that has attracted critical comment, the Stuffs are ritually humiliated.[44] The distinction between the miraculous rise of the chambermaid who remains loyal to the codes and structures of her betters, and the social performance of a couple of citizens, must be inscribed upon them.

The nature of the Stuffs' punishment, however, within a play so concerned with patterns of mobility, suggests not only the overwhelming desire to restore order but also the virtual impossibility of doing so. In a distorted version of a popular shaming ritual designed for unruly women, they are tossed in a blanket, then Pinnacia is stripped of her gown and sent home in a cart with Nick (her 'footman') beating a basin before her (4.3.88–99). But whereas popular rituals – 'rough ridings' or 'skimmingtons' – were designed for performance within the bounds of a geographically distinct community, such as a village, thereby affirming that community's values through means of negative definition, the Stuffs' punishment is stretched over twelve miles of highway.[45] On one level, this obviously enough extends the humiliation, situating them within the wider spatial frame that this play so consistently invokes. On another level, however, as the elite culture of the play prepares to close in on itself, the punishment of the Stuffs effectively releases them, and all they represent, into the anonymity of the highway and the city. Consequently, while the Stuffs are creatures of nightmare, ripe for stigmatization, the excessive project of social discipline imposed upon them betrays irrepressible anxieties at work in the play about the real forces of

[43] Sanders, '"Wardrobe Stuffe"', para. 23.

[44] Barton, *Ben Jonson*, p. 270; Sanders, '"Wardrobe Stuffe"', para. 23.

[45] On these traditional shaming rituals, see esp. Martin Ingram, 'Ridings, Rough Music and Mocking Rhymes in Early Modern England', in *Popular Culture in Seventeenth-Century England*, ed. Barry Reay (London and Sydney, 1985), pp. 166–97; and E. P. Thompson, *Customs in Common* (New York, 1991), pp. 467–538.

mobility in contemporary England. These forces have little to do with idiosyncratic desires to study gypsies, but very much more to do with commerce, economic competition, and social aspiration.

At the close, the effort to define a society ready to retreat into traditional values of family and place is undermined, more profoundly, from within. While the betrothal of Lovel and Frances is properly idealized, the fate of Goodstock's second daughter, Laetitia, is more problematic. Goodstock has raised her in the belief that she is a boy, and treated her as a stepson; however, dressed as a girl for the purpose of the sports, she attracts the carnal materialist Lord Beaufort, whose views serve throughout as a dramatic counterweight to the romance discourse of Lovel. Beaufort and Laetitia are duly married in a 'new stable', by a priest fetched from 'the next inn' (5.1.12, 19). When Frances argues that the secrecy of the matter has breached 'laws of hospitality', Beaufort claims in response the 'licence / Of all community' provided by the inn (5.4.5, 8–9). His assertion realizes on stage the arguments made about the inn by Lovel in the opening act, exposing the Parliament of Love as a mere game and insisting instead upon their circumstances. In an inn, he need answer to nobody. When Laetitia's identity is partially exposed – as a woman, but not yet one of noble blood – Beaufort, with similar force, disclaims the match and declares that he will have 'none of your Light Heart fosterlings, no inmates' (5.5.40). The word 'inmate' invokes clauses in the Poor Laws, denoting those trying to qualify for relief by illegally attaching themselves to a community. Technically, an 'inmate' is someone who dwells in a house without properly belonging.[46] Although he is quickly reconciled to the match once he is assured of her pedigree, it is noteworthy that Laetitia herself remains silent throughout all the revelations of the final scene. Perhaps more significantly, while it is Laetitia's mother who reveals the quality of 'blood' in Laetitia's 'veins', just seconds before this announcement she has, in her guise as poor Irishwoman, confronted Beaufort's aphorism, 'Let beggars match with beggars', with the rhetorical question, 'Is poverty a vice[?]' (5.5.65, 45, 56). For the father, Goodstock, the match is welcome; but to the mother the sense that Laetitia has been treated as a commodity – 'sold' or stolen – rankles to the end (5.5.9, 109). The audience cannot escape the suggestion that human relationships in the inn, as in English society more generally, are determined as much by commercial imperatives as by abstract values of birth and virtue.

---

[46] See esp. Steve Hindle, *On the Parish? The Micro-Politics of Poor Relief in Rural England c.1550–1750* (Oxford, 2004), p. 311.

Jonson's great Jacobean work of social satire, *Bartholomew Fair*, ends with the characters moving to an identifiable 'home', to share a festive meal. In *The New Inn*, by contrast, the characters remain within the inn. Journeys to respective homes are of course implicit in the various couplings of the final act; however, it remains unclear, to the end, exactly where in the country any of these people will actually live. Settlement, like the marriage of Lovel and Frances, is deferred. The inn itself, meanwhile, is given by Goodstock to Fly. In the moralized discourse of the cast-list, Fly is described as 'the parasite of the inn'; equally, though, he might be considered its manager, since he alone fully understands its operation, and its balance of legal and illegal business. Goodstock provides two conflicting histories for Fly: that he was 'assigned … in the inventory' when Goodstock purchased the inn; and that he was Goodstock's 'fellow gypsy' in his wanderings (2.4.17; 5.5.127). Either way, Fly is defined as essentially homeless. He stands as an index of the inn as a space of mobility and commerce: all the forces that the central characters are eager to leave behind, but that the play itself cannot.[47]

Jonson's play, written roughly in the middle of the period that is my concern in this book, articulates with remarkable clarity prevailing anxieties about emergent patterns of mobility. As I have attempted to demonstrate here, writers throughout the period were concerned with the ways in which the inexorable dynamics of human and mercantile mobility were corroding and remoulding traditional assumptions of social and economic order. The representation of inns and alehouses, as sites of chance encounter and enforced social mixing, in which traditional codes of hospitality collide with market forces, therefore inspired some of the period's most incisive interrogations of an emergent culture of mobility. While much of this writing may rightly seem conservative, as though restrained by traditional values of property and settlement, it is often striking in the ways that it registers change. Jonson himself is widely acknowledged for his achievements, in his city comedies, delineating his contemporary urban environment. Here I would suggest that he was equally concerned with domestic travel and formations of nationhood.

---

[47] Cf. Sanders, *Ben Jonson's Theatrical Republics*, p. 148.

PART II

Travellers

CHAPTER 4

The progress: royal travellers and common authors

This chapter is concerned with the politics of domestic mobility. It attends specifically to the effects of the circulation of individuals and information, and the associated consolidation of systems of communication, on the constitution of the English nation. For, despite the nation's poor roads and inadequately exploited rivers, transport historians have demonstrated rising 'levels of interaction and contact' across the country in the course of the early modern period.[1] Here I am concerned less with the facts of improving communications than with the politics of this phenomenon. On whose terms would these systems be established? Whose interests would they serve? Such questions may in turn direct our attention to critical shifts in the political culture of early modern England. They may help us to understand how, in Patrick Collinson's formulation of one of the central questions of Tudor and Stuart historiography, 9,000 parishes metamorphosed into 'a single political society'.[2] And they may lead to a reflection upon ongoing debates over the emergence in England of something resembling the 'public sphere' that Jürgen Habermas has identified in the latter decades of the seventeenth century.[3]

To lend a degree of clarity to this discussion, I want to focus on one highly politicized model of domestic travel: the royal progress. Throughout the early modern period the progress was the quintessential expression of a

---

[1] Mark Brayshay, *et al.*, 'Knowledge, Nationhood and Governance: The Speed of the Royal Post in Early-Modern England', *Journal of Historical Geography*, 24 (1998), 265. The narrative is common to many studies of the nation's transport and communications infrastructure. See, e.g., J. Crofts, *Packhorse, Waggon and Post: Land Carriage and Communications under the Tudors and Stuarts* (London, 1967); H. J. Dyos and D. H. Aldcroft, *British Transport: An Economic Survey from the Seventeenth Century to the Twentieth* (Leicester, 1971); W. T. Jackman, *The Development of Transportation in Modern England*, 3rd edn (London, 1966).

[2] *Elizabethans* (London and New York, 2003), p. 27.

[3] *The Structural Transformation of the Public Sphere: An Inquiry into a Category of Bourgeois Society*, trans. Thomas Burger (Cambridge, Mass., 1991). Scholars who have argued that a version of a Habermasian public sphere may be identified earlier in the seventeenth century, or even as far back as the sixteenth century, will be considered as appropriate below.

structure – as much imagined as real – in which authority was imposed upon the nation's myriad places by a central force. On progress, a monarch would enact his or her authority over the people and places of the land, at once realizing proprietorial claims and exercising judicial power. The progress entertainments, which took shape as a recognizable genre under Elizabeth, deploy a range of artistic strategies to articulate and celebrate these political myths. But the progress is also a model open to appropriation and transformation. Undoubtedly, the practical demise of the Elizabethan model was due largely to the very different characters of Elizabeth's early Stuart successors, James I and Charles I.[4] These men were less comfortable with the publicly staged theatricality of progress entertainments, and preferred the more controlled intimacy of the court masque. But the history of the idea, or discursive model, of the progress is also embedded in more fundamental political and cultural struggles, which can be traced throughout the early modern period. This is not a straightforward narrative of change; the shifts are far more subtle and complex than such a narrative would allow. But the cultural history of the progress, I want to suggest, promises insight not only into changing relations between monarchs and subjects, but also into relations between subjects and the spaces of their nation.

The chapter plots a selective path through a wealth of potentially relevant material. Temporally, it moves from the reign of Elizabeth to the collapse of monarchical rule in the 1640s. Although the conclusion glances forward to the latter decades of the seventeenth century, I believe that the core of the argument can be substantiated through a more concentrated study. In its range and selection of material, the chapter is equally particular. The first section concentrates on the reign of Elizabeth, considering the progress as a highly theatricalized performance of authority. This was a powerful model for the maintenance of her rule, though I suggest that it was ultimately unsustainable within an increasingly dynamic nation. The subsequent section moves from a consideration of authors who were themselves drawn into journeys by the Queen's movement, into a broader analysis of the progress as a model available for appropriation by aspiring authors. The final section considers radical transformations of the progress in the 1640s, particularly at key moments when Charles I was transformed into a fugitive within his own land. At the same time, and partly in direct response to the lack of central authority, popular voices asserted the value of a political consciousness constrained neither by political nor spatial bonds.

---

[4] See, e.g., David Bergeron's survey, *English Civic Pageantry 1558–1642* (London, 1971), pp. 65–121.

ELIZABETH AND THE POLITICS OF PLACE

Elizabeth was her nation's one truly legitimate traveller. Whereas her subjects all had their proper geographical places, for her the entire nation was her home. As William Harrison wrote in 1577, acknowledging the legal principle that all land belonged to the monarch:

all is hers, and when it pleaseth her in the summer season to recreate herself abroad and view the estate of the country and hear the complaints of the poor commons injured by her unjust officers or their substitutes, every nobleman's house is her palace.[5]

Coupled with these proprietorial rights was an assumption of centralized legal authority. Like the assize judges who routinely travelled the country, imposing a national code of justice upon the provinces, like the plethora of local officials bound in various ways to the interests of the centre, and like the system of royal posts that was designed to serve the interests of the sovereign, the progress represented, in the most overtly public and ceremonial manner, the visiting of royal power upon the places of the nation.[6] In a progress, monarchical authority, generally reliant as it was on the more mundane structures of the state, is physically enacted, while in the associated rituals and entertainments it is celebrated and mythologized. The history of interpretations of progresses, however, demonstrates a need to separate acts of mythologizing from underlying political tensions. Some early new historicist analyses were arguably too eager to embrace the former, informed by Clifford Geertz's seductive model of a monarch 'stamping a territory with ritual signs of dominance'.[7] By contrast, some of the more influential recent work has attended to local tensions, in the process revealing the progresses as altogether more fraught and dynamic exercises in governance.[8] Working within this context, I want to examine the spatial

[5] *The Description of England*, ed. Georges Edelen (Ithaca, 1968), p. 227. See also David Loades, *Power in Tudor England* (Basingstoke, 1997), p. 24.

[6] On the assize system, and its rise in significance at the expense of regional courts, see Loades, *Power in Tudor England*, pp. 28–30.

[7] 'Centers, Kings, and Charisma: Reflections on the Symbolics of Power', in *Culture and its Creators: Essays in Honor of Edward Shils*, ed. Joseph Ben-David and Terry Nichols Clark (Chicago and London, 1977), p. 153.

[8] See esp. Curtis Breight, 'Caressing the Great: Viscount Montague's Entertainment of Elizabeth at Cowdray, 1591', *Sussex Archaeological Collections*, 127 (1989), 147–66; Breight, 'Realpolitik and Elizabethan Ceremony: The Earl of Hertford's Entertainment of Elizabeth at Elvetham, 1591', *Renaissance Quarterly*, 45 (1992), 20–48; and *The Progresses, Pageants, and Entertainments of Elizabeth I*, ed. Jayne Elisabeth Archer, *et al.* (Oxford, 2007). For an overview of critical approaches, see R. Malcolm Smuts, 'Progresses and Court Entertainments', in *A Companion to Renaissance Drama*, ed. Arthur F. Kinney (Oxford, 2004), pp. 287–91.

dimensions of progresses and progress entertainments, considering the ways in which they sought to encode an ideology founded at once upon regal mobility and the geographical placement of her subjects, and the ways in which they exposed the limitations of, and challenges to, that ideology.

The progress was founded on the principle of the monarch's free and uncontested movement within her realm. At Elvetham in 1591 this principle was actualized, as 'six Virgins' removed 'blockes out of her majesties way', while a poet explained that 'Envie' had placed them 'in *Majesties* highway'.[9] While the glance towards 'envy' represents a conventional way of moralizing voices of dissent, the metaphor functions equally on a more literal level, suggesting the way in which Elizabeth defined the location and direction of her 'highway' in the course of her progress. One person's pathway is translated, in the process of her movement, to the level of a legal principle.[10] In actuality Elizabeth's movements were relatively constrained geographically, stretching in her most ambitious progresses only as far as Staffordshire, Lincolnshire, Bristol, Gloucester, Bath, Norwich and Worcester. As Mary Hill Cole demonstrates, the Queen 'strayed 90 to 130 miles from London only five times in her life'.[11] It is also evident that the appearance of free movement was in fact facilitated by meticulous planning by numerous court officials. The Surveyor of the Ways mapped out the best available routes, the Master of the Post ensured that the mobile court was connected to national and international information networks, teams led by a Gentleman Usher prepared houses to receive the Queen, the Yeoman of Her Majesty's Wardrobe of Robes dealt with the transportation of clothing, the Officers of the Removing Wardrobe of Beds saw to domestic furnishings, and so forth.[12] But the principle of unfettered movement remained compelling, reinforced in ceremonies and entertainments throughout Elizabeth's reign.

By comparison, Elizabeth's subjects were defined, in accordance with the period's prevailing social discourse, by place. Indeed the progresses were structured around assertions of distinctions between one county and another, one town and another, one estate and another. Boundaries were routinely observed. In her East Anglian progress of 1578, for example, she

---

[9] *John Nichols's 'The Progresses and Public Processions of Queen Elizabeth I': A New Edition of the Early Modern Sources*, ed. Jayne Elisabeth Archer, *et al.*, 5 vols. (Oxford, forthcoming). I am grateful to the editors for giving me access to completed texts before publication. Unfortunately, however, it was not possible to obtain page references before going to press.

[10] On the definition of 'highway', see above, p. 67.

[11] Mary Hill Cole, *The Portable Queen: Elizabeth I and the Politics of Ceremony* (Amherst, 1999), p. 24.

[12] Cole, *Portable Queen*, pp. 35–62; Zillah Dovey, *An Elizabethan Progress: The Queen's Journey into East Anglia, 1578* (Stroud, 1996) pp. 4, 8, 10.

was met as she crossed into Norfolk by 2,500 horsemen, including 600 gentlemen. Fifteen days later, when she left the county, many of the Norfolk gentry reassembled to bid her farewell.[13] Moreover, ceremonies of greeting, particularly at the boundaries of towns and private estates, typically involved the temporary abandonment of symbols of authority. The model was that of 'total prestation, the surrender of all the resources of an individual or community to the visiting sovereign'.[14] On James's progress of 1617, Sir Richard Hoghton of Hoghton Tower, Lancashire, even modelled his relationship with the King on the controversial system of wardship, under which land would legally pass to the control of the king if an heir was a minor. Here a household god declared to James: 'Wee render upp to thy more powerfull Guard / This House;—this Knight is thyne, he is thy Ward'.[15] (Sir Richard, in 1617, was forty-six years old.)[16] The emphasis on placement was reiterated in turn by the monarchs and their officers. William Cecil, Lord Burghley, for instance, used Elizabeth's visit to Norfolk to revise a list of 324 county gentlemen, with the locations of their houses.[17] Such priorities are further marked by his annotations to his personal copy of Saxton's *Atlas*: a volume which includes sporadic notes about itineraries and special arrangements for posts, but consistent details, county by county, of resident justices of the peace.[18]

For the duration of her visit, the ultimate source of authority in the nation, usually experienced by the populace in mediated forms, was temporarily impressed upon a place. In accordance with the prevailing arts of sovereignty, however, Elizabeth rarely exercised this authority in direct and tangible ways. Even when lavish gifts were made to her – as became standard in the course of her reign – the self-interest of the giver 'had to be cloaked in the language of deference, and specific suits uncoupled from the royal visit'.[19] But the monarch bore a powerful capacity to confer honour upon those she visited, in part simply through her presence and in part through her practice of granting knighthoods while on progress. Indeed chroniclers of progresses routinely provide lists of those knighted, thereby

---

[13] *John Nichols's 'The Progresses and Public Processions of Queen Elizabeth I'*; Dovey, *Elizabethan Progress*, p. 102.

[14] Felicity Heal, 'Giving and Receiving on Royal Progress', in *Progresses, Pageants, and Entertainments*, pp. 48–9.

[15] *The Progresses, Processions, and Magnificent Festivities of King James the First*, ed. John Nichols, 4 vols. (London, 1828), III.399.

[16] George C. Miller, *Hoghton Tower: The History of the Manor, the Hereditary Lords and the Ancient Manor-house of Hoghton in Lancashire* (Preston, 1948), p. 79.

[17] Dovey, *Elizabethan Progress*, p. 74.   [18] BL MS Royal 18.D.iii.

[19] Heal, 'Giving and Receiving', p. 52.

acknowledging this as a key function of the progress. She was also exposed to petitions of various kinds.[20] For David Zaret, the petition is a signal model of political interaction within an absolutist system. 'To petition is to enter a privileged communicative space,' he argues, 'analogous to privileges that follow admission to the "freedom" of a municipal corporation. Petitions afforded subjects limited immunity to norms that otherwise restricted public commentary on political matters.'[21] Based on the presumption of spontaneity, the delivery of a petition momentarily actualized the theoretically permanent and indissoluble bonds between monarch and subject. In 1578, for instance, Edward Downes, lord of the manor of Earlham, in Norfolk, approached the Queen, in an apparently unscheduled intervention, and addressed her in verse, 'with the intention of clarifying his tenure of the manor'.[22] And the petition also provided a model for more formal and less direct requests. Burghley, for example, used a number of Elizabeth's visits to Theobalds in the 1590s to stage elaborate appeals for the elevation of his son, Robert Cecil, coupled with expressions of his own desire for retirement.[23]

The mythologies of place enacted in progress entertainments were forged within this framework of profoundly spatialized power relations. In particular, especially in the latter half of her reign, Elizabeth was occasionally greeted by the fairy queen, a figure derived at once from medieval romance and popular mythology, though given still greater prominence by Edmund Spenser's epic poem. The fairy queen serves most commonly as a mythologized shadow-image of Elizabeth, theoretically placeless yet curiously bound to the places in which she appears. At Elvetham, for instance, she is clearly associated with local fairy lore, declaring that she 'abide[s] in places under ground', and 'every night in rings of painted flowers' she 'Turne[s] round, and carroll[s] out *Elisaes* name'.[24] The Queen's presence simply draws the fairy queen forth, realizing a mythology that, the logic of the entertainments insists, is inherent in the land itself. Similarly, savage men, or cognate figures such as Silvanus, find themselves drawn from the woods in order to pay homage to Elizabeth. At Bisham, Berkshire, in 1592, Silvanus

[20] Cole, *Portable Queen*, pp. 78–85.
[21] *Origins of Democratic Culture: Printing, Petitions, and the Public Sphere in Early Modern England* (Princeton, 2000), p. 88.
[22] Dovey, *Elizabethan Progress*, p. 68.
[23] Cole, *Portable Queen*, pp. 79–80; James M. Sutton, *Materializing Space at an Early Modern Prodigy House: The Cecils at Theobalds, 1564–1607* (Aldershot, 2004), pp. 79–128.
[24] *John Nichols's 'The Progresses and Public Processions of Queen Elizabeth I'*.

simply appeared before Elizabeth, mystified and professedly 'enchanted'.[25]
At Kenilworth, in 1575, he was more expansive about Elizabeth's effect:

> O Queene I must confesse,
>   it is not without cause:
> These civile people so rejoyce,
>   that you should give them lawes.
> Since I, which live at large,
>   a wilde and savadge man,
> And have ronne out a wilfull race,
>   since first my lyfe began:
> Doe here submit my selfe,
>   beseeching you to serve.[26]

The essential function of such a figure is to demonstrate the power of royal authority over apparently untamed nature. The acknowledgement of forces of incivility of various kinds – the term 'wilfull' being suggestive at once of untamed erotic forces, in accordance with the wider thematics of the Kenilworth entertainment, but perhaps also of a capacity for political dissent – hints at potential challenges and limitations to Elizabeth. Yet the motif of savagery tamed by nobility is strong and consistent.[27] Indeed he is only there, and thus in a position to outline the shadowy forces of savagery, because he has been tamed by Elizabeth.

Through the course of Elizabeth's reign, these strains of panegyric were increasingly underscored by the resources of the pastoral mode. At Elvetham, for instance, 'the Fairy Queene and her maids' danced around 'a garland made in the fourme of an imperiall Crowne', and sang:

> *Elisa* is the fairest Queene,
> That ever trod upon this greene.
> *Elisaes* eyes are blessed starres,
> Inducing peace, subduing warres.
> *Elisaes* hand is christall bright,
> Her wordes are balme, her lookes are light.
> *Elisaes* brest is that faire hill,
> Where vertue dwels, and sacred skill,
> O blessed bee each day and houre,
> Where sweete *Elisa* builds her bowre.[28]

The substitution of 'fairest Queene' for 'fairy queen' appropriates for the panegyric all the mythic associations of the latter, just as the fairy

---

[25] *Ibid.* [26] *Ibid.*

[27] On this motif more widely in Elizabethan culture, see Bergeron, *English Civic Pageantry*, p. 32.

[28] *John Nichols's 'The Progresses and Public Processions of Queen Elizabeth I'.*

queen and her maids willingly subject themselves to the 'imperiall Crowne'. At Bisham, rural fertility is more specifically encoded as a product of Elizabethan rule, as the shepherdess Sybilla declares to Pan that 'By her it is ... that all our Carttes ... are laden with Corne'. Significantly, this quality is aligned almost immediately with a political effect: 'We upon our knees, wil entreat her to come into the valley, that our houses may be blessed with her presence, whose hartes are filled with quietnes by her governement'.[29] Crucially, the quiet heart, an image embedded in a tradition of pastoral *otium*, is also a politically quiescent heart.

As these instances demonstrate, however, even when the entertainments are at their most overtly celebratory pitch they are not free of political tensions. Silvanus hints at latent challenges to Elizabethan civility, rooted in the nation's wilder landscapes; Sybilla suggests the necessity of a politics of submission in order to avoid the open conflict evident elsewhere in Europe.[30] Importantly, in many such instances it is the brute realities of local environments and localized politics that disturb the fabric of panegyric. In some cases tensions centred on codes of property. At Kenilworth, for instance, Elizabeth famously rebuked the Lady of the Lake, and in turn the estate's owner, Robert Dudley, Earl of Leicester, for claiming ownership of the ornamental lake. As George Gascoigne reported: 'It pleazed her highnes too thank this lady and too ad withall, we had thought indeed the Lake had been oours, and doo you call it yourz noow?'[31] At Theobalds, in 1591, a Gardener and a Molecatcher argued over the rightful ownership of a box of jewels purportedly discovered buried in the earth. The correct answer, leading to the presentation of a gift to Elizabeth, is that by the law of treasure trove 'all monye or Jewlls hidden in the earthe is the Queenes'. But this solution is overlaid with contrary legal argument, suggesting not only the rights of 'the Lorde of the soile by the custome of the manor', but acknowledging also the labourers' palpable desires for personal gain.[32] Submission here is an effort, with a calculable cost.

In other cases, topical details, embedded in local landscapes, intrude upon the panegyric. Louis Adrian Montrose, for example, has demonstrated the extent to which the pastoralized celebration at Sudeley in 1591 labours to suppress a context of agrarian change and local discontent.[33] More fundamentally, as Michael Leslie has argued, on any progress Elizabeth necessarily

[29] *Ibid.*   [30] Cf. William Leahy, *Elizabethan Triumphal Processions* (Aldershot, 2005), pp. 118–20.
[31] *John Nichols's 'The Progresses and Public Processions of Queen Elizabeth I'.*   [32] *Ibid.*
[33] '"Eliza, Queene of Shepheardes", and the Pastoral of Power', *English Literary Renaissance*, 10 (1980), 171–3.

exposed herself to a degree of unpredictability, by virtue of her situation within intractably local and often unknown landscapes. 'Using the fluidity of the landscape setting', Leslie writes, progress entertainments could 'enter into a debate with the monarch about where the center lay and who should occupy that position.'[34] Specifically, this could mean exposure to thinly veiled arguments against her government's policies, as happened in Sir Philip Sidney's entertainment, *The Lady of May*, in which a contest between a shepherd and a forester for the hand of a shepherdess was also an argument between the respective values of a pacific and militant stance towards the continental wars of religion.[35] That Elizabeth famously chose the wrong side, favouring the shepherd, did not negate the essential affront. It could also mean exposure to the more urgent needs of her poorer subjects, as when she found herself unexpectedly 'environed with a number of begging rogues' on a ride on the outskirts of London in 1581.[36] Elizabeth's land was also, albeit infinitely more tenuously, their land.

In such instances, the qualities of place, steeped as they inevitably were in local interests and struggles, proved stubbornly resistant to the form of authority encoded by the royal progress. Much recent critical attention has been devoted to one of the most fraught of all progress entertainments, staged at Cowdray, Sussex, in 1591 on the estate of Anthony Browne, first Viscount Montague.[37] Montague was a Catholic in a notoriously Catholic region, and criticism has rightly centred on the ways in which the pageants staged in the course of Elizabeth's visit presented an argument against the values of the repressive Protestant centre. At one point, Elizabeth was shown an oak tree, 'whereon her Majesties armes, and all the armes of the Noblemen, and Gentlemen of that Shire, were hanged in Escutchions most beutifull', while a wild man expounded the virtues of the local gentry.[38] This was a bold assertion of honour, and arguably a veiled suggestion that those on the apparent margins of the nation may prove more valuable to Elizabeth than those at the heart of power. As the wild man

---

[34] '"Something Nasty in the Wilderness": Entertaining Elizabeth on Her Progresses', *Medieval and Renaissance Drama in England*, 10 (1998), 62.

[35] *Sir Philip Sidney*, ed. Katherine Duncan-Jones (Oxford, 1989), pp. 5–13. For analysis of the text's politics, see esp. Louis Adrian Montrose, 'Celebration and Insinuation: Sir Philip Sidney and the Motives of Elizabethan Courtship', *Renaissance Drama*, n.s. 8 (1977), 3–35; Leslie, '"Something Nasty in the Wilderness"', 56–8.

[36] *John Nichols's 'The Progresses and Public Processions of Queen Elizabeth I'*; see further Leahy, *Elizabethan Triumphal Processions*, p. 86.

[37] See esp. Curtis Breight, 'Caressing the Great'; Elizabeth Heale, 'Contesting Terms: Loyal Catholicism and Lord Montague's Entertainment at Cowdray, 1591', in *Progresses, Pageants, and Entertainments*, pp. 189–206; Leslie, '"Something Nasty in the Wilderness"', 63–9.

[38] *John Nichols's 'The Progresses and Public Processions of Queen Elizabeth I'*.

says: 'Your majesty they account the Oke, the tree of Jupiter, whose root is so deeplie fastened, that treacherie, though shee undermine to the centre, cannot finde the windings.'[39] Curiously, the Queen was led to the tree by an altogether more rootless figure, a pilgrim. While the pilgrim is overtly secularized, having professedly 'travelled manie countries' in search of 'antiquities', he has otherwise no right to be roaming Sussex.[40] The wild man, for one, is unconvinced, suggesting that 'such a disguised worlde it is, that one can scarce know a Pilgrime from a Priest, a tayler from a gentleman, nor a man from a woman'.[41] To see this pilgrim as a straightforward representation of a Catholic priest, however, would be too narrow an interpretation.[42] More profoundly, the pilgrim represents, in his direct confrontation of Elizabeth, occult forms of knowledge of her own nation. Within this context it is significant that the pilgrim's movement, by contrast with the Queen's, is positioned as at once unauthorized and untraceable. Within the canon of progress entertainments, this stands as a rare instance of Elizabeth being confronted by a person who is genuinely itinerant, and experiencing the land in markedly different ways to the Queen herself.

Progress visits to towns were potentially problematic for similar reasons. Whereas access to estates could be controlled, towns were more open to the flows of people upon which they depended for their social and economic survival. C. E. McGee has argued that the trend, evident by the middle of Elizabeth's reign, towards towns employing court-based men to take charge of their progress pageants is indicative of a prevailing concern to suppress local interests in favour of merely mirroring those of the centre.[43] Hence, in two of Thomas Churchyard's commissions, Elizabeth's visit to Bristol in 1574 became dominated by military shows, while for her stay in Norwich in 1578 much of the mythic paraphernalia of the countryside was imported wholesale. But towns also gave more specific displays of how their inhabitants viewed their significance within the nation. As Elizabeth left Sandwich, Kent, in 1573, for instance, she viewed a performance of local industry: 'upon a scaffold made uppon the wall of the scole howse yarde were dyvers children englishe and dutche to the nomber of cth or vi score, all spynning of fyne bay yarne'.[44] And in Norwich, one pageant involved

---

[39] *Ibid.* See Leslie, '"Something Nasty in the Wilderness"', 68.
[40] *John Nichols's 'The Progresses and Public Processions of Queen Elizabeth I'.* On pilgrimage, see further below, pp. 177–8.
[41] *Ibid.*   [42] Cf. Breight, 'Caressing the Great', 154.
[43] 'Mysteries, Musters, and Masque: The Import(s) of Elizabethan Civic Entertainments', in *Progresses, Pageants, and Entertainments*, pp. 104–21.
[44] *John Nichols's 'The Progresses and Public Processions of Queen Elizabeth I'.*

painted images of weavers working at their looms, producing different kinds of local cloth, in front of which a child expounded upon the production of wealth from labour.[45] Such displays could be yoked to Elizabeth's own agenda: as at Bristol, where a personification of the city pronounced that,

> We venter goods and livs ye knoe,
>   and travill seas and land.
> To bring by trafick heaps of wealth,
>   and treasuer to your hand.[46]

But towns, and the 'trafick' upon which they depended, were more complex than such a model allows, shaped as they were by combinations of individual desires and economic exchanges over which the monarch held little influence. Dutch cloth-workers, for instance, at both Sandwich and Norwich, suggested by their mere presence a porous model of nationhood, at odds with orthodox models of enclosure and placement.[47] For this was a nation, despite all contemporary assertions to the contrary, that was becoming as dependent upon national and international flows of capital and labour as it was upon the sovereign authority of the Queen.

Such limitations were clarified by occasional petitions from the citizens of towns suffering from economic problems. The monarch was not entirely without influence in the face of such appeals, especially given the highly regulated nature of trade and industry in the sixteenth century. At Stafford in 1575, for example, Elizabeth agreed both to renew the local capping industry's monopoly, thereby protecting it from competition, and to shift the assizes back to the town.[48] At Worcester on the same progress, however, citizens and monarch alike struggled to comprehend forces of economic change. The cloth industry was in such decline that, whereas once 380 'grett loomes' had supported 8,000 people, now there was demand only for the produce of 160 looms.[49] In the town's official address, the citizens tried to attribute their 'unlooked for trobles' to factors over which the Queen, in her roles as legal authority and military protector, may have some control. The troubles were thus caused, variously, by 'the breache of faytheles merchauntes', or 'the nomeber of pyrates upon the seas'. Yet, even as the citizens presented their monarch with a 'poore peece [i.e. purse] & small porcion

---

[45] *Ibid.* [46] *Ibid.*

[47] Curiously, in a rare instance of a financial gift from the Queen in the course of a progress, she sent £30 back to the Dutch and Walloon communities in Norwich shortly after her own departure from the city. The Dutch community, however, had given her a cup allegedly worth £50. (Dovey, *Elizabethan Progress*, pp. 77, 87.)

[48] Cole, *Portable Queen*, p. 111.

[49] *John Nichols's 'The Progresses and Public Processions of Queen Elizabeth I'.*

therin conteyned', the speech betrays an anxiety that the mysterious forces of 'trafyque' may not bend to Elizabeth's 'pryncely providence'.[50] Interestingly, across the period appeals to Elizabeth and her successor came to focus not so much on hopes that the monarch might bring back lost trade, but rather that he or she might help to improve the nation's commercial infrastructure. In 1573, for instance, the people of Rye appealed for help clearing their silted harbour, while on James's 1617 progress to Scotland he was petitioned by the citizens of both Lincoln and York about the poor state of their rivers.[51] Here, the monarch is positioned not as the only authorized traveller, binding a nation together by the act of movement, but as an authority who might facilitate England's quotidian flows of people and goods. In the cultural history of domestic travel in England, this distinction is critical.

The appeals of towns such as Lincoln and York brought into confrontation two fundamentally different experiences of mobility. The royal progress theatricalized travel, from its elaborate pageants down to its finer details of transportation. Poor roads, for instance, were routinely repaired to ease the journeys of a monarch, while efforts were also made to clear roads and towns of beggars and vagrants.[52] But other kinds of spatial imperatives and other forms of spatial knowledge pressed insistently upon the experience of the progresses, and as a result leave their traces on entertainments and pageant texts alike. In an entertainment at Sudeley, for instance, the 'Cutter of Cootsholde' (a sheep-shearer, and thus set subtly apart, as an itinerant labourer, from the shepherds), produces an almanac. While the almanac informs the group of Elizabeth's birthday, prompting an extended expression of 'wonder', the Cutter did not buy it for this reason. Instead, he says, 'I ever carrie it, to knowe the hye waies, to everie good towne, the faires, and the faire weather.'[53] For him, in other words, the book's value is that it facilitates popular acts of travel. In the wake of the Elizabethan progresses, I want now to suggest, such popular imperatives of mobility underpinned

---

[50] *Ibid.* On the shifting fortunes of the cloth industry in Worcester, see Alan D. Dyer, *The City of Worcester in the Sixteenth Century* (Leicester, 1973), pp. 109–19.

[51] Cole, *Portable Queen*, pp. 107–8; *Progresses, Processions, and Magnificent Festivities of King James the First*, III.265, III.271.

[52] On the repair of roads, see esp. Philip Harrison and Mark Brayshay, 'Post-Horse Routes, Royal Progresses and Government Communications in the Reign of James I', *Journal of Transport History*, 18 (1997), 124. On the removal of beggars and vagrants, see esp. Cole, *Portable Queen*, pp. 163–4; Bergeron, *English Civic Pageantry*, pp. 99–100.

[53] *John Nichols's 'The Progresses and Public Processions of Queen Elizabeth I'.*

various appropriations and transformations of the royal model, which posited in turn very different models of spatial politics.

PROGRESS TEXTS AND COMMON AUTHORS

On a progress, each of the estimated 30 to 350 people travelling with the court was recorded in the Bouche of Court and the Book of Diet.[54] These documents identified those people who were authorized to be with the travelling party, defining their roles in relation to the monarch. The status of the authors of progress entertainments, by comparison, was more complicated. Some would be sent ahead of the main party, thereby enjoying a degree of independence in their shaping of an entertainment. Most would be employed by hosts – towns or the owners of estates – and may as a result, as suggested above, bring local interests into conjunction with the imperatives of panegyric. Moreover, especially when bringing their achievements into print, some sought to found their own reputations as authors upon their involvement in the events. These matters have been considered by others. Notably, Wendy Wall has examined the possibilities for 'different kinds of textual authorization' created by the publication of entertainment texts, focusing on the examples of Sidney and Gascoigne.[55] Daryl W. Palmer has taken a step further, into the realm of popular print, arguing that a number of writers appropriated for their own purposes 'authorized representations of pageantry'.[56] Working within this context, I want here to focus on the way in which the progress serves as both a rationale and model for acts of authorship. Crucially, it provides a model of legitimate, and marketable, mobility. This is apparent, I suggest, in the career of one of the most prominent, though critically neglected, of pageant-authors, Thomas Churchyard. And it is extended in turn by popular writers with no direct experience of progresses: men such as William Kemp and John Taylor.

For Churchyard, an association with progress entertainments marked a pivotal moment in his audacious project to create for himself an identity as a professional writer. After an early career as a soldier, Churchyard wrote a range of militaristic and topical texts, and contributed to *A Mirror for Magistrates*. Though never more than a marginal figure at court, he was

---

[54] Cole, *Portable Queen*, pp. 42–3.
[55] *The Imprint of Gender: Authorship and Publication in the English Renaissance* (Ithaca and London, 1993), pp. 111–67 (quote at p. 115).
[56] *Hospitable Performances: Dramatic Genre and Cultural Practices in Early Modern England* (West Lafayette, Indiana, 1992), pp. 119–55 (quote at p. 120).

commissioned to devise the Bristol entertainment of 1574, which he subsequently published as just one item of his miscellaneous volume, *The Firste Parte of Churchyardes Chippes*.[57] This appears in retrospect a somewhat modest effort, in which Churchyard positions himself principally as a reporter of events; however, it makes Churchyard the first identifiable deviser of a pageant entertainment, and doubtless helped to secure his reputation for such work.[58] Significantly, as David Bergeron has noted, when he published his account of the Norwich entertainment of 1578 he transformed his approach.[59] *A Discourse of The Queenes Majesties Entertainement in Suffolk and Norffolk*, rushed into print in the same year as the progress, centres attention almost as much on Churchyard himself as on Elizabeth. The title-page declares that the text is 'Devised by THOMAS CHURCHYARDE, Gent. with divers shewes of his own invention sette out at *Norwich*'. From the outset it juxtaposes the principal narrative of the progress with that of Churchyard's own experience, as he was 'called' to Norwich three weeks ahead of the court to devise the central entertainments, and struggled to bring these to fruition, despite the contingencies of the weather and mysterious 'crossing causes in the Citie'.[60]

The narrative of his efforts culminates in his desire, on Elizabeth's final day in Norwich, 'to do somewhat might make the Queene laugh'.[61] Since his planned allegorical entertainment of the previous day had been thwarted by rain, Churchyard hurriedly transformed his boy-actors from nymphs of the water into fairies. These boys waited with Churchyard by the road out of town, and leapt through a hedge as she passed, dancing and delivering speeches in verse. The text describes the effect:

> Their attire, and comming so strangely out, I know made the Queenes highnesse smyle and laugh withall. And I hearing this good hope, being apparelled like a water Sprite, beganne to sounde a Timbrell, and the rest with me ... And although I had no great harting, yet as I durst, I ledde the yong foolishe *Phayries* a daunce, which boldnesse of mine bredde no disgrace, and as I heard said, was well taken.[62]

The authorial self-referentiality, which emerges as a characteristic of Churchyard's work, captures both the necessary boldness and the ultimate success of his makeshift device. The effect not only figures Churchyard as a

---

[57] (1575), fols. 100v–110v.   [58] Bergeron, *English Civic Pageantry*, p. 26.

[59] 'The "I" of the Beholder: Thomas Churchyard and the 1578 Pageant', in *Progresses, Pageants, and Entertainments*, pp. 142–59.

[60] *John Nichols's 'The Progresses and Public Processions of Queen Elizabeth I'*. Bergeron notes that this was the first time that a printed pageant text had borne the deviser's name ('The "I" of the Beholder', p. 147).

[61] *John Nichols's 'The Progresses and Public Processions of Queen Elizabeth I'*.   [62] *Ibid.*

successful courtier, adeptly balancing boldness and deference, but also looks outward to the audience of the printed text, claiming before them an unquestionable measure of authority. In what is presented as a test of his powers, Churchyard made the Queen laugh.

Churchyard reflected again on his relation to Elizabeth in a New Year's Day entertainment staged at Hampton Court, probably in 1594.[63] This piece centres attention on a painter, whose 'most skill' is to 'showe at full, trym Townes and stately Towers'.[64] The poem about the painter, which was presumably recited before a series of painted images, describes his paintings of a series of English, Welsh and Irish towns. After producing these works, however, the painter is drawn to court. Here, 'peeping throw' the 'Presence Chamber doore', he sees a number of female courtiers, 'like Goddesses divine', and is prompted further – like a frustrated Actaeon – to speculate about what he is not able to see: 'If such faire flowrs quoth he, in Presence men may find, / In Privey-chamber sure, some faire sweet saints are shrind'.[65] If the painter is interpreted as an authorial figure, as seems unavoidable, the effect of this image of an artist is curiously double-edged. On the one hand, he is positioned on the margins of the court, tantalizingly out of reach of the one person whose approval would justify his labours. On the other hand, the weight of the text leading up to this pregnant image pulls in another direction, suggesting the value of the painter's experience and travel through the nation. As a reflection on authorship, the text thus juxtaposes two competing sources of authority, just as it seeks to reconcile two divergent models of nationhood. For Churchyard, at this stage over seventy years old, it epitomizes one of the dominant tensions of his career.

This image of authorship helps to contextualize a book Churchyard wrote several years earlier. *The Worthines of Wales* (1587) appears loosed from any discernible generic ties, yet it stands as one of the most compelling essays in British travel-writing produced in the sixteenth century. It claims some connection with an Elizabethan interest in Welsh history, and also with the fledgling genre of chorography.[66] (It is unlikely, though, that Churchyard would have encountered Camden's *Britannia*, first published in Latin in 1586, by the time he was writing.) But it is otherwise a quirky, idiosyncratic piece, loosely structured around a survey of particular shires of Wales, but including historical and geographical digressions, and passages of panegyric on likely patrons. It is mostly in verse, of different metrical

---

[63] *Ibid.*   [64] *Ibid.*   [65] *Ibid.*
[66] On Welsh history, see esp. Humphrey Llwyd, *The Breviary of Britayne*, trans. T. Twyne (1573); and Caradoc of Lancarvon, *A Historie of Cambria, now called Wales*, trans. Humphrey Llwyd (1584).

forms, though it includes some purportedly historical documents, in prose, in both Latin and English. What holds it together is precisely what Churchyard had discovered, through his work on pageants, could provide a foundation for authorship. The text relies, that is, on individual experience. At more than one point Churchyard expounds upon this approach:

> The eye is judge, as Lanterne cleere of light,
> That searcheth through, the dim and darkest place:
>
> ...
> But where no face, nor judging eye doth come,
> The sence is blynd, the spirit is deaffe and dome:
> For wit can not, conceive till sight send in
> Some skill to head, whereby we knowledge win.   (sig. C3r–v)

And the eye is of course dependent upon the author's travel, which Churchyard posits as more valuable for his purposes than research in the works of former 'good Authors' (sig. *4r). Even within the emergent context of chorography, this stands as a particularly bold claim. Significantly, in the dedication he directs these efforts back to Elizabeth, as his own greatest patron and the sovereign authority over both England and Wales. Yet Elizabeth, unlike Churchyard, never reached Wales. It is the poet, rather than the monarch, who claims the power to describe and interpret the land, as he tells Elizabeth: 'I have travayled sondry times of purpose through [Wales], and what is written of I have beheld, and throughly seene' (sig. *2v).

In a thematic that is fundamental to Churchyard's representation of space, he insists further that travel is not merely a source of pleasure, but a matter of labour. He pauses on occasion to address himself, as though goading himself onward:

> Is bodie tyerd with travaile, God forbid,
> That wearie bones, so soone should seeke for rest:
> Shall sences sleepe, when head in house is hid,
> As though some charme, were crept in quiet brest.   (sig. G3v)

Subsequently, deploying a strain of georgic imagery later developed by Spenser, he urges: 'Put hand to Plough, like man goe through with all, / Thy ground is good, run on thou canst not fall' (sig. L2v).[67] And such lessons are also projected outward, in his assessment of the Welsh people. Wales is depicted as 'a Countrey rich at will', which promises to make the

---

[67] On Spenser's recurrent use of the figure of the ploughman to represent authorial labour, see esp. Anthony Low, *The Georgic Revolution* (Princeton, 1985), pp. 35–70.

Welsh 'full quickly wealthie' if they are prepared to 'take paynes to plye the Plough' and labour in the 'sweat of [their] browes' (sigs. F2v–F3r). Furthermore, this wealth is imagined as itself dependent upon mobility, as goods are channelled through the routes of traffic, centring on Shrewsbury:

> This Towne with more, fit members for the head,
> Makes *London* ritch, yet reapes great gayne from thence:
> It gives good gold, for Clothes and markes of lead,
> And for Welsh ware, exchaungeth English pence.   (sig. K3v)

In his Bristol entertainment, considered above, the city had boasted to Elizabeth how its engagement in 'trafick' brought 'heaps of wealth and treasuer to your land'. *The Worthines of Wales*, by comparison, makes the point about economic process in more abstract terms, concerned less with a central source of authority than with the transportation of goods and money across Wales and England, at the behest of countless individual subjects. From this perspective the English capital becomes 'A fountaine head, that many Condits serve', in a process of circulation as vital as the flow of rivers to the sea (sig. K3v).

Churchyard's shift of emphasis, from the mobile monarch to the laborious mobility of commoners, establishes in turn a context within which to set another cluster of journey texts which emerged at the end of the Elizabethan period. In these texts, commoners undertake domestic journeys that are rendered noteworthy by some particular, quirky challenge. Most notably, of those recorded in print, Richard Ferris rowed by sea from London to Bristol, while Will Kemp, Shakespeare's first stage-clown, morris-danced his way from London to Norwich.[68] And, at the tail-end of the tradition, the London waterman John Taylor (whose later works of travel-writing I will consider at greater length in Chapter 6) seized upon the model as a way of establishing his career, publishing an account of a walk to Edinburgh in which he carried no money and swore never to beg for food or shelter.[69] There are no direct links between these writers and Churchyard; yet, like *The Worthines of Wales*, their pamphlets are created in part out of the purloined fabric of progress texts. Kemp's narrative of his singular 'progresse', *Kemps Nine Daies Wonder*, as Palmer observes, not only 'adopts a royal genre', but follows the path of his monarch, as described in Churchyard's 1578 work.[70] Taylor, whose *Pennyles Pilgrimage* is

[68] *The Most Dangerous and Memorable Adventure of Richard Ferris* (1590); *Kemps Nine Daies Wonder* (1600).

[69] *The Pennyles Pilgrimage* (1618); in *All the Workes* (1630), I.121–39.

[70] *Kemps Nine Daies Wonder* (1600), sig. A2v; Palmer, *Hospitable Performances*, p. 127.

the other text I want to consider in any detail here, is by comparison multiply parasitic, narrating a trip, from London to Edinburgh, recently taken not only by King James but also by James's leading court poet, Ben Jonson.[71]

For all their awareness of the model of the progress, Kemp and Taylor alike reposition themselves, attending to the economics of both travel and authorship. Hence, while each man is determined to demonstrate the public profile of his journey, particularly by noting the hordes of people who followed him out of London (and, in Kemp's case, shadowed him all along his route), each is also concerned to renegotiate relations between traveller and audience. The approach is calculating, even entrepreneurial. Indeed, since each man is travelling on the basis of wagers their journeys are essentially commercial exercises, and followers and readers alike are treated as customers. In Kemp's case, as Max W. Thomas argues, this attitude underpins the translation of a traditional act of communal celebration, the morris dance, into something approaching the status of a 'fungible commodity', as Kemp moves relentlessly and independently through space rather than observing bounds of place and associated codes of festivity.[72] It also informs his overtly mercantile attitude to the gift. He states, for instance, that 'Sir Thomas Mildmay standing at his Parke pale, received gently a payre of garters of me: gloves, points, and garters, being my ordinary marchandize, that I put out to venter for performance of my merry voyage' (sig. B1v). In other words, the gift, like the journey, is an investment, ventured in expectation of reward. Appropriately, at the end of the pamphlet, having detailed the Norwich mayor's promise of a lifetime pension of forty shillings per year, Kemp pauses to consider, in a self-satisfied tone, 'what profit I have made by my Morrice' (sig. D2r). For both Kemp and Taylor, moreover, the commercial imperative had a significant textual dimension. Kemp claims that his pamphlet is necessary in order to secure his reputation, in the process correcting versions of his journey circulated by 'impudent ... Ballad-makers' (sig. D3r). For Taylor, meanwhile, whose journey itself proved less lucrative than that of his predecessor, the fashioning of authorial authority arguably exceeded in significance the more immediate desire for return from his

---

[71] On James's progress of 1617, see *Progresses, Processions, and Magnificent Festivities of King James the First*, III.255–436. On Jonson's journey of 1618, see Ian Donaldson, *Jonson's Walk to Scotland* (Edinburgh, 1992); and James Knowles, 'Jonson in Scotland: Jonson's Mid-Jacobean Crisis', in *Shakespeare, Marlowe, Jonson: New Directions in Biography*, ed. Takashi Kozuka and J. R. Mulryne (Aldershot, 2006), pp. 259–77.

[72] '*Kemps Nine Daies Wonder*: Dancing Carnival into Market', *PMLA*, 107 (1992), 511–23.

backers.[73] This was not a simple process, since Taylor learned to trade on a reputation for buffoonery and clownishness; however, it was essential to his subsequent career. It was thus to some extent fortuitous that the commercial failure of the journey provided a further opportunity to launch himself into print, as he published in the following year a poem in which he '*satyrically suited 800 of his bad debters, that will not pay him for his returne of his journey from Scotland*'.[74]

The attention in these texts to individual opportunists travelling through the nation also informs their representations of hospitality. The royal progress, as discussed above, was in part an enactment of bonds between the monarch and her subjects. By contrast, Kemp's text translates this discourse into a new register, typically figuring hospitality as an endorsement of his own success, in his task and also in his public identity. At one inn, Kemp's arrival sets the host 'stammering' as 'he began to study for a fit comparison', before eventually declaring that Kemp was 'even as welcome, as the Queenes best grey-hound'.[75] Whatever the man may actually have said, Kemp's decision to record his welcome in precisely these terms not only plays on the text's understated analogy with the progress, but also underscores the author's novel status as he reshapes the royal model into something more akin to a prize-sport. Taylor's text offers an extended play on another form of hospitality: that of Catholic mendicancy. He is a secular pilgrim, travelling across his nation and testing whether those he meets along the way are capable of recognizing the peculiar, almost indefinable qualities which make him worthy of support. Much of that support comes from members of the gentry and nobility; indeed, in his account of his time in Scotland he is keen to point out his connections with members of James's court, as part of his life-long project of defining himself as (to quote the title-page of the 1618 edition of *The Pennyles Pilgrimage*) 'the Kings Majesties *Water-Poet*'.[76] Yet, despite his venture's overt repudiation of a commercial economy, he also attends repeatedly to sites of commercial hospitality. Taylor assumes the right to judge hosts – and, by implication, to assess their inns for his readers – on the basis of their response to him. Hence, to take one instance, he approves of 'Master *Taylor*, at the Sarazens head' in St Albans, who 'Unask'd (unpaid for) me both lodg'd and

---

[73] On Kemp's position in relation to the 'Ballad-makers', see David Harris Sacks, 'London's Dominion: The Metropolis, the Market Economy, and the State', in *Material London, ca. 1600*, ed. Lena Cowen Orlin (Philadelphia, 2000), pp. 40–1.

[74] *A Kicksey Winsey: or a Lerry Come-Twang* (1619); in *Workes*, II.35–43.

[75] *Kemps Nine Daies Wonder*, sig. C1v.   [76] Cf. Knowles, 'Jonson in Scotland', p. 267.

fed'.[77] This form of judgement is essentially nonsensical, since it requires innkeepers to act against the commercial basis on which their houses operate. If a host demands payment from Taylor, he is dismissed as churlish. Yet it also typifies the peculiar, paradoxical status of the venture, which positions Taylor as at once special and deserving of support, in the model of a progressing monarch, and fundamentally common, tracing the paths taken by countless numbers of his countrymen.

In their efforts to translate acts of domestic travel into works of literature, writers such as Churchyard, Kemp and Taylor were working against the weight of powerful cultural orthodoxies. Legitimate roles for commoners on the road were severely limited. This is part of Taylor's point in his playful invocation of the proscribed model of pilgrimage, and it is a point that Churchyard, in particular, confronts altogether more studiously. For the purposes of such efforts, established models, such as that of the royal progress, provided valuable 'materials' and 'codes', available for appropriation and subtle transformation.[78] These texts are not, as a result, transgressive or subversive. They do not endorse the unfettered movement of commoners; rather, they insist that something special about the journey or the journeyer legitimizes the enterprise, just as royal progresses depended on the unique nature of their central figure. Nonetheless, these texts stand as pivotal exercises in the representation of common mobility, positioning the individual traveller as a source of authority, and the act of travel as a labour worthy of financial reward. Their authors are fascinated by their nation's networks of communication, and they glance knowingly beyond their own journeys to a regime of circulation in which even the unwelcoming innkeepers will make a person welcome 'for your money'.[79] Indeed they begin to imagine England as a space, in Taylor's terms, infinitely amenable to 'painfull industry'.[80]

THE WANDERING KING

Beggars wander through land to which they have minimal connection; monarchs progress through land over which they assert proprietorial and legal authority.[81] For a few years in the 1640s, however, this essential distinction within the dominant social discourse of space broke down. On more than one occasion during this period of civil war, King Charles

[77] *Workes*, I.123–4.   [78] Cf. Palmer, *Hospitable Performances*, p. 132.
[79] Cf. Sacks, 'London's Dominion', 41; Taylor, *Workes*, I.124.   [80] *Workes*, I.133.
[81] On representations of beggars, see above, p. 91.

fled across his country in disguise. At other times he was held as a prisoner, was forcibly moved from one place to another, or was required to dwell in palaces which had been redefined as the property of the parliament. Not only was he not recognized as the ultimate owner of the whole nation, he did not even own Hampton Court. The shock of this should not be overstated. The English were familiar with images of impotent, displaced kings from the pages of chronicle histories, and also from the history play. Even in these sources, however, the image held a fundamental mystery, and this was only intensified in the 1640s, when there was no pretender but rather an unprecedented contest between the monarch and parliament. In the present context, a consideration of texts which reflect upon Charles's journeys, from royalist poetry to parliamentarian newsbooks, leads to an engagement with some of the major issues in studies of seventeenth-century political culture. The discussion must touch, most notably, on shifts in political theory, the impact of printed newsbooks, the emergent significance of individual opinion, and the development of a public sphere.

In royalist panegyric of the early 1640s, one defensive reaction to the King's difficulties was to propound a discourse of ubiquity. For example, several poems contributed to *Irenodia Cantabrigiensis*, a Cambridge University collection published to celebrate Charles's return from Scotland in 1641, insist on the essential distinction between the travel of a king and that of his subjects. For one writer:

> Princes in this respect are Gods, I see;
> Since even They must Omnipresent be,
> If not in person to inculcate aw,
> Yet by the pow'rfull presence of a law.[82]

John Cleveland, who would become more perturbed about Charles's movements in the 1640s than any other royalist poet, adopted at this point a similar position:

> Return'd? I'll ne'r believe 't; First prove him hence;
> Kings travel by their beams and influence.
> Who says the soul gives out her gests, or goes
> A flitting progresse 'twixt the head and toes?
> She rules by Omnipresence, and shall we
> Denie a Prince the same ubiquitie?[83]

---

[82] T. Yardley, 'On his Majesties Journey to Scotland, as Also on his Happy Return', in *Irenodia Cantabrigiensis*, sig. K4r.

[83] *The Poems of John Cleveland*, ed. Brian Morris and Eleanor Withington (Oxford, 1967), pp. 2–3 (ll. 1–6). (In *Irenodia Cantabrigiensis* the poem is at sigs. L1v–L2r.)

Cleveland's poem, in particular, is forged out of the language of the 'progresse', as it anxiously weighs Charles's fraught trip to Scotland with the models established by his predecessors.[84] The formalities of a monarch's movement – such as the 'gests', or official itinerary – are thus figured merely as unnecessary trappings. Indeed physical movement itself, within the terms of this logic, becomes virtually irrelevant. But the strains on such a logic become increasingly pressing as the poem continues, teasing away at the paradox of ubiquity in a series of conceits:

> Yet as the tree at once both upward shoots,
> And just as much grows downward to the roots,
> So at the same time that he posted thither
> By counter-stages he rebounded hither.   (ll. 9–12)

Charles did, effectively, 'post' back and forth to Scotland, just as the royal post shuttled its way daily across the British nations. But that is not what Cleveland is trying to say. He is using the analogy of the royal postal system – as he uses that of a tree growing upward and downward at the same time – to support his model of ubiquitous authority. The argument and the diction, however, never quite coalesce. By the close of the sentence, the verb 'rebounded' leaves the unfortunate impression of a monarch with all the autonomy of a tennis ball.

    Five years later, when Charles fled in disguise from Oxford, only to be captured within eight days, royalist poets were forced to look more critically at the staple tropes of panegyric. Cleveland's consideration of this 'strange journey', 'The Kings Disguise', has attracted attention for its analysis of a king 'participat[ing] in his own occlusion'.[85] Henry Vaughan's 'The King Disguised: Written about the Same Time that Mr John Cleveland Wrote His', by comparison, is even more acute in its attention to the spatial dimensions of Charles's transgression.[86] The poem begins: 'A King and no King! Is he gone from us, / And stol'n alive into his coffin thus?' (ll. 1–2). This positions Charles's flight as a bleak negation of the progress. To be 'gone' is to depart from his geographical place but also to take leave of his political place, stealing away into a living death.[87] Subsequent lines struggle to distinguish the peripatetic king from a mere vagrant:

---

[84] On this poem, see James Loxley, *Royalism and Poetry in the English Civil Wars: The Drawn Sword* (Basingstoke, 1997), pp. 142–3.

[85] *Poems*, pp. 6–9 (quote at l. 117). Loxley, *Royalism and Poetry*, p. 138. See also Gerald Hammond, *Fleeting Things: English Poets and Poems, 1616–1660* (Cambridge, Mass., 1990), pp. 84–6.

[86] Vaughan, *The Complete Poems*, ed. Alan Rudrum (New Haven and London, 1976), pp. 327–8.

[87] The imagery is indebted to the opening line of Cleveland's 'The Kings Disguise' ('And why so coffin'd in this vile disguise').

> Wolves did pursue him, and to fly the ill
> He wanders (Royal Saint!) in sheep-skin still.
> Poor, obscure shelter! if that shelter be
> Obscure, which harbours so much Majesty. (ll. 7–10)

Like Cleveland before him, Vaughan seeks to align Charles with a prophecy, that had circulated in the preceding years, of a mysterious 'white king'. According to one exposition of the prophecy, the white king 'shall obscure himselfe for a certaine time or some dayes or weeks after … his escape', and 'men shall commonly say; there the White King is; in such a place; here; there; no where; or yonder he is'.[88] But the poem never quite manages to reconcile myth and reality, as it ponders the implications of regal wandering and obscurity. The central paragraph concedes the underlying anxieties most openly:

> But I am vexed, that we at all can guess
> This change, and trust great *Charles* to such a dress.
> When he was first obscured with this coarse thing,
> He graced *plebeians*, but profaned the King.
> Like some fair Church, which zeal to charcoals burned,
> Or his own Court now to an ale-house turned. (ll. 27–32)

Ostensibly, the final line functions as the second half of a couplet of twinned similes, forged in an effort to comprehend actions which the poet urges himself to 'trust'. Yet topicality leaks into the passage. While the preceding line relies comfortably on a staple of anti-puritan satire, the image of a court 'turned' to an alehouse wrestles in vain with the brute facts of Charles's journey. According to the political theory that underpinned the royal progress, the location of the court was entirely dependent upon the location of the monarch. Vaughan's nightmare vision, however, is of location undoing the mysteries of royalty. In the syntax of the poem, Charles does not turn an alehouse into a court; instead the alehouse effects the transformation upon the monarch and his courtiers. As much as the poem seeks to set this image in its proper place, as it figures Charles as a 'Royal Riddle' and turns upon his enemies, the spiralling implications of a disguised, wandering king are too profound to be quashed.

Other writers developed extended narratives of Charles's movements. John Taylor was by the mid-1640s a veteran of print culture, having published his *Workes* in 1630 and continuing apace thereafter, not

---

[88] William Lilly, *A Prophecy of the White King* (1644), p. 12. For an outline of the texts associated with the myth, see the editor's headnote to Cleveland's 'the Kings Disguise' (*Poems*, p. 87).

only with travel pamphlets but also with a series of pieces of anti-puritan and pro-royalist polemic. He even tried his hand at conventional panegyric, publishing a poem celebrating the return of Charles to 'his own House', Hampton Court, in the summer of 1647.[89] More interestingly, however, the following year he sought to combine travel-writing and royalist polemic, in a pamphlet describing his own journey to visit Charles on the Isle of Wight. *Tailors Travels from London to the Isle of Wight* struggles, against the weight of the genre that Taylor had shaped for himself, to position the stationary king at the heart of the narrative. Unlike most of his other travel texts, therefore, this pamphlet describes a direct, linear journey to and from a particular place, where Taylor declares that 'all my Earthly blisse' was that Charles 'gave me straight his Royall hand to kisse' (p. 10). Moreover, Taylor's own journey is paralleled by a number of others narrated within the pamphlet, including those taken by several commoners seeking cure, by the royal touch, of the king's evil (pp. 10–12). But the text is also, irrepressibly, a narration of Taylor's own travels. It begins – like so many of his works – by conceding his 'intent to get some Silver in this Iron Age', and describing his arrangements made with his 'Customers', or financial supporters (t.p.). Moreover, like the pamphlets to which those backers had become accustomed, it presents the author 'merrily' pursuing his course, and includes comic narratives of his trials along the way, such as 'a dirty tale' of being dumped in the mud (pp. 5, 8). The imprisoned king, therefore, cannot hold his evident position at the heart of the narrative.

Taylor is also determined not to be seen to be writing news. A prefatory poem states:

> This pamphlet is not stuft with Triviall Bables,
> Or vaine prodigious undigested fables:
> This is no *Mercury* (with scoffs and jeeres)
> To raise debate, and set us by the eares,
> As if poore *England* had not yet endur'd
> Sufficient plagues; but she must be assur'd,
> By New, New, Newes, of New frights, and new foes,
> And future mischiefes worse then present woes.   (p. 5)

For Taylor, news is an unreliable agent of dissension, designed purely 'To raise debate, and set us by the eares'. His reaction is not uncommon, within a period in which the flow of printed newsbooks reached unprecedented levels, and their outspoken political stances helped to clarify divisions

---

[89] *The Kings Most Excellent Majesties Wellcome to his owne House* (1647).

within the state.[90] Until the 1640s, in fact, the publication of domestic political news had been strictly controlled. Earlier forms of printed news, such as reports of crimes or, indeed, narratives of royal progresses, were occasional and relatively unconcerned with political debates.[91] While the circulation of news in manuscript had gathered pace in the early seventeenth century, and while the publication of 'corantoes', principally concerned with events on the continent, had flourished in the 1620s, the distinct news explosion of the 1640s unquestionably shocked many observers. As Taylor perceives, news effected a shift in the centre of authority, away from the King and towards the 'intelligence' of individual news-gatherers.[92] Moreover, it provided a forum for the expression of individual opinion. As Joad Raymond argues, 'Opinion was one of the things that invaded England in 1640–1642, most notably in the guise of books and pamphlets.'[93] For Habermas, opinion is also one of the foundation-stones required for the construction of a public sphere.[94]

Throughout the middle years of the 1640s, newsbooks shadowed the movements of Charles, speculating on his motives and exposing him to ridicule for his loss of control. At the time of his 1646 flight from Oxford, for instance, Marchamont Nedham's *Mercurius Britanicus* declared that Charles had 'shifted away privately in the habit of a *Serving-man*, and (if all be true) as *Jack Ashburnhams* man, with a Cloak-bag behind him ... a deserved posture for all Princes that endeavour to make their *subjects slaves* by the sword'.[95] A year earlier, after the battle of Naseby, Nedham had opened one issue of *Mercurius Britanicus* in an affected state of perplexity:

Where is King *Charles*? What's become of him? The strange variety of opinions leaves nothing certain: for some say, when he saw the Storm comming after him as far as *Bridgwater*, he *ran away* out to his *dearly beloved* in *Ireland*; yes, they say he *ran away* out of his own *Kingdome* very *Majestically*: Others will have him erecting a new *Monarchy* in the Isle of *Anglesey*: A third sort there are say he hath hid himselfe. I will not now determine the matter, because there is such a deale of uncertainty; and therefore (for the satisfaction of my Countrymen) it were best to send a *Hue and Cry* after him.[96]

---

[90] On this development, see esp. Joad Raymond, *The Invention of the Newspaper: English Newsbooks 1641–1649* (Oxford, 1996).

[91] Raymond, *Invention of the Newspaper*, p. 6; on progress texts as news, see Natalie Mears, *Queenship and Political Discourse in the Elizabethan Realms* (Cambridge, 2005), pp. 154–8.

[92] On the significance of 'intelligence', see Raymond, *Invention of the Newspaper*, p. 161.

[93] 'Introduction: Networks, Communication, Practice', in *News Networks in Seventeenth-Century Britain and Europe*, ed. Raymond (London, 2006), p. 4.

[94] *Structural Transformation of the Public Sphere*, pp. 89–102.

[95] *Mercurius Britanicus*, no. 128 (27 April–4 May 1646), pp. 1095–6.

[96] *Mercurius Britanicus*, no. 92 (28 July–4 August 1645), p. 825.

The proclamation of hue and cry, employed to trace fugitive criminals, represents the authority of the state brought to bear upon a subject who has temporarily eluded its structures of legal and spatial discipline. For Nedham to imagine turning this machinery upon the King is therefore a treacherously arch piece of satire, and it is unsurprising that this passage prompted a reprimand from the House of Lords.[97] The unavoidable implication is that a king who cannot be traced is not a king at all: just as the suggestion of a monarchy contracted to the Isle of Anglesey is a mere parody of a monarchy that represents and controls the entire nation. The terms of the suggested hue and cry, which Nedham proceeds to provide, underscore the function of the newsbook, stating that anyone who locates Charles should '*give notice to* Britanicus, *and you shall be well paid for your paines*'. This remains an exercise of scurrilous fantasy; however, it is remarkable for the clarity with which it claims for news itself, as a fledgling institution within the state, the power not only to trace but ultimately to discipline the King. The newsbook here actively represents the interests of the nation's citizens.

The development of news thus involved a dispersal of authority, and this process had spatial as well as social dimensions. As others have argued, across the early modern period news itself became a vital cohesive force, furthering 'a sense of the integration of local and national'.[98] In the period of the Civil War, one of the most audacious and damaging acts of Charles's opponents was the interception and publication of his private letters after his defeat at Naseby in 1645.[99] The effects of this were manifold. By translating private correspondence into news, to be picked over endlessly by commentators such as Nedham, it exposed the King to criticism as both a man and a politician. Yet it also epitomized the King's loss of control over the nation's structures of communications. Indeed no single act would more sharply exemplify the long-term shift whereby the postal network metamorphosed from a privilege of the sovereign into a fundamentally public resource.[100] More generally, newsbooks in the 1640s at once represented and embodied the spread of information, not merely from the centre to the periphery, but in more complex and haphazard ways. Newsbooks

---

[97] Joad Raymond, 'Marchamont Nedham', *ODNB*.

[98] Richard Cust, 'News and Politics in Early Seventeenth-Century England', *Past and Present*, 112 (1986), 69; cf. Raymond, *Invention of the Newspaper*, p. 16.

[99] *The King's Cabinet Opened* (1645). See further Loxley, *Royalism and Poetry*, pp. 129–32; Derek Hirst, 'Reading the Royal Romance: Or, Intimacy in a King's Cabinet', *The Seventeenth Century*, 18 (2003), 211–29.

[100] On the common assumption, across Europe, that the system of posts was 'a privilege of the sovereign', see Paul Arblaster, 'Posts, Newsletters, Newspapers: England in a European System of Communications', in *News Networks in Seventeenth-Century Britain and Europe*, p. 20.

transformed the gathering and circulation of intelligence from a process controlled by the state into one directly involving the state's citizens. The newsbook was as a result ideally shaped to the interests of a nation wrenched into unprecedented levels of mobility by the forces of war. It not only brought information to those involved in the fighting, but enlisted them as active agents in the gathering of news.

In this respect it is appropriate that news insistently valorized figures so often seen as objects of fear and loathing: mobile commoners. The figure of the unfixed and unidentifiable revealer of hidden truths had a long history in pamphlet literature and manuscript libel, stretching back to the Elizabethan Marprelate tracts and including evasively mythical speakers such as 'Tom Tell-Troth'.[101] Like Churchyard in his writings, as considered above, such authorial personae were founded on assumptions of the essential value of individual experience. For Churchyard, 'The eye is judge'; Taylor, similarly, sets out for Edinburgh wanting 'to be an eye-witnes'.[102] But while these particular men sought to subordinate individual knowledge to the authority of their royal patrons, in the 1640s the same foundation for discursive authority was deftly turned against the King. This is evident in Nedham's facetious request for help finding Charles. It is equally evident in the titles of pamphlets and newsbooks, from both sides of the political divide: including *The Parliament Scout* (1643–5), *The Spie* (1644), and *The Parliaments Post* (1644). Moreover, while the massive social instability of the Civil Wars inevitably passed, the privileging of the unsettled individual searching for intelligence would endure in the nation's developing news culture. Indeed here, as much as anywhere else in the early modern period, we may observe the critical process through which subjects transformed themselves into citizens.

Charles II was also forced into disguise and flight across the country, after his abortive attempt to claim the throne in 1651 at the Battle of Worcester. Unlike his father's experiences, however, Charles II's flight was not only successful but also subject to historical revision on the restoration of the monarchy in 1660. Numerous texts at this point reflected on the details of Charles's disguise, his journey through the 'by-ways', and his hiding in secret rooms previously used to protect Catholic priests.[103] His survival

[101] See McRae, *Literature, Satire and the Early Stuart State* (Cambridge, 2004), pp. 101–2.
[102] *Worthines of Wales*, sig. C3r; *Workes*, I.121.
[103] See esp. *Boscobel: Or, the History of His Sacred Majesties Most Miraculous Preservation after the Battle of Worcester* (1660), quote from p. 38. For a collection of poetry on the Restoration, see *The Return of the King: An Anthology of English Poems Commemorating the Restoration of Charles II*, ed. Gerald Maclean, http://etext.virginia.edu/toc/modeng/public/MacKing.html.

could be figured as miraculous, or a product of providence; in the words used as a refrain in one ballad, 'God in mercy would not destroy' him.[104] Accounts centred attention on the 'royal oak', a hollowed tree in which Charles took shelter at one point. By the Restoration, in fact, the oak was said to have become a tourist attraction, on the model of the pilgrimage, and that as a result it had 'been depriv'd of all its young Boughs by the visiters of it, who keep them in memory of *His Majesties* happy preservation'.[105] Royal authority, this discourse suggests, is imprinted upon the landscape: as unmistakably in 1660 as it had been in the reign of the Elizabethan progress.

But the long-term shifts in the politics of mobility, traced through the course of the present chapter, are unmistakable. The key political settlements of the latter half of the seventeenth century whittled away the authority of the monarch, abolishing many of the mechanisms of arbitrary rule and rescinding the remnants of feudalism. Never again, as a result, would the monarch be able to claim, as Elizabeth had done, to possess the entire nation. Similarly, as demonstrated above, the Crown lost control of the nation's networks of communication. The post system, by the end of the seventeenth century, was principally and unassailably a vehicle for the transmission of information by private citizens.[106] News, though generally stripped of the outer layers of vituperation evident in the 1640s, developed into a regular and reliable business. And individuals, as demonstrated throughout this book, moved from place to place, in ever growing numbers. One poem on the Restoration imagines church bells across the nation proclaiming news of the event 'to all the Parishes': an image at once of news networks being returned to the control of the Crown and people being settled in their proper places.[107] This, however, was little more than royalist fantasy.

These developments might prompt a reflection, finally, on the spatial dynamics of the public sphere. In Habermas's account of the development of a public sphere in England, much was dependent upon the emergence of new kinds of urban sites, such as coffee houses, which 'institutionalized' nascent conceptions of the 'public'.[108] Citizens, in other words, depended upon places for the exchange of information and ideas. Other scholars, particularly those concerned with news and pamphlet culture, have questioned this key premise of Habermas's work, and as a result have argued that

---

[104] J. W., *The Royall Oak* (1660).   [105] *Boscobel*, p. 53.
[106] See esp. Brayshay, *et al.*, 'Knowledge, Nationhood and Governance', 283–4.
[107] *Iter Australe* (1660), p. 17.
[108] *Structural Transformation of the Public Sphere*, pp. 31–43 (quote at p. 36).

the origins of a public sphere, or multiple public spheres, may be traced back into the early decades of the seventeenth century, or even into the reign of Elizabeth.[109] In the current context, attention to the practical and discursive model of the royal progress has underpinned a reassessment of the politics of domestic mobility, which may add substance to existing criticisms of Habermas on this point. The cultural history of the progress, from the reign of Elizabeth through to the middle of the seventeenth century, is a narrative of the dispersal of political interaction across the nation. It is a narrative of the corrosion of absolutist myths, and the emergence of new figures of placeless and inquisitive citizens. And it there-fore situates domestic mobility – of individuals and information alike – as fundamental to the constitution of the emergent public sphere.

---

[109] See esp. Halasz, *The Marketplace of Print: Pamphlets and the Public Sphere in Early Modern England* (Cambridge, 1997); McRae, *Literature, Satire and the Early Stuart State*, pp. 85–113; Mears, *Queenship*; *The Politics of the Public Sphere in Early Modern England*, ed. Peter Lake and Steven Pincus (Manchester, 2007); Joad Raymond, 'The Newspaper, Public Opinion, and the Public Sphere', in *News, Newspapers, and Society in Early Modern Britain*, ed. Raymond (London and Portland, 1999), pp. 109–40; Zaret, *Origins of Democratic Culture*.

CHAPTER 5

Tourism: Celia Fiennes and her context

To use the word 'tourism' to describe forms of travel within England in the early modern period is anachronistic. The *Oxford English Dictionary* traces the first use of the term, in its modern meaning of 'travelling for pleasure', to the early nineteenth century, while recent theorists define practices of tourism as bound to the modern age, bringing as it did 'improvements in transport systems ... and the development of organized tours'.[1] Yet the history of individuals travelling for reasons other than business or economic necessity stretches back through the ages. In early modern England it was undoubtedly an unusual, even troubling phenomenon; indeed accounts left by such travellers commonly include references to being questioned or challenged along the way.[2] The suspicion was reasonable enough, since tourists travelling within their own country neither conformed to any available models, nor followed any predictable routes. For a culture that was profoundly anxious about manifestations of human mobility, the journeys of such people simply made no sense. Within this context, I want to attend to texts of various kinds written by domestic tourists, considering how they perceive and represent their journeys. How, in particular, do they articulate their motivations and purposes? And how do they ascribe meaning to demonstrably inessential acts of travel?

There is no obvious body of texts to sustain these lines of enquiry. It is fair to assume that most tourists left no textual traces of their journeys at all, while those who did record their experiences rarely sought to circulate their works beyond circles of families and friends.[3] Moreover, such works

---

[1] *OED*, 'tourism'; Adrian Franklin, *Tourism: An Introduction* (London, 2003), pp. 40–1; Chloe Chard, *Pleasure and Guilt on the Grand Tour: Travel Writing and Imaginative Geography 1600–1830* (Manchester, 1999), p. 215.

[2] See, e.g., *A Relation of a Short Survey of the Western Counties*, ed. L. G. Wickham Legg, Camden Miscellany 16 (London, 1936), p. 5; 'Thomas Baskerville's Journeys in England, Temp. Car. II', *Reports of the Historical Manuscripts Commission, 13th Report, Appendix II* (London, 1893), p. 287.

[3] Given that so few tourists sought to print their accounts, it is likely that many such texts remain undiscovered, particularly in family and county archives. Since this research represents only one chapter of the present book, I decided to look no further than printed sources and manuscripts in the British Library.

consistently concede a degree of ambivalence about the traveller's novel enterprise. Edward Browne, for instance, records his return home to East Anglia with the comment that, by comparison with the other places he and his companions had been, the city of Norwich 'seem'd ... to deride our rambling folly'.[4] Similarly, the man we know only as Lieutenant Hammond, who wrote two of the best extant travel journals as records of summer tours in the 1630s, reflected doubtfully upon his 'peregrinating Travells'.[5] For all these notes of uncertainty, however, there was an undeniable development in travel-writing across the period. Increasingly, tourists presented their experiences in more direct and confident ways, embracing the journal as the preeminent textual form for the representation of the mobile subject within national space. One index of this shift is the work of Daniel Defoe, which I will consider below in the Epilogue. Another is the publication, a couple of decades earlier, of James Brome's *Travels Over England, Scotland and Wales* (1700).[6] Brome may in fact never have undertaken more than a fraction of the journeys he relates, and for this reason barely figures in the present study. The crucial point here, however, is that an author in the final decade of the seventeenth century might perceive the journal – as opposed, say, to a chorography or a natural history – as the best available form for a 'true and impartial Account' of his nation.[7]

Indeed, given that travel literature was on the eve of arguably its greatest phase, running through the course of the eighteenth century and beyond, it would be easy enough to trace narratives of emergence and development. Such an approach might make many useful connections with extant scholarship on forms of eighteenth-century domestic travel, from the journeys of Defoe to the aesthetic tourism of the latter half of the century. A further benefit of such an approach would be that it would offer a strategy for dealing with the extraordinary lack of a research context for the material at hand. To research the literature of domestic tourism between Chaucer and Defoe is to work in a peculiar critical vacuum.[8] Nevertheless, while

---

[4] 'Journal of a Tour', in Sir Thomas Browne, *Works*, ed. Simon Wilkin, 4 vols. (1836), I.22–42 (quote at I.42).

[5] *A Relation of a Short Survey of 26 Counties*, ed. L. G. Wickham Legg (London, 1904), p. 123; on the identity of the author, see pp. xviii–xix. Cf. John Evelyn's use of 'pererration', defined by the *OED* as 'An act or instance of wandering' (*Diary*, ed. E. S. de Beer, 6 vols. (Oxford, 1955), III.142).

[6] This text had been published – in an imperfect, pirated version, Brome claimed – six years earlier, as *The Historical Account of Mr R. Rogers's Three Years' Travels over England and Wales*.

[7] *Travels*, sig. A3r; Anita McConnell and Vivienne Larminie, 'Brome, James', *ODNB*.

[8] Some exceptions include: Barbara Korte, *English Travel Writing from Pilgrimages to Postcolonial Explorations*, trans. Catherine Matthias (Basingstoke, 2000), pp. 66–91; Esther Moir, *The Discovery of Britain: The English Tourists* (London, 1964), pp. 24–46; Joan Parkes, *Travel in England in the Seventeenth Century* (London, 1925).

remaining sensitive to the valuable ways in which studies of eighteenth-century literature and culture have analyzed and theorized travel-writing, I want in general to avoid the temptation of teleology. The texts at hand are important not merely because they might lead us to Defoe, but because of the ways in which they reflect upon relations between subjects and space in their own time. What is happening in works of domestic travel-writing across the early modern period, I suggest, is a reassessment of what it meant to know the English nation. Spatial knowledge is claimed, with increasing assurance, as a product of individual engagement with space, with all the challenging exigencies and unpredictable encounters that such engagement demanded. Tourism thus comes in turn to enact a new relationship between the individual and the nation. The domestic tourist, gathering experience with every mile of land traversed, is reshaped into a model of the active citizen, within a socially and economically dynamic nation.

The chapter works its way towards an extended engagement with the most important travel journal of the seventeenth century, the account of a series of journeys undertaken by Celia Fiennes in the final decades of the seventeenth century. I argue that Fiennes is important not merely for the degree of detail she provides about the land, but equally for the extent to which she articulates, more clearly than any previous traveller, an identity and purpose for the domestic tourist. Fiennes's work, however, demands to be situated within a much wider context. This chapter therefore begins with a consideration at once of the motivations underlying acts of domestic travel, and of the cultural and textual models available to people exploring their native land. The following section examines a group of journey poems, which stands as the most coherent corpus of domestic travel texts of the period. These poems, for all their trappings of coterie exclusivity, and for all their efforts to represent elite travellers as essentially distinct and detached from the environments through which they move, grapple in illuminating ways with the challenge of turning domestic journeys into poetry. The final section examines prose journals, considering a range of texts, but particularly focusing on the work of Fiennes. These texts, I suggest, position the tourist in the landscape in a freshly assertive and assured manner, validating the desire – which had seemed, just a generation or two earlier, little more than peculiar – for direct knowledge of domestic space. At a time, that is, when travelling was still widely assumed to mean movement beyond one's nation, these texts find value in moving more widely, and looking more carefully, within national borders.

MODELS AND MOTIVATIONS

For at least 150 years after the Protestant Reformation, which brought an abrupt end to practices of pilgrimage – within England as well as beyond its shores – there were no obvious and authoritative models for domestic tourism. In this respect this period presented unique challenges to those wanting to explore their country and to record those acts of exploration. Indeed there is no question that exercises in the collection and organization of spatial knowledge, especially in the earlier part of this period, were commonly met with a degree of unease, if not open hostility. Therefore, before I engage with the work of those who developed new strategies for representing domestic tourism, I want briefly to consider the context within which such writers worked, considering the models of travel available to them, and the ways in which these changed over the period. While much effort has been devoted by cultural and literary historians to debates over the value of foreign tourism, I would suggest that too little attention has been paid to equivalent debates over domestic journeys.[9]

The Protestant assault on pilgrimage dovetailed with wider attacks, in social discourse of the Tudor and early Stuart eras, on the causelessly mobile individual. Even before the Reformation the pilgrim was increasingly being represented as a person motivated in part by secular curiosity, at a time when this quality was widely perceived, in Barbara M. Benedict's words, as 'the mark of threatening ambition'.[10] Moreover, as Christian Z. Zacher demonstrates, curiosity was understood, on the authority of Saint Augustine and other patristic writers, as 'a kind of wandering'. It might manifest itself in forms of verbal waywardness, such as gossiping and tale-telling, or in forms of spatial presumption, such as travel.[11] Hence the eradication of what had for centuries been one of the few acceptable forms of travel was achieved with remarkable ease. While the desacralization of the post-Reformation English landscape was undeniably a long and complex process, which we are only now learning to understand, the eradication of pilgrimage itself was more distinct and immediate.[12] This brought important practical implications, such as the dismantling of structures of

---

[9] On the debates over foreign tourism, see esp. Chard, *Pleasure and Guilt*; Justin Stagl, *A History of Curiosity: The Theory of Travel* (Chur, Switzerland, 1995).

[10] Barbara M. Benedict, *Curiosity: A Cultural History of Early Modern Inquiry* (Chicago and London, 2001), p. 2.

[11] *Curiosity and Pilgrimage: The Literature of Discovery in Fourteenth-Century England* (Baltimore and London, 1976), pp. 34–5.

[12] See Alexandra Walsham, *The Reformation of the Landscape* (Oxford, forthcoming).

hospitality directed towards the sustenance of pilgrims on the roads.[13] It also contributed to a reassessment of the nation's sites of interest and attraction. Thus, as I will consider further below in my discussion of travel journals, travellers still visited Canterbury Cathedral, but found sources of interest other than the remains of the shrine of Thomas à Becket, which had been destroyed at the order of Henry VIII. And they commented with disdain, through to the end of our period, on the sight of ragged Catholics – no better than rogues – drawn to holy wells.

Within this context, acts of tourism were inherently problematic, and required justification within wider systems of value. Most notably, this tension shaped the genre of chorography, which was founded on countless acts of domestic travel, tracing back to those of John Leland.[14] William Camden, whose *Britannia*, more than any other text, gave definition to chorography, was reputed to have been addicted to antiquarian expeditions. As a student in the 1560s, one biographer wrote, 'it was not in his power to keep within doors: the bent of his own Genius was always pulling him out'.[15] Yet, while his own preface announces that he has 'travailed over all England for the most part', the text itself seems unsure how to articulate the individual experience of travel.[16] In Chapter 1 I considered the ways in which chorographies commonly construct perambulations of counties by following the paths of rivers, rather than the routes which a human traveller would more commonly be required to take.[17] Camden's method, however, is less simplistic than those adopted by some of his successors. To take his perambulation of Gloucestershire as an example, he generally observes the convention, tracing the courses of the Severn and its tributaries. Elsewhere, with linking phrases such as 'From thence we come to …' and 'Now proceed we forward …', he imaginatively draws the reader along on a journey, while at other points he specifically positions himself in the landscape (pp. 360, 364). He writes, for instance, that 'I had sight of *Duresley* reputed the auncientest habitation of the *Barkleyes*', and 'I have seene that notable Roman high-way … called the *Fosse*' (pp. 364, 366). Such images of the author as traveller typify a tension at the heart of chorography, between patterns of order rooted in history on the one hand, and the exigencies of human agency on the other hand. Knowledge,

---

[13] Jonathan Sumption, *Pilgrimage: An Image of Mediaeval Religion* (London, 1975), p. 198.
[14] On Leland, see further above, pp. 3–7.
[15] Thomas Smith, 'Life of Camden', in Camden, *Britannia*, ed. and trans. Edmund Gibson (1695), sig. B1v; quoted in Graham Parry, *The Trophies of Time: English Antiquarians of the Seventeenth Century* (Oxford, 1995), p. 22.
[16] *Britannia* (1610), sig. π4r.   [17] See above, pp. 29–33.

however passingly, is posited as a product of individual engagement with the land.

Chorography typically seeks to resolve such tension by privileging history over geography. The *Britannia* locates nationhood primarily in the ancient past; in his preface, Camden says that he aims, through antiquarian research, to 'restore antiquity to Britaine, and Britain to his antiquity' (sig. π4r). In his county descriptions he also acknowledges narratives of genealogy, a concern which would come to dominate chorography in the early Stuart period. For all the obvious tensions between antiquarianism and genealogy, each prioritizes historical models of order over the more complex and dynamic realities of the present. Space is treated as a backdrop to history; the land is assumed 'as the central element of historical stability', underpinning 'a static spatial (and hence social) order'.[18] As a result, the only truly legitimate lines of enquiry into the nation are back through time: exercises, in Camden's terms, of restoration. There were, of course, other models of chorography. Most notably, William Harrison's 'Description of England' is thematically structured, and analytical in its approach to the structures of his contemporary nation.[19] Harrison's strategies echo through the tradition as a minor, essentially conflictual strain; Camden, for instance, regularly pauses to note the principal industries and agricultural systems in a county, while John Norden and others attend more rigorously to social structures and economic practices.[20] Yet, like the mobile author himself, across the chorographical tradition the struggles and interventions of contemporary men and women are typically rendered peripheral, providing an easy background for the essential business of historical research.

By comparison, the only acts of tourism accepted at this time as genuine and meaningful were those that involved travelling abroad, typically to continental Europe. Indeed what became known as the Grand Tour developed, in the decades following the Protestant assault on pilgrimage, out of a humanist effort to legitimize human curiosity, harnessing it for the benefit of the state.[21] Such travel, undertaken 'not ... for personal, private ends, but to make the gentleman profitable to his prince and

---

[18] Bernhard Klein, *Maps and the Writing of Space in Early Modern England and Ireland* (Basingstoke, 2001), p. 144.

[19] *The Description of England*, ed. Georges Edelen (Ithaca, 1968).

[20] Andrew McRae, *God Speed the Plough: The Representation of Agrarian England, 1500–1660* (Cambridge, 1996), pp. 245–53.

[21] Scholarship on continental travel differs on the date at which it becomes appropriate to use the term 'Grand Tour'. Some use it to describe all continental journeys undertaken by elite Englishmen from the mid-sixteenth century onwards (e.g. Chard, *Pleasure and Guilt*), whereas others focus only on a period from the latter half of the seventeenth century, when tourism was centred on the refinement of

commonwealth', was founded upon the collection and organization of information.[22] It was posited as a fundamentally rational exercise in empiricism, gathering data in order to construct reliable images of contemporary states. Some manuals for the traveller, in fact, include page after page of questions, or tables which promise to organize data under headings and subheadings.[23] In time, however, as the tourist's route through Europe became increasingly regularized, and the value of any information he might gather became less obvious, the purpose of such long and expensive journeys was reassessed. The work of Thomas Coryate, in the early years of the seventeenth century, was pivotal in this regard. Coryate roughly stuck to established paths; however, travelling alone and often on foot, with neither the time nor the resources of the elite tourist, his trip assumed the form of an accelerated and socially debased version of the Grand Tour. On his return to London, and in his audacious publication, *Coryats Crudities* (1611), he established his identity not as one gathering information in the service of the state, but as an individual engaging with other lands, in ways specific to his own character and circumstances. This text prioritizes the eye of the observer and the unpredictability of human encounters over facts of topography and history. Indeed, as Anthony Parr has argued of the *Crudities*, 'at the same moment' that continental travel 'was becoming routine it was also disclosing its idiosyncratic potential, its surplus value, the little experiences and odd perceptions that the dull reason of the advice manuals could never comprehend'.[24] Coryate suggested the pleasure of going where others had been before, and experiencing with one's own eyes – and encountering with one's own body – the pronounced wonders of Europe. Though Coryate's work as an author remains unique, his attention to the subtle pleasures and unpredictable challenges of an individual's engagement with space clarifies key aspects of the tourist's experience. He would be remembered, throughout the seventeenth century, by travellers within England.[25]

Within this context, efforts to turn away from the continent, towards a fresh exploration of domestic space, were inevitably problematic. For James Howell, the contrast was stark; to be moved by 'a desire of *Travell*', he wrote in 1650, was to refuse 'to be bounded, or confined within the shoares and

---

the individual traveller (e.g. Stagl, *A History of Curiosity*, p. 82; Sara Warneke, *Images of the Educational Travellers in Early Modern England* (Leiden, 1995), pp. 1, 49). Since this debate has little bearing on my own arguments, I propose to refer throughout to continental travel as the Grand Tour.

[22] Michelle O'Callaghan, *The English Wits: Literature and Sociability in Early Modern England* (Cambridge, 2007), pp. 128–9.

[23] See, e.g., Robert Dallington, *A Method for Travell* (1605); Jerome Turler, *The Traveiler* (1575).

[24] 'Thomas Coryat and the Discovery of Europe', *Huntington Library Quarterly*, 55 (1992), 586.

[25] See further below my discussion of John Taylor (pp. 216–33).

narrow circumference of an *Island*. In his view, it was a mark of 'mean and vulgar spirits, whose *Soules* sore no higher than their *Sense*' to 'love to hover ever about home'.[26] To be bound to one's homeland, as to be bound to one's household, was thus no condition for the elite male. Admittedly, some writers on the subject of travel argued either that the young man 'should be first well acquainted' with his own country, or that a domestic tour should be taken after returning from the continent.[27] Most commonly, however, it was assumed that such knowledge would be derived from books, such as Camden's *Britannia*, John Speed's *Theatre of the Empire of Great Britaine*, or works of chronicle history.[28] Though seemingly obvious as a cheap alternative, or supplement, to the Grand Tour, few writers even attempted to endorse it in the same terms. Henry Peacham, despite being troubled that many Englishmen on the Grand Tour were evidently encountering 'strangers' who could 'say more of England then they', celebrated the pleasures of 'Riding with a good Horse and a good Companion, in the Spring or Summer-season, into the Countrey' not in his authoritative conduct manual, *The Compleat Gentleman*, but in a shorter tract titled *The Worth of a Peny*. Such travel, moreover, was presented as a mere 'recreation', highlighted by the 'mirth' to be derived from encounters with 'Maids, and Market Wenches'.[29] And even John Evelyn, who travelled widely in his own country as well as in continental Europe, posits his most extensive domestic journeys as principally recreational, motivated by invitations from his wife's family and a desire 'to shew her, the most considerable parts of her native Country, who from her childhood had lived altogether in France'. He admits his own 'curiosity' only as a secondary consideration.[30]

Yet Evelyn's journal, despite these notes of hesitation about his project, assumes a place in relation to renewed efforts, evident across the seventeenth century, to legitimize tourism within England. Antiquarian expeditions remained popular throughout the seventeenth century, and culminated in the fresh research organized by Edmund Gibson, but undertaken by individuals throughout the country, for the new edition of Camden's *Britannia* in 1695.[31] Other men pursued more specialized lines of enquiry. John Weever's *Ancient Funerall Monuments*, for instance, is presented as the

---

[26] *Instructions and Directions for Forren Travell* (1650), p. 7.
[27] Edward Leigh, *Three Diatribes or Discourses* (1671), p. 6; cf. Henry Peacham, *The Compleat Gentleman* (1622), p. 202. *Aubrey on Education: A Hitherto Unpublished Manuscript by the Author of 'Brief Lives'*, ed. J. E. Stephens (London and Boston, 1972), p. 136.
[28] Howell, *Instructions*, p. 11; Joseph Hall, *Quo Vadis? A Just Censure of Travell as it is Commonly Undertaken by the Gentlemen of our Nation* (1617), pp. 33–5.
[29] *Compleat Gentleman*, p. 202; *Worth of a Peny* (1641), p. 30.   [30] *Diary*, 3.117.
[31] See Parry, *Trophies of Time*, pp. 331–57.

product of the author's 'painefull expences' devoted to 'travels' throughout England. Seeing the 'sacred Sepulchres of worthie, famous personages', and visiting the places they inhabited, he claims, 'doth move and stirre us up as much, or more, then the hearing of their noble deeds, or reading of their compositions'.[32] In other texts, contemporary England was posited as an object of enquiry alongside, or in place of, continental countries. Fynes Moryson, for example, though he writes at much greater length of his continental travels, also includes a brief description of journeys through England and his native Scotland.[33] Meanwhile, as Englishmen were travelling abroad, so foreigners were visiting England and recording their experiences. The *Itinerarium* of Paul Hentzner, for instance, tracing journeys through Germany, France, England and Italy, was published in Latin from Nuremberg in 1612.[34] Later in the century, Francis Misson compiled *Mémoires et observations faites par un voyageur en Angleterre*, a detailed and analytical text organized into a series of alphabetical entries.[35] Such texts, even when not translated into English (as Misson's was, in 1719), doubtless filtered back into England, contributing to an emergent culture of enquiry.[36]

The most important influences, however, were linked to the widespread agenda of research into the natural world inspired by the new philosophy movement. This was initiated by the work of Francis Bacon, but gathered pace in the latter decades of the seventeenth century, especially under the aegis of the Royal Society. Just as humanism had underpinned an earlier programme of investigation into foreign lands, the new philosophy refocused the gaze of an intellectual elite on domestic space. John Ogilby's road-atlas, *Britannia*, considered in Chapter 2, was a by-product of this, since it was intended to be just one part of a much wider investigation of the nation.[37] Others, closer to the intellectual heart of the Royal Society, developed more detailed outlines for research. Robert Plot, for instance, issued a broadside, dense with text, in 1679, titled, *Enquiries to be propounded to the most Ingenious of each County in my Travels through England and Wales, in order to their History of Nature and Arts*. Its questions were arranged under headings for 'heavens and air', 'waters', 'earths and minerals', 'stones', 'metals, &c', 'plants' and 'husbandry'. Other men, somewhat more realistically, pursued specialized lines of enquiry. John Ray, for example, author of one of the travel journals I will consider below, was on

---

[32] (1631), t.p., sig. π5v, p. 40.   [33] *Itinerary* (1617), I.272–4; III.136–52.
[34] Hentzner, *Travels in England in the Reign of Queen Elizabeth*, trans. R. Bentley (London, 1892).
[35] (The Hague, 1698).   [36] Misson's work was translated as *Memoirs and Observations*.
[37] See above, pp. 79–82.

the road principally to gather information for his *Catalogus plantarum circa Cantabrigiam nascentium* (1660).[38] Others still, such as Evelyn and those associated in various ways with Samuel Hartlib, attended to local practices of agriculture and mining.[39] Such investigative projects positioned domestic travel not as a poor, even emasculating, alternative to the Grand Tour, but as an heroic and virtually inexhaustible endeavour. They were also bound to the era's predominant commitment to social and economic improvement. Spatial knowledge, therefore, was envisaged as directly applicable to the business of manipulating and transforming space.

But this was no straightforward revolution. Ambivalence about mobility prevailed throughout the seventeenth century, and there are no texts of domestic travel which might be aligned simply and unproblematically with the agenda of men such as Ogilby and Plot. Indeed even Plot's own work retains a strong commitment to orthodox models of social order. His *Natural History of Oxford-Shire* (1677), one of two county studies that he produced, unquestionably transforms the chorographical model in accordance with a Baconian model of investigation. The book is concerned, he writes, not only with 'the advancement of a sort of *Learning* so much neglected in *England*, but of *Trade* also' (sig. b3v). Yet it maintains a conventional focus on the county as a fixed and stable unit, and also a concern with existing structures of property. On the prefatory map, which includes 'ancient *Ways*' but not contemporary roads, Plot uses heraldic arms to signify ownership, arguing that 'the *Gentry* hereby will be somewhat influenced to keep their *Seats*, together with their *Arms*, least their *Posterity* hereafter, not without *reflexions*, see what their *Ancestors* have parted with' (Fig. 5.1). In fact, in the range of travel-writing to be considered below, the agenda of the new philosophy is at best evident in diluted and indirect forms. It was more often appropriated by gentlemen investigating ways of improving their own lands, or combined with more traditional interests, such as antiquarianism. One person setting off for a tour of the West Country, for instance, prepared a kind of guide-book in advance, with notes about what he should see that are organized under the following headings: 'Ancient Coines, Urnes, Medicinal waters, the severall Oares of Metals, Mminerals, unusual Buildings, Gamasies in stones, or Plants, or any other Curiosities in Art, or Nature'.[40] Such breadth of

---

[38] Ray's journals are published in *Memorials of John Ray*, ed. Edwin Lankester (London, 1846), pp. 121–205. Cf. an earlier piece of botanical research, Thomas Johnson's *Iter Plantarum Investigationis ergo Susceptum a Decem Socijs, in Agrum Cantianum* (1629).

[39] See esp. Stan A. E. Mendyk, '*Speculum Britanniae*': *Regional Study, Antiquarianism, and Science in Britain to 1700* (Toronto, 1989), pp. 136–45.

[40] BL MS Sloane 2789, fols. 2r–7r. I have been unable to ascribe a meaning to 'Gamasies'.

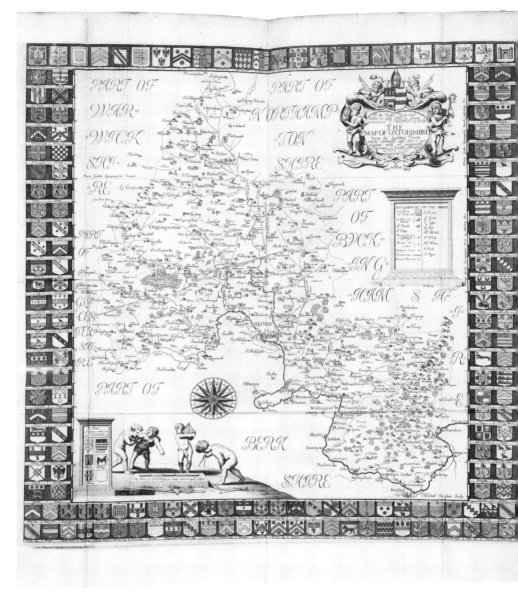

Fig. 5.1 Map of Oxfordshire in Robert Plot, *Natural History of Oxford-Shire* (1677).

interests, rather than anything more methodical, was entirely characteristic of domestic tourists of this time.

The key motivation, for this traveller as for any other, was curiosity. The pursuit of physical 'Curiosities in Art, or Nature', or the exercise of one's intellectual powers of curiosity, impelled travel from Leland through to the eighteenth century. Gradually, curiosity was liberated from the constraints of Medieval religious and intellectual orthodoxy, to become the crucial motivating force for acts of tourism. The models and motivations of domestic tourism were thereby revised and extended, as new forms of investigation, underpinned by new codes of curiosity, became imaginable. This struggle to reconceptualize and reposition curiosity informed acts of domestic travel-writing throughout the early modern period. In the following sections of the chapter it remains to consider the writings of those few people who sought, in various ways, to articulate the pleasures of travel within their own land, translating their curiosity into new kinds of texts.

JOURNEY POEMS

The tradition, or minor genre, of the journey poem represents the only concerted effort before the eighteenth century to fashion a distinct literary approach to domestic tourism.[41] The journey poem may be traced from Richard Eedes's *Iter Boreale* of 1583, through works of the early and mid-seventeenth century by poets such as Richard Corbett and Richard Brathwaite, to Restoration pieces by Charles Cotton, Jeremiah Wells and others.[42] A number of these poems self-consciously announce their kinship; after Eedes, two more were titled 'Iter Boreale', two 'Iter Australe', one 'Iter Orientale' and another 'Iter Lancastrense'.[43] It was also a tradition rooted in

[41] This grouping of poems has received little sustained critical treatment. Perhaps the most important exception is Felicity Henderson, 'Erudite Satire in Seventeenth-Century England' (unpublished Ph.D. dissertation, Monash University, 2002), pp. 55–90.

[42] Corbett, 'Iter Boreale', in *Poems*, ed. J. A. W. Bennett and H. R. Trevor-Roper (Oxford, 1955), pp. 31–49; Brathwaite, *Barnabe Itinerarium* (1636; reissued with facing-page English translation two years later); Cotton, 'A Journey into the Peak. To Sir Aston Cockain' and 'A Voyage to Ireland in Burlesque' (*Poems*, ed. John Beresford (London, 1923), pp. 270–2, 293–309); Wells, 'Iter Orientale', in *Poems upon Divers Occasions* (1667), pp. 76–110. Brathwaite's poem, which claims a tangential, arguably parodic, relation to the genre will be discussed in Chapter 6 (pp. 212–13).

[43] Corbett, 'Iter Boreale', in *Poems*, pp. 31–49; Thomas Master, *Iter Boreale* (1675); Thomas Bispham, *Iter Australe* (1658); Nicholas Oldsworth, 'Iter Australe', in *Poems*, ed. John Gouws (Tempe, Arizona, forthcoming); Wells, 'Iter Orientale'; Richard James, *Iter Lancastrense*, ed. Thomas Corser, Chetham Society Old Series 7 (1845). The title 'iter boreale' was also adopted for other types of poem, the most notable of which was Robert Wild's 1660 poem in praise of General George Monck and his role in the restoration of monarchy.

a socially and intellectually exclusive, masculine culture.[44] Several poems, including that by Eedes, are in Latin, while others were designed for circulation in manuscript circles rather than for print. Almost all of them are connected in some way to the University of Oxford. Yet, although they are unquestionably arcane in many respects, these poems are critical to any explanation of the cultural expectations and literary conventions of domestic travel in the seventeenth century. More than any other literature before the work of Fiennes, they reflect upon the motivations of the domestic tourist, and the nature of his engagement with the society and landscape of his nation. Their authors are concerned to distinguish tourism from other forms of travel, and to position it – however hesitantly and unconvincingly – in relation to continental tourism. As a result, for all their articulation of anxieties, and for all their clubby erudition and social bigotry, these poems lend a degree of shape to the nascent enterprise of domestic tourism.

The poems and journeys alike are characterized by an affected purposelessness and directionlessness. Although Horace's Satire I.v, an account of a voyage to Brundisium with Virgil, Maecenas and others, provided a degree of authority, poets commonly played on the novelty and purportedly haphazard quality of their work. 'Quo te Musa pedes?' asks Thomas Bispham in the first line of his 1658 poem, *Iter Australe* (p. 1). Similarly, Eedes defensively posits his 'Musa … loquaci' ('chattering muse') as a product of a tedious journey, and at the end of the poem imagines this 'rude' and 'rustic' spirit fleeing at the sight of Oxford.[45] In their accounts of journeys, the poems rarely acknowledge plans or goals; landmarks may be discussed as they are encountered, but this is a different matter to actually setting out with a list of such destinations in hand. To some extent, there appears in fact to have been a genuine degree of concern about the value of representing such sites. Indeed Corbett, in his 'Iter Boreale', a poem which achieved an extraordinary currency in manuscript circulation, explicitly resists the obvious temptation to describe the urban architecture of Leicester, stating that, for 'those great Landmarkes I referr / To *Camdens* Eye, Englands *Chorographer*' (ll. 81–2). For Corbett, in other words, after Camden there was no point describing the land; England was a space, by definition, that was already known. This assumption, though obviously limiting, underwrites the poet's attention to individual experience as opposed to enduring physical realities. These poems are about *uses* of

---

[44] Cf. Henderson, 'Erudite Satire', p. 65.

[45] ll. 21, 654–68; translations from Eedes, *Iter Boreale*, ed. and trans. Dana F. Sutton (2003), www.philological.bham.ac.uk/eedes/.

space, recording the acts of those who assume the licence, as English men with sufficient free time and money, to move at will through their nation. They are poems of sociability, memorializing acts which bind a group. Like the country-house poems of the same era, they endorse hospitality and acts of patronage, yet they are generally less concerned with places than with mobility, and less concerned with hierarchical relations than with those between equals.

By the end of the seventeenth century, it appears to have become accepted that such acts of domestic travel might be represented in terms of burlesque.[46] Cotton, in fact, evidently felt by 1670 that he could assume this connection, titling one of his journey poems 'A Voyage to Ireland in Burlesque'.[47] As Timothy Raylor has demonstrated, the concept of burlesque was gradually taking shape in the middle of the seventeenth century, before ultimately assuming its modern form as 'a genre of imitation or caricature'. In this period it was understood primarily as a style rather than a form. Like the contemporary concept of 'drollery', which faded out of literary culture by the end of the century, burlesque was understood as a mode of ridicule and derision, often destructive or 'morally dubious' in character.[48] Importantly, burlesque offered authors of journey poems the necessary resources to manage anxieties about the value of domestic tourism. For, by comparison with those of their peers travelling on the continent, domestic tourists were doing something not only culturally different, but widely assumed to be inferior, often because they could afford to do no more. Within this context, burlesque serves two main functions. On the one hand, the mode's scattergun violence propels the journey poem's fundamental effort to distinguish the elite and leisured tourist from commoners. On the other hand, characteristic traces of self-disgust betray to the coterie readership, in coded and generally manageable ways, shared anxieties about involvement in the peculiar business of domestic tourism.

This distinctive approach to travel-writing is justified by reference to existing practices in both literature and the visual arts. Cotton suggests a debt to a native textual tradition, as he invokes: 'Oh Couriate [i.e. Coryate]! thou traveller fam'd as Ulysses, / In such stupendious labour as this is'.[49] In doing so he was presumably thinking as much of the commendatory poems in *Coryats Crudities*, written by many of the leading poets of the early

---

[46] Cf. Henderson, 'Erudite Satire', p. 72; Timothy Raylor, *Cavaliers, Clubs, and Literary Culture: Sir John Mennes, James Smith, and the Order of the Fancy* (Newark, 1994), p. 130.

[47] *Poems*, pp. 293–309. The poem may be dated, roughly, by Cotton's reference to being 'forty years old' (p. 293).

[48] *Cavaliers*, pp. 113, 116–17.   [49] 'A Voyage to Ireland in Burlesque', *Poems*, p. 293.

seventeenth century, as of the text itself. As Raylor has suggested, these poems may be seen as 'an important, yet ignored source for the burlesque'.[50] In them, Coryate was decidedly *not* 'fam'd as Ulysses'; his journey was figured as altogether pedestrian, and therefore a matter of comedy rather than heroism. Gradually, over the following decades, this kind of attitude towards the representation of travel assumed fresh clarity. Richard Flecknoe, whose poem *The Diarium, or Journall* (1656) predates by two years the *OED*'s first recorded use of 'burlesque', underscores the social politics of such writing. He compares 'your Burlesque, or Drolling Poem' to the art of Brueghel, on account of its representation of 'Grotesque & fantastick figures'. He explains: 'That I use broad words sometimes, 'tis but conform to the pattern I imitate: *Brughel* representing, without any dishonesty, here a *Boor* shiting, there a *Boorinne* pissing, to render the vulgar more ridiculous' (sig. A3r–v). Burlesque is thereby unashamedly confirmed as a 'deeply conservative' technique of social distinction, ideally suited to an elite performance of leisure, with all of its coterie posturing and contrived excesses.[51]

Consequently, while humour at the expense of servants and other commoners was informed by the model of Horace's Satire I.v, it becomes decidedly more aggressive in many of the seventeenth-century poems. Wells, for instance, describes the 'Heathenish crew' of waggoners encountered along the road: 'The Waggoners such *Centaures* were, that they / Knew nothing but their Horses and their Way; / To cry Gee Tib and Ball is all they ken, / Men only to their Beasts, and Beasts to Men'.[52] For William Richards, whose prose *Wallography* has much in common with the journey poems, the 'dregs of mankind' he finds in one village are dismissed as 'wild Savages'.[53] There is a blunt political charge to such attacks. To define commoners as ignorant and inarticulate, within their native space, imaginatively disenfranchises them, by contrast to the educated and leisured travellers. Given the degree of unease betrayed by the poems, about spaces that were demonstrably alien and unsettling – despite conventional claims to the contrary – this was an obvious enough strategy. Perhaps the most consistent butts of burlesque, meanwhile, are those whose spatial knowledge gave them a discomfiting degree of authority over the travellers. The employment of local guides was necessary in places across the country, requiring the elite tourist to place himself in the hands of a commoner, often at considerable cost. Cotton was one of several writers to resist this power dynamic in his verse, giving a burlesque description of one guide:

---

[50] *Cavaliers*, p. 122.   [51] *Ibid.*, p. 120.   [52] 'Iter Orientale', *Poems*, p. 84.
[53] *Wallography; Or The Britton Describ'd* (1682), pp. 6–7.

> With a head like a nutmeg, and legs like a spider;
> A voice like a cricket, a look like a rat,
> The brains of a goose, and the heart of a cat.

This guide, he notes,

> demanded great vails [tips],
> For conducting me over the mountains of Wales;
> Twenty good shillings, which sure very large is;
> Yet that would not serve, but I must bear his charges.[54]

Burlesque here asserts social and cultural otherness, along a simple binary of high and low. For the traveller, recalling the unease of this relationship, its resources of socially coded detraction offer a strategy for the management of authorial anxiety.

Hence also the significance, in these poems, of inns. Wherever possible, the elite traveller avoided inns, and the journey poems often lavish praise on those people who afforded the authors accommodation in private homes. Inns, by contrast, as I argued in Chapter 3, commercialize hospitality. They were places open, by law, to anyone capable of paying the required fees, and in the seventeenth century they were particularly important to the growing numbers of people involved in internal trade. In the journey poems, travellers fret about the social ambiguity of the space, all too keen to assert their own unusual status as travellers of leisure. In this context, previous visitors to an inn become important; Flecknoe, for instance, decries an inn in Mitcham, 'Where none but *Carrier* ere had been' (pp. 40–1), whereas the 'best cheere' that Corbett derives from his stay at the Bull's Head in Nottingham is that 'his *Grace of Yorke* had lodged there' (l.168). The point of such notes is partly to draw qualitative distinctions between inns, but partly also to mask, wherever possible, the fundamentally commercial nature of the environment. Corbett, more than anyone else, worries about this matter. At one point he drily recalls a contemporary proverb, that '*A handsome* Hostesse makes the Reckoning *deare*'; at another he notes the rise of an ostler to the status of innkeeper, tracing a trajectory of social advancement that underlines the commercial dynamics of the trade (ll. 286, 173–84).[55] Elsewhere, after devoting ten lines to the 'scandalous' act of a tapster in Leicester, charging a group of '*Divines*' the sum of '*seav'ne and sixpence* [for] bread & beere', he recoils, declaring: 'Away, my Muse, from this base subject, know / Thy *Pegasus*

---

[54] 'A Voyage to Ireland in Burlesque', *Poems*, pp. 304–5.
[55] Morris Palmer Tilley, *A Dictionary of the Proverbs in England in the Sixteenth and Seventeenth Centuries* (Ann Arbor, 1950), H730.

nere strooke his foote soe low' (ll. 99–100). But what his poem registers, even as he resists its implications, is the fact that in the inn he is translated from divine to consumer, on what he describes as 'A journey not so soon conceiv'd as spent' (l. 6). This shift naggingly unveils the economic relations between him and those he encounters. To an innkeeper, a tourist is no different, because no less valuable, than any other kind of guest.

Another characteristic response to this situation is to accentuate, or comically exaggerate, the nature of touristic consumption. This is in fact another quality of burlesque, underwriting the predominant attention in the poems to corporeal rather than intellectual concerns. For Corbett, the travelling party of scholars in 'Iter Boreale', 'having lesse to do / With *Augustine* then with Galen in vacation, / Chang'd studyes, and turn'd bookes to recreation' (ll. 2–4). Tourism, in other words, involves a devotion to the pleasures of the body. The recurrent scenes of drunkenness in the poems thus signify both the financial means and the social quality of the tourists, distinguishing them from those whose engagement with space is determined more by mercantile interests. Indeed in one of the most notorious but also most influential of the journey poems, John Mennes's 'To a friend upon a journey to Epsom Well', excretion figures as a more violent assertion of distinction.[56] The speaker in this poem looks sardonically upon those who visit Epsom Well genuinely seeking cures for their diseases, and dwells rather on the excremental remains of their efforts at purgation. The poem culminates in the speaker participating in a shitting contest, in which 'he that gaines the glory here / Must scumber furthest' (p. 6). Having duly broken the longstanding record, the attendant 'ask'd me name' and

> writ
> In yellow Letters, who 'twas shit,
> Which still stands as a Monument,
> Call'd Long-taile, from the Man of *Kent*.   (p. 7)

The shit of the gentleman-poet, disdainfully foisted upon the landscape, and duly monumentalized and memorialized, might almost be said to epitomize the approach to social space assumed by these poems. The poem implicitly mocks more purposeful forms of tourism, such as those who visit spas in the interests of their health, or those who visit churches to record funeral monuments, asserting by contrast a casual consumption and exploitation of space.

This approach infects the poems, even when their authors turn to more conventional forms of description. Objects of curiosity are rarely sought,

---

[56] *Musarum Deliciae: or, The Muses Recreation* (1656), pp. 3–7.

but rather tend to impinge upon the texts as though by accident. Corbett and his party, for instance, miss out on a tour of Kenilworth Castle because 'The Keeper … was from home', then encounter instead the statue of Guy of Warwick:

> who there stands
> Ugly and huge, more then a man on's hands:
> His helmett steele, his gorgett male, his sheild
> Brass, made the Chappell feareful as a Field.
> And let this answere all the *Popes* complaints,
> Wee sett up *Gyants* though wee pull downe *Saintes*.   (ll. 361, 271–6)

The final couplet, with its double-edged satire on puritan iconoclasm and the dubious popular historical narratives which have produced this 'humble *Shrine*' (l. 369), is typical of Corbett's poem. The point is that religion and history alike are unreliable in the country. At Bosworth, subsequently, a drunken innkeeper confuses his supposed narrative of the death of Richard III with his memories of Shakespeare's play and its most famous actor: 'For when he would have sayd, King *Richard* dyed, / And call'd, a horse, a horse; he, *Burbidge* cry'de' (ll. 351–2). By comparison, true cultural value is located firmly back home in Oxford. As in several of the other journey poems, the return to a site of enclosed community, in which standards of value directly correlate with physical space, is critical.[57] This manoeuvre, common in conservative traditions of satire, affirms the boundaries of virtue and civility, which have been threatened though never overturned by experiences in the wider world.[58] Corbett's party return at the close, 'just with soe much ore / As *Rawleigh* from his Voyage, and noe more' (ll. 507–8).

Some poems, however, stretch the constraints of the genre, embracing more openly the curiosity that increasingly gave shape to prose journals of the same period. Most notably, Richard James's *Iter Lancastrense*, which he describes himself as a 'journall poem', dwells on the tourist's pursuit of knowledge and experience (l. 389). At one point an old fisherman identifies tourism as a product of the men's economic status:

> you gentlemen at ease,
> Whoe money have, and goe where ere you please,
> Are never quiett; wearye of the daye,
> You now comme hether to drive time away.   (ll. 127–30)

---

[57] Cf. the return to Oxford in Eedes's *Iter Boreale*; and the closing panegyrics on country estates and their owners in Bispham's *Iter Australe* (p. 23) and James's *Iter Lancastrense* (pp. 12–13).
[58] Cf. Henderson, 'Erudite Satire', pp. 88–9.

Whereas other poets might embrace an urge 'to drive time away', however, James seeks rather to justify the status that his money purchases, pursuing interests in antiquarianism and natural history. He describes, for instance, a visit to the remains of a Roman road between York and Chester, while he casts a sceptical eye over St Winifred's Well in Shropshire, which continued to attract visitors over a century after it had officially been stripped of its status as a holy well. For James, the mysteriously coloured stones in the well, held in local myth to contain the blood of St Winifred, required a more scientific evaluation:

> From natures secretts poets storyes faine;
> Naught els of poets doe these monks retaine.
> This faire cleere springe, which courses through the hills
> Conveys summe mettall tincture in hir rills,
> Which they make staine of blood.   (ll. 233–7)

James thus translates a site of religious veneration into an object of scientific enquiry, open to the gaze of the educated traveller. Curiosity, rather than mere social disgust, gives the traveller a powerful measure of control over the landscape he encounters.

Compared to the weight of the minor tradition considered here, James represents a new approach to touristic consumption. For most of the journey poets, consumption is figured as a matter of self-assertion, and is commonly articulated in terms that betray forms of antagonism and aggression. It is a way, above all, in which they define bonds of community, as though in opposition to the perceived barbarism of their native land. But these poems are also more complex than they may initially appear, and they function at their best as subtle reflections on the experience of domestic tourism. As I am arguing throughout this chapter, the practices of tourism were gradually shifting, towards new forms of enquiry and consumption, and new ways of positioning the travelling subject within the nation. As I will argue further below, such tourists were consuming time and space, and reconfiguring the domestic landscape in the process.

TRAVEL JOURNALS

The basic coordinates of the travel journal are the specificities of dates and places, so that in its barest form it becomes little more than an itinerary. But while some seventeenth-century journals of domestic tours begin or end with itineraries, or conclude with lists of places visited or calculations of mileage covered, the textual dilation into the form of a journal essentially privileges the individual engagement with space. The journalist directs his or her course, confronts the challenges of navigation, and describes sites perceived to be of interest. Some travel journals are included within longer diaries; however, most of those to be considered here are framed as independent texts, and are of particular interest for this reason. These texts were kept by different kinds of people, often with quite distinct interests and objectives, and as a result they vary considerably. Moreover, while most of the texts were carefully prepared, since none of them was actually brought to print it becomes difficult to make judgements about intended audiences and actual readers.[59] Although these facts raise obvious interpretative challenges, making it difficult to talk in any helpful way about a genre or a body of texts, it is also crucial to any understanding of the literature of domestic tourism. For, while many of the journey poems considered above are almost stifled by their commitment to generic models and exclusive reading communities, the extant prose journals are altogether more diverse in style and content, registering different kinds of engagement with domestic space. The form enables, rather than constrains, novel responses and representations. It is therefore not necessarily surprising that the best journal of all, a text which I consider in detail in the latter half of this section, was written by a woman.

For all their elements of heterogeneity, the journals are consistent, and consistently enlightening, in their attention to the essentially paradoxical situation of the domestic tourist, exploring space that is by definition familiar. They are records of individuals, to adopt Edward S. Casey's term, embroiled in the places they visit.[60] By extension, they lend clarity and meaning to national space itself: not only by asking, constantly, what sites or features of the land justify exploration, but also by reflecting upon the functions of human mobility. At their best, I want to argue, they bring the traveller's experience of the land into alignment with freshly dynamic conceptions of nationhood. In the work of Fiennes, in particular, the tourist, freshly appreciated as a new kind of consumer – and a new kind of citizen – is positioned within a nation that is represented as dependent upon the circulation of people, merchandise, information and ideas.[61]

---

[59] For the purposes of this discussion I have consulted roughly a dozen pieces, some in modern editions and some in manuscript. While I would not claim this as exhaustive research, it encompasses all sources that are referenced with any kind of regularity in comparable studies, and is unquestionably representative of a sparse and disparate range of material.

[60] *Getting Back into Place: Toward a Renewed Understanding of the Place-World* (Bloomington and Indianapolis, 1993), p. 276.

[61] All references to Fiennes's journals are from *The Illustrated Journeys of Celia Fiennes 1685–c.1712*, ed. Christopher Morris (Stroud, 1982).

Curiosity, within this model, is liberated from centuries of suspicion, and valorized as a key determinant of national development.

On 22 July 1654 John Evelyn visited the 'stupendious Monument' of Stonehenge. Like countless other tourists before and since, he walked around the site, counted the stones, and considered how and why it came to be built. Like somewhat fewer others, he then produced a hammer and applied 'all [his] strength' to the eventually fruitless project of 'break[ing] a fragment'. Disappointed, he attributed the 'duritie' of the stones to 'their long exposure'.[62] Although it would be an exaggeration to claim that tourists routinely attacked sites that have since become national monuments, this scene finds parallels in a number of the journals. A famous hawthorn bush at Glastonbury, traditionally thought to be miraculous on account of the fact that it flowered at Christmas, was one target. In 1635 Sir William Brereton 'brought away many branches and leaves, and left the first letters of my name thereon upon record', noting that 'the tree and bark is much decayed … by this practise of those that visit it'.[63] Twenty-seven years later – although the intervening period was notable more for the iconoclastic furies of the mid-century than for tourism – the botanist John Ray noted that 'the stump of the old Christmas thorn is now quite dead and gone.[64] What links such acts is a desire on the part of the tourist to mark one's presence upon sites perceived to be of national importance. As such, they invite comparison with the act of writing a journal, recording an individual's unique experiences within an essentially familiar environment. These are responses, of different yet cognate kinds, to the questions faced by all tourists in the domestic landscape. Why travel within England? Why not instead stay at home with a copy of Camden's *Britannia*? And what is the relation between individual experience and public knowledge?

In confronting these questions, tourists were clearly aware of the extent to which existing models required revision. Evelyn, one of the few journalists to be considered here who had previously toured continental Europe, pauses on occasion to draw comparisons, or to remark on his nation's claims to distinction. The practice of those living in caves in Nottingham, noticed by numerous travellers of the period, is thus compared to 'the manner … about *Tours* in *France*', while Salisbury Cathedral is praised as 'the

[62] *Diary*, III.116.
[63] *Travels in Holland, the United Provinces, England, Scotland and Ireland 1634–1635*, ed. Edward Hawkins, Chetham Society (Manchester, 1844), p. 174.
[64] *Memorials*, p. 182. Alexandra Walsham, 'The Holy Thorn of Glastonbury: The Evolution of a Legend in Post-Reformation England', *Parergon*, 21 (2004), 1–25.

compleatest piece of *Gotic*-Worke in *Europe*'.[65] Yet for most domestic tourists the Grand Tour, with its increasingly consistent itinerary and package of common experiences, was little more than a shadowy presence.[66] It helped to contextualize the traveller's experience, but did not offer clear structures or directions. Similarly, although travellers commonly followed the footsteps of pilgrims, who had criss-crossed the land, just generations before them, to visit various shrines, holy wells and other sites, they keenly appreciated the need to revise Catholic systems of value. In Canterbury Cathedral, which had been the most important of all English pilgrimage destinations, Hammond paused at the place where the 'sayd rich Shrine' of 'that great adored Saint, Thomas of Becket' had stood, acknowledging the history of adoration and 'oblations'. Then, in the face of a perceived absence, of both physical presence and spiritual significance, he describes the architecture and 'rich high Windowes', before cataloguing all the other notable monuments in the building.[67] Visitors to holy wells also used their journals to examine and justify their interest. Many, like the poet Richard James (considered above), sought scientific explanations for phenomena that had traditionally been seen as miraculous, thereby contrasting their own investigative powers with the 'ignorant blind zeale' of the papists who continued to be drawn to these sites.[68] Others, such as Fiennes, embraced the contemporary interest in the medicinal qualities of such wells, treating them alongside the numerous other English spas attracting tourists at this time.

More importantly, these texts are committed to the construction of new standards of value. Hammond, who is more expansive – or less discriminate – on this point than others, defines his task as being 'to take a view of the Cities, Castles, and cheife Scytuations' of the counties in his path.[69] At the end, he resorts to quantification:

And it was some comfort to us, that it was soe with us, after wee had marched 800. and odd Miles; quarter'd safely in, and pass'd through 26. famous Shires, and County's; billeted hansomely in 15. fayre, and strong Cittyes; Sally'd through about 40. neat and ancient Corporations; fac'd and Scal'd as many strong, goodly, and defensible Castles; doubled, and offered up our Devotions in 13. ancient rich, and magnificent Cathedralls; view'd in them, and in other hansome, neat Churches, above 300. rich, sumptuous, Tombes, and Monuments.[70]

---

[65] *Diary*, III.125, III.113.
[66] On the consistency of the Grand Tour, even from early in the seventeenth century, see John Stoye, *English Travellers Abroad 1604–1667: Their Influence in English Society and Politics*, revised edn (New Haven and London, 1989), pp. 322–3.
[67] *Relation of a Short Survey of the Western Counties*, pp. 12–13.
[68] *Illustrated Journeys of Celia Fiennes*, p. 158.
[69] *Relation of a Short Survey of 26 Counties*, p. 1.   [70] *Ibid.*, pp. 123–4.

And his enumeration continues, listing rivers, bridges, forests, chases, parks and universities. The following year, 'to round in the residue of this famous Island, which hee ... the last Summer left out', he set off again, working his way around the southern coastline, from Norwich to Somerset.[71] Yet even this apparently exhaustive approach is guided by certain principles. Hammond, like most of his fellow tourists, admired places that were evidently solid and substantial in the present, though equally rooted in history. Moreover, when he enters towns he attends methodically to coordinates of time and space, noting structures of local government and spatial organization and then attending to the transcription of monuments. The latter task, aligned to the antiquarian agenda that underpinned so much tourism in the seventeenth century, was unquestionably considered by him, as for so many of his peers, to be 'something of a duty'.[72]

Others were more limited in their commitment of time and consequently more focused in their geographical range. In such journals, Hammond's obsession for spatial coverage gives way to an emergent sense of identifiable tourist routes. Samuel Pepys, to take as an example the century's most meticulous diarist, was a regular traveller in the course of his work, but took only one purely recreational journey within England, a 1668 tour of the West Country.[73] The principal objects of this tour were Oxford, Stonehenge, Bath, Bristol and Avebury. At Oxford he bought a printed guide to Stonehenge, which he duly found 'as prodigious as any tales I ever heard of them and worth going this journey to see' (IX.226, IX.229–30). Along the way he also engaged in what were becoming standard tourist activities, such as experiencing the King's Bath – despite some distaste at the idea of 'so many bodies together in ... the same water' – and viewing funeral monuments (IX.233). Unlike many of the other tourist accounts considered in this chapter, Pepys's suggests little sense of enthusiasm or discovery; instead, it documents a man performing a role, having reached the sort of social level at which such a performance might be expected of him. He is dutifully following a path, rather than forging his own route. The key point, in the present context, is that such paths, with all their trappings of guides and guidebooks, inns and diversions, were gradually becoming established.

Across the land, tourists such as Pepys were looking for indices of Englishness. In the following century, as tourist routes became more clearly entrenched, attention was increasingly focused on the aesthetics and values

---

[71] *Ibid.*, p. 1.   [72] Parry, *Trophies of Time*, p. 13.
[73] Parkes, *Travel in England*, p. 280; *The Diary of Samuel Pepys*, ed. Robert Latham and William Matthews (11 vols., London, 1970–83), IX.224–43.

of grand country estates.[74] In the seventeenth century, as the experience of Pepys suggests, the category of valued sites was somewhat more open and contested. It certainly included country houses, but also stretched to sites that were less exclusive, and therefore indicative of different models of nationhood. Stonehenge was one. Ongoing debates over the origins of Stonehenge were in part debates over the foundational narratives of England, a matter of import not simply to antiquarians but equally to travellers seeking ways of assessing the structures of their nation.[75] Unusually striking natural sites, meanwhile, gathered around them different kinds of national discourses. The Peak District, for instance, with its collection of 'wonders' that was codified quite early in the period, at once attracted and challenged the elite tourist.[76] Tourists consistently comment on the difficulty of the topography, while Fiennes complains bitterly about the inn at Buxton Well, which forced travellers to share beds (p. 108). And narratives of popular history offered the tourist other models of Englishness again. Like Corbett, many were attracted to sites connected to Guy of Warwick, while at Arundel Castle Hammond had the supposed sword of Bevis of Southampton, 'which is 2. yardes Long and 2. inches broad … drawne against me (though not in anger)'.[77]

The experiences of such travellers, however, equally demonstrate the unnerving challenges inherent in the construction of national identities. Discourses of wonder, which were by the seventeenth century quite well established for the representation of foreign sites, metamorphosed in a domestic setting.[78] One of the principal Wonders of the Peak, for instance, was a formation known as the Devil's Arse: a term shunned by some as impolite, but embraced by others for its comic potential. Edward Browne, for instance, recalls:

At the bottome of the backside of a high rocky mountain, bipartite at the top and perpendicularly steep from thence to the leavell of the ground, wee beheld a vast hole or den which was presently understood by us to bee the anus, into which by the helpe of light and guides wee did not onely enter, but travailed some space up the *intestinum rectum*, and had made further discovery of the intralls had the way been good, and the passage void of excrement; but the monster having drunke hard

---

[74] Carole Fabricant, 'The Literature of Domestic Tourism and the Public Consumption of Private Property', in *The New Eighteenth Century: Theory, Politics, English Literature*, ed. Felicity Nussbaum and Laura Brown (New York and London, 1987), pp. 254–75.
[75] See Parry, *Trophies of Time*, pp. 281–7.
[76] Trevor Brighton, *The Discovery of the Peak District: From Hades to Elysium* (London, 2004), pp. 31–40.
[77] *Relation of a Short Survey of the Western Counties*, p. 31.
[78] On the concept of wonder, see esp. Lorraine Daston and Katharine Park, *Wonders and the Order of Nature 1150–1750* (New York, 1998).

the day before, did vent as fast now, and wee, thinking it not good sayling up Styx against the tide; after some inspection ... wee returned again to the upper world.

While others tried hard to sustain it, the category of wonder collapses here, undermined by strains of burlesque, familiar from the journey poems. Unsurprisingly, this strategy is informed in part by social tensions, since Browne's description leads directly to an encounter with people who live in the caves, and claim that they would '[scorn] to change theirs for any mortal mansion having greater accommodations in this their commonwealth'.[79] Such people pose pointed challenges to the tourist's familiar codes of property and aesthetics.

Similarly, Hammond's engagement with popular history brought him into proximity not so much with essentialized qualities of heroism, but rather with opportunistic commoners. At Robin Hood's Well, near Skelbrooke in Yorkshire:

according to the usuall, and ancient custome of Travellers, [we] were in his rocky Chaire of Ceremony, dignify'd with the Order of knighthood, and sworne to observe his Lawes: After our Oath we had no time to stay to heare our Charge, butt discharg'd our due Fealtie Fee, 4d. a peece to the Lady of the Fountaine, on we spur'd with new dignitie to Pomfret.[80]

The unmistakable strain of irony interwoven through this description, from its portentous reference to the 'ancient custome of Travellers' to the closing claim to a 'new dignitie', bespeaks a degree of unease familiar to tourists. Hammond is participating in an essentially harmless, commodified performance, which bears little relation at all to Robin Hood. Yet it appears to challenge him, as it challenged other early modern tourists, not only to reflect upon the relation between Robin Hood myths and his own nation, but also to consider the relation between a leisured traveller and the dubious 'Lady of the Fountaine' to whom he has just given four pence. While poets of the period employed burlesque to accentuate their difference from such people, a journal-entry such as this acknowledges more subtle and unshakeable connections – of national identity, at least, if not a commitment to the ideals of an outlaw knight – across lines of social degree. Englishness, as a result, becomes somewhat less a matter of heroic historical narratives, and rather more a matter of uneasy social encounters, embedded in the immediacy of time and space.

Travellers typically assert a greater sense of control when viewing the land from a distance. In these recurrent set-piece descriptions of views, or

---

[79] [Thomas Browne], *Works*, I.33.   [80] *Relation of a Short Survey of 26 Counties*, p. 13.

'prospects', travellers articulate not only ideals of beauty in their native landscape, but equally perceptions of their own relation to the country. Indeed, as opposed to the innumerable unsettling experiences of travel, the prospect invites reflections upon perspective and underlying structures of order. As others have demonstrated, for the eighteenth-century tourist the country house was established as a cynosure of beauty, representing an ideal relation between nature and civilisation. Moreover, views from country houses were increasingly managed and manipulated, in order to underline the significance of the house and its owner as a centre of moral value and political authority.[81] Unsurprisingly, these perceptions and discourses can be traced back through the preceding centuries. At one point, travelling in Northamptonshire, Hammond comments that 'many pleasant, delicate, rich Scytuations of Lords, knights, ladies and Gentlemen', some of which he lists in the margin, 'render[ed] the time not irkesome to weary Travellers'.[82] Elsewhere his account, like almost all others, comments on the prospects from estates to which he gained access. Similarly, Fiennes appreciated views such as that from Sir George Pratt's house at Coleshill, Oxfordshire, which 'gives a great prospect of gardens, grounds, woods that appertaine to the Seate, as well as a sight of the Country at a distance' (p. 47). And Evelyn commonly discusses both architecture and landscape design; he notes, for instance, that the garden at Wilton, which he describes at length, is 'esteem'd the noblest in all *England*'.[83]

Yet Evelyn devotes still more attention to different kinds of prospects altogether. Indeed one universally consistent approach to space, throughout the journals, is to seek out, as both practically useful and aesthetically significant, wide and unfettered views of the land. In towns and cities, views from church spires are particularly valued, while in the countryside prospects which offer a sight of multiple counties are considered equally significant. Evelyn, for instance, decrees that one prospect from the Malvern Hills, purportedly offering a view of at least nine counties in both England and Wales, is 'one of the goodliest Vista's in *England*'.[84] Further north, not far from Chester, Edward Browne came across 'a prospect as delicious as almost England can afford', stretching from the Welsh mountains to southern Lancashire.[85] For John Barrell, in his influential analysis of attitudes towards landscape and landscape art in a period from the latter half of the

[81] Tom Williamson and Liz Bellamy, *Property and Landscape: A Social History of Land Ownerhip and the English Countryside* (London, 1987), p. 128.
[82] *Relation of a Short Survey of 26 Counties*, p. 84.   [83] *Diary*, III.114.
[84] *Ibid.*, III.119.   [85] [Thomas Browne], *Works*, I.36.

eighteenth century, such panoramic views are associated with a capacity to 'comprehend the order of society and nature'. By extension, they epitomize truly disinterested citizenship, founded upon the ownership of property.[86] Donna Landry, concerned with a period stretching back into the seventeenth century, similarly links such approaches to prospect as 'synonymous with dominion, and with a commanding view from the heights of that dominion'.[87] But the seventeenth-century travel journals suggest a subtly different politics. Although, in practical terms, most were written by men and women who owned property, they essentially privilege a form of spatial knowledge that is dependent more upon mobility than settlement. The knowledge accorded by a particular position in the landscape – a position which is theoretically open to any traveller – becomes emblematic of the tourist's sense of enfranchisement. The individual who can stand in one place and identify one county from another, or one street from another within a town, and who can subsequently carry these visions home and recall them on the page of a journal, is a person who appreciates that he or she belongs to something bigger than a local community.

Without question, the extant travel journals form an awkward and disparate body of texts. Yet their responses, to challenges and questions faced by all tourists in the period, articulate important new perceptions of the functions of travel. These perceptions are in part political. The traveller's claim to a stake in his or her nation, founded as much upon knowledge and experience as upon property and placement, suggests a potentially powerful justification for tourism. They are also, in part, aesthetic, committed to the construction of codes of beauty within both urban and rural landscapes. And they are in part economic, reaching out towards emergent discourses of national development, and suggesting the importance of human mobility and the spatial knowledge it entails. Turning, at this point of the chapter, to an extended reading of one particular journal will facilitate a more concentrated analysis of the complex relations between these different kinds of perception. Although it would be an exaggeration to claim Fiennes's text as representative of the wider body of travel journals, she responds to common challenges by fashioning the period's most coherent justification of domestic tourism.

---

[86] 'The Public Prospect and the Private View: The Politics of Taste in Eighteenth-Century Britain', in *Landscape, Natural Beauty and the Arts*, ed. Salim Kemal and Ivan Gaskell (Cambridge, 1993), pp. 81–102 (quote at p. 90).

[87] *The Invention of the Countryside: Hunting, Walking and Ecology in English Literature, 1671–1831* (Basingstoke, 2001), p. 4.

Celia Fiennes (1662–1741) undertook a series of journeys between 1685 and c.1712, in the course of which she visited every county in England. She travelled almost exclusively on horseback, with a small number of servants (perhaps two or more), hiring guides when necessary and accepting the company of friends and relatives when offered (e.g. pp. 159, 191). Her travel diaries are framed with a conventional female modesty topos, suggesting that they were neither 'designed' for publication, nor ever 'likely to fall into the hands of any but my near relations' (p. 32); however, she comfortably refers to the text as a 'Book' (pp. 32, 33), and conceives of its value in didactic terms.[88] Her prefatory address 'To the Reader' concludes with an exhortation to 'the studdy of those things which tends to improve the mind and makes our Lives pleasant and comfortable as well as proffitable' (p. 33). The fact that she addresses the journal 'to all, but especially my own Sex', demonstrates an underlying desire to reposition women, effectively barred as they were from continental tourism, within a domestic culture of mobility (p. 33).[89] In the final pages of this chapter, I want to consider at once the unique qualities of this text, particularly its attention to issues of gender, and also its status as the most eloquent example of a wider genre of travel-writing. As I argue, Fiennes seizes upon the relation between civility and mobility, positing a nation endlessly amenable to the tourist's curious investigation, and infinitely capable of transformation in the interests of social and economic development.

In her preface, Fiennes addresses the purpose of travel and the consequent value of her text:

Something may be diverting and proffitable tho' not to Gentlemen that have travelled more about England, staid longer in places, might have more acquaintance and more opportunity to be inform'd. My Journeys, as they were begun to regain my health by variety and change of aire and exercise, soe whatever promoted that was pursued; and those informations of things as could be obtein'd from inns en passant or from some acquaintance, inhabitants of such places, could furnish me with for my diversion, I thought necessary to remark: that as my bodily health was promoted my mind should not appear totally unoccupied, and the collecting it together remain for my after conversation (with such as might be inquisitive after such and such places) to which might have recourse; and as most I converse with knows both the freedom and easyness I speak and write as well as my deffect in all, so they will not expect exactness or politeness in this book, tho' such embellishments might have adorned the descriptions and suited the nicer taste. (p. 32)

---

[88] On the composition of the manuscript, and its relation to an earlier draft, see Christopher Morris, 'Introduction' to Fiennes, *Illustrated Journeys*, p. 10.

[89] On the rarity of women touring continental Europe, see Antoni Maczak, *Travel in Early Modern Europe*, trans. Ursula Phillips (Cambridge, 1995), pp. 140–2.

Fiennes's claim of poor health, as others have noted, may well be a mere pretext for her unconventional passion; although she regularly visited mineral spas, there is no evidence that she suffered from any serious medical condition.[90] Yet whatever the veracity of this rationale, it is worth attending to its textual consequences. Her claim to be travelling for the good of her health legitimizes her position within the domestic landscape. While she may not overtly contest the knowledge of 'Gentlemen that have travelled more about England', nor trespass upon their preferred textual forms, such as chorography or cartography, she negotiates a cultural position for the journal, with its individualized collection of information and observation. According to her account in the preface, she moved as though at random, and collected scraps of information along the way, merely for her 'diversion'. Consequently, the country unfolds before her in a sequence of local detail and chance occurrence, and it is this process that she determines to present to the reader, disavowing authorial arts of 'exactness or politeness'.

Fiennes's capacity for self-directed movement underpins the subject position that the text constructs for the tourist. Like others of the period, as considered above, she was attracted to positions within the landscape which gave her a wide view of the land. Some of these are from private estates; however, others are from public sites, such as the 'vast prospect of the Country at least 30 mile round' afforded from the tower of York Minster, or the more humble 'delighting' prospects to be viewed along the roads of East Anglia (pp. 90, 82). Moreover, on several occasions she implicitly contrasts her own status, as one capable of viewing and understanding the land in this way, with people who are perceived as being trapped within their local environments. In one case:

I passed by some woods and little villages of a few scattered houses, and generally the people here are able to give so bad a direction that passengers are at a loss what aime to take, they know scarce 3 mile from their home, and meete them where you will, enquire how farre to such a place, they mind not where they are then but tell you so farre which is the distance from their own houses to that place. (p. 135)

Patriarchal discourse commonly situates women in relation to a domestic sphere, and Fiennes herself rehearses this model elsewhere, sarcastically noting that the local women are 'especially' bound to the home, and 'so may be term'd good housekeepers' (p. 102). Yet the fundamental dichotomy here is articulated in terms of spatial knowledge. Fiennes may not know her

---

[90] Morris, 'Introduction', pp. 18–20; Margaret Willy, *Three Women Diarists: Celia Fiennes, Dorothy Wordsworth, Katherine Mansfield* (London, 1964), p. 10.

way, but she has a clear appreciation of the relations between one place and another, and ultimately between places and the nation. These local people, by contrast, are place-bound: relegated, by their ignorance, to the margins of civil society. The traveller, as a person capable of appreciating the nation's space and participating in its cultural and political life, emerges as a figure of the true citizen.

From this position, Fiennes further asserts the citizen's standards of taste and decorum. Of Blith Abbey in Yorkshire, for example, she comments approvingly that 'the Gardens are very neate and after the London Mode of Gravel and Grass walks and Mount' (p. 89). While other travellers were motivated by a desire to unearth the nation's history, Fiennes looks rather to the future, as she repeatedly valorizes 'new' styles of architecture and decoration. The 'London Mode', a phrase suggestive of urbanity and modernity, becomes a reliable standard of aesthetic value. In Hereford, by comparison, she describes the estate of Stoke Edith, held by the parliamentary speaker Paul Foley, as a property standing tantalizingly on the verge of transformation: 'its a very good old house of Timber worke but old fashion'd and good roome for Gardens but all in an old form and mode, and Mr. Folie intends to make both a new house and gardens; the latter I saw staked out' (p. 65). Equally, she brings the polite traveller's standards to bear upon the towns and villages in which she stays. Of Alford in Somerset, for example, she complains that there was 'no good accommodation for people of fashion, the Countrey people being a clounish rude people' (p. 43). At Ely she describes a room infested with 'froggs and slow-worms and snailes', and attributes the problems to the slovenliness of the town's inhabitants:

its true were the least care taken to pitch their streetes it would make it looke more properly an habitation for human beings, and not a cage or nest of unclean creatures, it must needs be very unhealthy, tho' the natives say much to the contrary which proceeds from custom. (p. 141)

'Custom' is figured here as a source at once of poor sanitation and unpleasant appearance; cleanliness, by contrast, becomes an index of both regional prosperity and moral dignity. Peterborough, where 'the streetes are very clean and neate well pitch'd and broad as one shall see any where', thus 'looks like a very industrious thriveing town' (p. 144). The 'pitching' (roughly equivalent to 'paving') of streets is accorded significance throughout her journeys, and becomes indicative of a settlement in which a traveller might not only lodge comfortably, but through which she might pass in comfort. A pitched street is a street which links a town to the nation's routes of circulation and exchange.

Within this environment, a key motivating force for the traveller of leisure, within Fiennes's own terms, is curiosity. As discussed above, curiosity was a troublesome, problematic force throughout the early modern period, and it is noticeable that the journey poems and most of the journals avoid the word, seeking instead other ways of justifying travel. But a gradual transformation in attitudes towards curiosity can be traced back into the late Middle Ages. As others have demonstrated, this shift lent fresh legitimacy to acts of foreign travel; indeed humanism increasingly equated the foreign tourist's curiosity with laudable processes of investigation, and came in turn 'to value mobility over stability'.[91] In more general usage, it has been argued that by the second half of the seventeenth century positive uses of the word outweighed negative occurrences. Curiosity, as a result, 'temporarily became central to the construction of both desire and knowledge in various discourses'.[92] For Fiennes, this shift lent legitimacy to her project. To be sure, given her degree of access to aristocratic households, Fiennes was no stranger to a culture of relatively passive encounters with items deemed to be 'curiosities'. Visiting Burghley House, itself 'eminent for its Curiosity', for instance, she encountered 'a Glass-case full of all sorts of Curiosityes of amber stone, currall [coral] and a world of fine things'.[93] She comments that 'My Lord Excetter in his travells was for all sorts of Curious things if it cost him never so much' (pp. 83–4). But her modes of enquiry were characteristically more active and independent. Curiosities may for her be found anywhere in the landscape: from the garden at York, where she sees 'all manner of Curiosityes of Flowers and Greens', to the hill at Shuckburgh where she is presented with a fossilized 'Curiosity they dig up … thereabout' (pp. 93, 116).

The primary impetus of curiosity links with Fiennes's endorsement of the period's ethos of improvement, impelled as it was by a Baconian commitment to enquiry and experimentation. She announces at the outset that the traveller's curiosity should extend beyond 'pleasant prospects' and 'good buildings', to consider also 'different produces and manufactures of each place' (p. 32). Accordingly, as part of what has been described elsewhere as a 'leitmotif' of her text, she consistently seeks to observe local trade and industry in action.[94] She provides detailed observations, for instance, of

[91] Stagl, *History of Curiosity*, p. 49.
[92] Neil Kenny, *Curiosity in Early Modern Europe: Word Histories* (Wiesbaden, 1998), p. 13.
[93] On cabinets of curiosity as representing 'the key site of early modern curiosity', see Alexander Marr, 'Introduction', in *Curiosity and Wonder from the Renaissance to Enlightenment*, ed. R. J. W. Evans and Alexander Marr (Aldershot, 2006), p. 9.
[94] Korte, *English Travel Writing*, p. 72.

industries such as salt production, lace-making, silk-weaving and paper milling (pp. 69–70, 117, 119–20, 120). Nothing frustrates her more than a lack of information. At Newcastle-under-Lyme she is 'defeated in [her] design' to observe china production, which had ceased due to lack of clay, while at Maidstone she merely notes with annoyance that she 'could not learn what particular thing that was their staple Commodity' (pp. 156, 124). This approach is not especially novel; Camden's county descriptions, for instance, routinely record distinctive local products. But Fiennes moves beyond the implicit constraints of Camden's model, as she also notes instances of innovation, and ingenious uses of local conditions. At Colchester, for example, 'the low grounds all about the town are used for the whitening their Bayes [baize] for which this town is remarkable' (p. 132). At Pontefract, she observes

a fruitfull place fine flowers and trees with all sorts of fruite, but that which is mostly intended is the increasing of Liquorish [Liquorice], which the Gardens are all filled with, and any body that has but a little ground improves it for the produce of Liquorish, of which there is vast quantetyes, and it returns severall 100 pounds yearly to the towns. (p. 103)

Such comments evidence not only an appreciation of the importance of local specialization within the framework of an expanding national economy, but also a perception that the knowledge gained through travel may facilitate such developments. Indeed Fiennes advises gentlemen, and 'especially those that serve in parliament, to know and inform themselves the nature of Land, the Genius of the Inhabitants, so as to promote and improve Manufacture and Trade suitable to each and encourage all projects tending thereto' (p. 32). Although she prudently acknowledges the gender codes which direct women to travel for pleasure and men to travel for profit, her text in fact repeatedly struggles against this division.

Fiennes's text also turns her standards of endeavour against those who are not flourishing within the competitive economy. Indeed manifestations of poverty are routinely attributed to the failure of individual enterprise. She comments of people around the border of Scotland and England, for instance, that they 'seem to be very poor people which I impute to their sloth' (p. 173). Moreover, here as elsewhere, moral rebuke is conflated with aesthetic disgust. The solution, as observed in Norwich, is to impose the discipline of labour on the poor; here, there are

3 Hospitalls for boys girls and old people who spinn yarne, as does all the town besides for the Crapes Callimanco [Calico] and Damaskes which is the whole business of the place; indeed they are arrived to a great perfection in their worke so

fine and thinn and glossy their pieces are 27 yards in length and their price is from 30 shillings to 3 pound as they are in fineness; a man can weave 13 yards a day, I saw some weaving. (p. 137)

While the tourist's attention focuses immediately on the beautiful object, her sense of satisfaction derives largely from the fact that the labour of the poor can be transformed into a valuable commodity. The extent to which labour may be assimilated for the polite traveller as an item of curiosity is epitomized in the final comment, which deftly juxtaposes Fiennes's act of observation with the man's day of productive toil. His placement within a workhouse, just as much as her own freedom to observe, signifies for Fiennes the nation's economic strength and cultural values.

This image of the tourist as observer of a specific act of production, repeated in different contexts throughout Fiennes's journal, is also indicative of her effort to make economic sense of tourism. Some tourists have relatively straightforward economic agendas. Brereton, for instance, compares agricultural practices on estates that he visits with those on his own property, while Baskerville goes out of his way to buy grafts of a particular kind of apple tree to take home with him.[95] Yet Fiennes, more than any other tourist, shifts attention, decisively and unashamedly, to consumption. No other journal pays such close attention to food. On the Isle of Purbeck, for instance, she ate 'the best lobsters and crabs boyled in the sea water'; at Burrow Bridge, she bought 'Craw fish 2 pence a Dozen'; of her stay in Carlisle, she grumbles that '2 joynts of mutton and a pinte of wine and bread and beer' cost her twelve shillings; and on more than one occasion she describes challenging encounters with oatcakes (pp. 40, 95, 172, 163–4, 167). Costs are remarked upon throughout; inns, and on occasion whole towns, may be endorsed as 'good … for travellers' or dismissed as 'very dear' (pp. 90, 140). Yet Fiennes appreciates herself as a consumer not merely of goods and services, but more generally of information and experience, and in her observation of local industries and living conditions she is consistently determined to situate herself within the land. At a glass-works, for instance, she spins some glass, while at a mint she stamps a half-crown (pp. 88, 92). In Cornwall, meanwhile, she stops to visit one of the county's typical 'poor cottages', and is surprised to find it 'clean and plaister'd, and such as you might comfortably eate and drink there, and for curiosity sake I drank there, and met with very good bottled ale' (p. 208).

Such experience is aligned more carefully elsewhere with pleasure. Country houses, with their carefully framed prospects, unquestionably

---

[95] Brereton, *Travels*, e.g. p. 172; 'Thomas Baskerville's Journeys', p. 293.

bring her pleasure; the 'visto' at Ingestre, Staffordshire, for instance, 'through the house and so to the gardens and through a long walke of trees of a mile through the parke to a lodge or summer house at the end ... lookes very finely' (p. 155). But she also enjoyed visiting clean and modern towns, which she often described as 'neat' or 'pretty'; such towns, she writes, give 'great pleasure to the travellers to view' (p. 145). Indeed it is significant that this comment – along with others in the journals, such as a description of a 'very pleasant' ride along the Trent – locates pleasure in the experience of moving through space (p. 86). Travel, in other words, is not for her a 'destination-oriented' encounter with one enclosed and aestheticized place after another, but an unfolding engagement with space.[96] On occasion, movement is aligned further with her pursuit of a particular consumerist experience. Her search for a certain kind of West Country tart, for instance, which she had maintained through Devon and Somerset, is finally concluded in Cornwall, at her St Austell inn:

> its an apple pye with a custard all on the top, its the most acceptable entertainment that could be made me; they scald their creame and milk in most parts of those countrys and so its a sort of clouted creame as we call it, with a little sugar, and soe put on top of the apple pye; I was much pleased with my supper. (p. 204)

The journey poems, considered above, regularly depict the tourist's pursuit of pleasure in terms of burlesque, articulating thereby a sense of unease about such an endeavour. Fiennes, by comparison, is at once more thorough and more consistent, appreciating not only the widespread nature of touristic consumption, but also its potential contribution to the national economy.[97] The woman travelling in search of local delicacies emerges from the page as a vital and dynamic economic agent.

This perception of consumption helps to contextualize Fiennes's approach to what would become, in subsequent centuries, one of the quintessential actions of the tourist: the collection of souvenirs. Given that items specifically marketed as souvenirs did not exist, Fiennes had to construct for herself codes of value and significance. More often than not, she opts not so much for recognizable consumer items, but for raw materials of local industries. Hence at Wigan she is shown a form of coal that can be polished like marble; and, she notes, 'I bought some of them for Curiosity sake' (p. 161). Later, at a Cornish tin-mine, she observes the process of smelting,

---

[96] Cf. Anne Wallace's delineation of contrasting approaches to travel-writing (*Walking, Literature, and English Culture: The Origins and Uses of Peripatetic in the Nineteenth Century* (Oxford, 1993), pp. 37–43).
[97] Cf. Fabricant's argument about eighteenth-century domestic tourism as a form of consumption ('Literature of Domestic Tourism', 261).

noting of the finished product that 'its a fine mettle thus in its first melting looks like silver; I had a piece poured out and made cold for to take with me' (p. 205). This image of a gentlewoman riding along the lanes of the West Country, cherishing in her luggage an ingot of tin, is richly suggestive. Circles of elite men were at this time travelling the country, collecting and exchanging antiquities; male tourists such as Evelyn and Brereton, meanwhile, were hacking away at national landmarks. But Fiennes was taking home a hunk of metal. Its significance to her was partly as a memento of a particular experience. At Oxford, in fact, she went a step further, having her name printed on a sheet of paper at the university press (p. 55). Yet it also signifies for her a particular form of nationhood, founded not only on industry and ingenuity, but equally on trade and human circulation. Hence, whereas a classic item of curiosity may well have been an object without a clear use, for Fiennes the ingot of tin is valued for its multiplicity of uses.[98] It stands for her not only as a reminder of a dynamic and productive nation, but equally of her contribution to it, as a particular kind of early modern tourist.

For Fiennes, as for other tourists of her century, knowledge underpins nationhood. A generation or two before her, Hammond had concluded his second and final journal with the rhetorical question, 'who can want that commendable Ambition to know their owne Country aright?'[99] Fiennes, in her preface, argues similarly that domestic travel promises to 'form such an Idea of England, add much to its Glory and Esteem in our minds and cure the evil itch of over-valueing foreign parts' (p. 32). This direct challenge to contemporary gentlemen taking the Grand Tour is unique among the journals considered here. While many male tourists within England perhaps felt themselves to be uncomfortably exposed to the retort that they travelled at home merely because they could not afford to travel abroad, Fiennes was arguably on more secure ground. Her point was that, as a woman and therefore someone constrained from continental tourism, she was developing a knowledge of England that many of her male peers were rejecting. Some members of the House of Commons, she continues, were 'ignorant of anything but the name of the place for which they serve in parliament' (p. 33).

Moreover, Fiennes's 'Idea of England' is not to be understood as an itinerary of significant or wondrous sites, after the model of the Grand Tour, but something altogether more dynamic. In this respect she clarifies a fundamental commitment to mobility and process that underpins all the journals considered here. Admittedly, her perception of the nation was

---

[98] Benedict, *Curiosity*, p. 3.   [99] *Relation of a Short Survey of the Western Counties*, p. 96.

more strictly delimited than many others of the time; her visit to Scotland left her with a distinct sense of otherness, and a determination to reinscribe national borders (pp. 173–4). Yet, within these geographical parameters, her journal's conception of England effectively resolves the anxieties and uncertainties so evident in the journey poems. Fiennes, more than any of the other journalists, is alert to the business of mobility: from the roads 'full of carriers' in Somerset, through Exeter's 'vast trade' in serge which 'turns the most money of a weeke of anything in England', to the fact of towns rising and falling – even to the extent of becoming 'ruinated' and 'disregarded' – as a result of economic forces (pp. 196, 197, 209). She was also attentive to the importance of what would subsequently become known as the nation's transportation infrastructure. She notes, for example, efforts to improve navigation on the Avon downstream of Salisbury, measures taken in Devon to adapt their methods of transport to the poor roads, and the way in which certain places have been developed 'for the conveniency of the road' (pp. 75, 41, 52).

In all these respects, in fact, Fiennes might be seen as prefiguring the work of Daniel Defoe. Yet while Defoe, as I will argue in the Epilogue, perceives himself fundamentally as a surveyor of trade and industry, Fiennes is more subtle in her attention to the wider motivations and functions of tourism. She epitomizes an era in which tourists saw no reason to distinguish between aesthetic and economic motivations. Indeed for the mobile citizen, enfranchised by the very act of travel, aesthetics and economics were equally significant constituents of nationhood. She is also typical of travelwriting in the century before Defoe in retaining her focus on the individual within the landscape, allowing more general perceptions of mobility and national identity to emerge suggestively, on the basis of particular experiences. While others were unnerved by the pleasures and demands of the body within space, Fiennes sets them at the foundation of her makeshift model of touristic consumption. For all these reasons, Fiennes, more than any previous writer, makes sense of the enterprise of tourism. She defines a place within the nation for the domestic tourist: as a seeker of pleasure and experience, information and ideas.

CHAPTER 6

Traffic: John Taylor and his context

When early modern writers wrote of the activities of 'trade' or the business of 'merchants', they referred, almost invariably, to international forms of commerce. By comparison, discourse on internal trade was rudimentary, hobbled throughout the period by concerns about the propriety of transferring goods across the country in the interests of individual profit. The most common term to describe internal trade, 'traffic', was itself often used in morally charged ways, to suggest underhand practices or illicit exchanges.[1] Yet traffic was effecting revolutionary changes in England, undergoing a process of intensification that brought about 'the growing commercial integration of the regional economies of England and Wales'.[2] This growth of traffic, in terms of both the volume of merchandise traded and the distances covered, also assumed a central place within broader patterns of economically motivated domestic mobility. Internal migration became increasingly common, drawing many individuals further and further from their places of birth.[3] The movement of information relating to business accelerated.[4] And the movement of capital and credit became ever more fluid, aided particularly by a range of structural innovations that have been labelled a 'financial revolution'.[5] Traffic was therefore at once a catalyst and

---

[1] 'Dealing or bargaining in something which should not be made the subject of trade' (*OED* 2d). The *OED* dates this meaning no earlier than 1663; however, this is somewhat conservative, as usages of 'traffic' to mean 'deal in sex' were prevalent several decades earlier (Gordon Williams, *A Dictionary of Sexual Language and Imagery in Shakespearean and Stuart Literature*, 3 vols. (London and Atlantic Highlands, 1994), *sub* 'traffic').

[2] Keith Wrightson, *Earthly Necessities: Economic Lives in Early Modern Britain* (New Haven and London, 2000), p. 176. See further J. A. Chartres, *Internal Trade in England 1500–1700* (London, 1977).

[3] See esp. *Migration and Society in Early Modern England*, ed. Peter Clark and David Souden (London, 1987).

[4] Chartres, *Internal Trade*, p. 41.

[5] See esp. Henry Roseveare, *The Financial Revolution, 1660–1760* (London and New York, 1991). On the informal, though equally significant, development of interpersonal credit networks, see Craig Muldrew, *The Economy of Obligation: The Culture of Credit and Social Relations in Early Modern England* (Basingstoke, 1998).

the most visible index of England's changing patterns of domestic mobility. As David Rollison has argued, it was 'the agency which above all others exemplifies the decline of localism and the unification of England'.[6]

The intensification of traffic is a thematic strand that has run throughout this book, most notably shaping the chapters in Part I. In this final chapter I want to attend to these issues in a more concentrated manner, focusing above all on one particular author who stands as a pivotal figure within early modern discourse on domestic travel. Indeed John Taylor, the Thames waterman and self-styled 'water-poet' of seventeenth-century England, has threatened on occasion to take over this book. Taylor was born in Gloucester, but was drawn to London where he worked, in his own words, as 'a mechanicke Waterman' on the Thames, before painstakingly carving out an identity for himself as an author.[7] In the course of his career he was concerned with mobility in almost any form, including the intro-duction of coaches to London streets, the process of the water cycle (in which 'nature in a circle runs about'), and the country's emergent systems of internal trading.[8] Here, I want to centre attention on a series of some fourteen pamphlets, spanning a period from the late 1610s into the 1650s, which describe his own travels, undertaken almost exclusively within England and Wales.[9] These texts are heterogeneous, including various combinations of news, narratives of his own contrived adventures, digres-sive comic anecdotes, and exhortations to economic improvement. What holds the project together is the singular figure of the industrious author, travelling the nation's roads and waterways like countless other commoners, and expecting financial reward for his acts of work. As a result, his pam-phlets, for all their qualities of experimentation and indirection, create the outlines of a discourse of traffic, figuring the nation as a space of infinite opportunities and potential connections, open to the initiative and industry of its inhabitants.

The chapter's concentration on one author is based partly on the grounds that Taylor was exceptional in so many ways, and partly on the belief that an

---

[6] *The Local Origins of Modern Society: Gloucestershire 1500–1800* (London and New York, 1993), p. 46.

[7] *The Praise of Hemp-seed* (1620), reprinted in *All the Workes* (1630), III.61. (The texts in Taylor's mid-career collected volume are generally reasonable reproductions of the originals, though I have checked longer quotes against the earlier publications. The pagination in *Workes*, in three distinct sequences, is occasionally unreliable, but generally provides an easier form of referencing than by gatherings.) On Taylor's life, see Bernard Capp, *The World of John Taylor the Water Poet, 1578–1653* (Oxford, 1994).

[8] See, e.g., *The World Runnes on Wheeles* (1623), in *Workes*, II.232–44; *The Praise, Antiquity, and Commodity of Beggerie, Beggers, and Begging* (1621), in *Workes*, I.95–102; *Taylor on Tame-Isis* (1632), p. 9.

[9] The domestic journeys are collected in *Travels in Stuart Britain: The Adventures of John Taylor, The Water Poet*, ed. John Chandler (Stroud, 1999).

intensive analysis of one writer can on occasion offer a point of entrance into broader cultural debates. Such an approach also provides scope to clarify some of the key strands of argument running throughout the book. The first section, then, considers the challenges presented to contemporary authors by the rapid growth of traffic, and suggests that in a number of his early works Taylor seized upon this context as a way of framing his unique authorial career. The subsequent section extends this analysis, examining the ways in which his methods of travelling and publishing established a new kind of authorial identity, founded at once on the force of his personality and the labours which he insists are deserving of reward. And the final section considers the ways in which Taylor, working unashamedly through the gaze of an industrious commoner, reassessed the meanings of domestic space. In the following century, as I will suggest in the Epilogue, Daniel Defoe surveyed and theorized internal trade; England, he declared, was 'the wonder of all the world of trade'.[10] By comparison, Taylor *experienced* traffic. He turned himself into a living embodiment of it, describing its effects not only upon his own identity, but on that of his nation.

THE CHALLENGE OF TRAFFIC

My analysis of journey poems in Chapter 5 overlooked one of the most idiosyncratic – and notoriously popular – pieces associated with this minor genre. Richard Brathwaite's *Barnabae Itinerarium* was published in Latin in 1636, then in a second edition in 1638 with an English translation on facing pages. It has been described as a piece of 'carnivalesque satire', parodying the more erudite journey poem by presenting the narrator as a womanizer and a drunk, stumbling his way across the countryside in a series of geographically specific journeys.[11] The fourth and final part of the text, however, takes an unexpected turn. Here Barnabee begins by cataloguing the various places he has visited, bidding 'farewell' to each, before announcing his transformation into a radically different kind of traveller. 'I am now become a Drover', he declares, and proceeds to describe his trading in horses at fairs across the north of England (sig. 2A3r). The function of this turn is inscrutable. On one page, a declaration that 'Smell of gaine my sense benummeth' suggests straightforward satire, directed against those involved in trade; on another, a

[10] *The Complete English Tradesman*, 2nd edn (1727), p. 321.
[11] Felicity Henderson, 'Erudite Satire in Seventeenth-Century England' (unpublished Ph.D. dissertation, Monash University, 2002), pp. 83–8.

commitment to transform himself, embracing interests of 'thrift' and 'favour', indicates a more positive attitude (sigs. 2A3r, Y6r). I do not propose to argue one way or the other; instead, I simply wish to note the novelty of Brathwaite's exercise. He seems almost to tease his readers, who have all too few generic guidelines to help them to make sense of a poetic representation of a horse-trader. This, I suggest, is precisely the cultural context within which Taylor positioned himself, as he tried more purposefully to create a new model of authorial identity, and new kinds of texts.

The problem for Taylor – or, indeed, for any truly reformed Barnabee – was that orthodox social and spatial models were so profoundly committed to values of place and settlement. Within such models, manifestations of traffic were either ignored or carefully constrained. Market towns, for instance, had an accepted status as 'the normal place of sale and purchase', and their very existence was dependent upon the incessant movements of people and goods.[12] Contemporary commentators, however, insisted on the limits of such traffic. Hence William Harrison argues that, thanks to the establishment of weekly markets across the country, 'no buyer shall make any great journey in the purveyance of his necessities, so no occupier shall have occasion to travel far off with his commodities'. Here England's systems of marketing are supposedly designed to *restrict* the need for travel. When Harrison continues the passage by acknowledging those who decide to go further afield, 'to seek for the highest prices', it is clear that he is describing a corruption of the system, rather than the system itself.[13] Indeed, even up to Harrison's time it was possible to perceive instances of marketing beyond the local market town as exceptional, and potentially corrosive of existing social and economic relationships.[14] Activities involved in food production, in particular, were thus perceived principally as 'social rather than economic activities', and the most common form of marketing was the sale of surplus produce, rather than production specifically geared towards the market.[15]

These values underpinned a complex array of laws designed to control internal marketing. In Chapter 2 I considered the uncertain status of petty traders, involved in the business of moving consumer goods around the

[12] Alan Everitt, 'The Marketing of Agricultural Produce', in *The Agrarian History of England and Wales*, Vol. IV: *1500–1640*, ed. Joan Thirsk (Cambridge, 1967), p. 467; David Rollison, 'Exploding England: The Dialectics of Mobility and Settlement in Early Modern England', *Social History*, 24 (1999), 10.
[13] *The Description of England*, ed. Georges Edelen (Ithaca, 1968), p. 246.
[14] See esp. Wrightson's survey of the country's 'overlapping spheres of commercial activity' (*Earthly Necessities*, pp. 93–8 (quote at p. 93)).
[15] Joyce Oldham Appleby, *Economic Thought and Ideology in Seventeenth-Century England* (Princeton, 1978), p. 27.

country.[16] More generally, markets and marketing functioned under the eyes of both local and national authorities. Within particular market-towns, traders often required licences, measures and weights were carefully monitored, and prices were often determined for the marketplace as a whole rather than left to be settled by individual negotiations.[17] Within the nation as a whole, the government commonly sought to prevent or restrain the circulation of agricultural produce, particularly in times of dearth. Most notably, Books of Orders, issued recurrently from the Elizabethan through to the Caroline eras, imposed emergency measures such as price-fixing and enforced sales of stored corn.[18] Offences against the market were encompassed in a specialized vocabulary of mercantile disorder: forestalling, engrossing, regrating, and so forth. As noted at various points throughout this book, such legislative efforts assumed a place within a broader governmental project to control mobility. Furthermore, the state attempted to control the circulation of capital, particularly through its laws on usury. Although this legislative project had waned by the early decades of the seventeenth century, anxieties about the ethics of money-lending remained powerful throughout the early modern period.[19]

Yet such laws, and the accompanying discourse evident throughout the period, are indices not of an unproblematic system, but of values creaking under unprecedented pressures. Throughout the early modern period, the overall rise in the national population, and the increasing pattern of clustering in urban areas, placed fresh demands on structures of traffic. Rising levels of consumption, particularly of new consumer goods, stimulated industry and trade alike.[20] And at the centre of all these processes stood London, the irrepressible expansion of which was steadily reorienting patterns of traffic across the nation. These forces of change affected the nature as well as the volume of traffic. Regional industrial specialisms were becoming ever more pronounced, in response to rising demands for particular goods, especially from towns and cities. Further, the nation's 'networks of internal commerce' were 'elaborated and tightened', reflecting the increasing degree of economic integration, and the movement of merchandise across greater distances.[21] Conceptions of the market, as a result,

---

[16] See above, pp. 101–11.   [17] Everitt, 'Marketing', pp. 486–8.
[18] Paul Slack, 'Books of Orders: The Making of English Social Policy, 1577–1631', *Transactions of the Royal Historical Society*, 5th series, 30 (1980), 1–22.
[19] See esp. Norman Jones, *God and the Moneylenders: Usury and the Law in Early Modern England* (Oxford, 1989).
[20] Muldrew, *Economy of Obligation*, pp. 32–5; Wrightson, *Earthly Goods*, pp. 296–300.
[21] Wrightson, *Earthly Goods*, p. 173.

became increasingly abstract.[22] Fairs, which were less regular and more specialized than markets, existed throughout the period; however, the fact that they were also less regulated than markets made them more responsive to expanding demand, and many therefore grew in significance.[23] Moreover, as noted in Chapter 2, increasing volumes of traffic were no longer channelled through markets and fairs at all, but were arranged informally by an emergent army of professional traders.[24] Traffic, under the weight of these changes, was assuming unsettlingly new shapes.

Given the palpable impact of these developments, there was surprisingly little effort devoted, in contemporary discourse, to making sense of traffic. J. A. Chartres has noted that the attention of economic historians has overwhelmingly been drawn to external trade; however, in this respect they are doing no more than following the lead of writers at the time.[25] Books such as *The Circle of Commerce* and *The Treasure of Traffike*, understood now as central to the 'mercantilist' debate of the seventeenth century, are virtually oblivious to the nature and effects of internal trade.[26] Without question this debate was transforming perceptions of economic relations: introducing a sense that commerce might have 'its own regularities', and laying the foundations for endorsements of the 'liberty' of trade.[27] The nascent 'discourse of national economy', however, was forged by focusing on England as a unit set in relation to other nations, rather than by dwelling on internal structures and dynamics.[28] Similarly, in literary texts a merchant is invariably a man involved with trade across the sea. These are not unproblematic figures, by any means; Shakespeare's *Merchant of Venice* is just the best known of a number of plays concerned with the relation between traditional social morality and the rules of the marketplace. But the image of the merchant as heroic adventurer was equally prevalent, especially in the wake of Richard Hakluyt's monumental *Principal Navigations, Voyages, Traffiques and Discoveries of the English Nation*.[29] By comparison, moving within one's own country and trading with one's own countrymen remained activities that were at once all too common and all

---

[22] See esp. Jean-Christophe Agnew, *Worlds Apart: The Market and the Theater in Anglo-American Thought, 1550–1750* (Cambridge, 1986), pp. 17–56.

[23] Everitt, 'Marketing', p. 534.   [24] See above, pp. 101–11.   [25] *Internal Trade*, pp. 9–11.

[26] Edward Misselden, *The Circle of Commerce* (1623); Lewes Roberts, *The Treasure of Traffike, or, A Discourse of Forraigne Trade* (1641). For valuable analyses of the cultural significance of mercantilism, see: Jonathan Gil Harris, *Sick Economies: Drama, Mercantilism, and Disease in Shakespeare's England* (Philadelphia, 2004); Mary Poovey, *A History of the Modern Fact: Problems of Knowledge in the Sciences of Wealth and Society* (Chicago and London, 1998), pp. 66–91.

[27] Appleby, *Economic Thought*, p. 47; Poovey, *History of the Modern Fact*, p. 75.

[28] Harris, *Sick Economies*, p. 2.   [29] 3 vols. (1599–1600).

too problematic, epitomizing as they did the gathering challenges to traditional economic values.

Popular literature, such as that produced by Taylor, presents a more fruitful seam of representations. Textual forms such as pamphlets and ballads were more insistently concerned with the lives and activities of the commoners who constituted their audience, and were as a result more likely to be drawn to details of local practices rather than more abstract relations between national economies. The work of Taylor was forged in this context. By roughly the middle of the 1620s, and certainly by the time of the publication of *All the Workes* in 1630, Taylor had constructed not only a recognizable authorial persona but also certain distinctive types of texts. His pamphlets of domestic travel represent the most notable products of this achievement; however, his earlier works, in which he was trying at once to define his status and to find appropriate forms for representations of economic processes, are equally significant in the present context. Some critical attention has been devoted to the ways in which Taylor sought to position himself in relation to Thomas Coryate, whose *Crudities* (1611), an exhaustive relation of his continental tour accompanied by a wealth of mock-heroic commendatory verses penned by London wits, became a milestone in early modern travel-writing.[30] Certainly this model appears to have weighed heavily on Taylor's mind in his very early years of authorship, in which he produced two of his own narratives of continental journeys.[31] Further approaches – including my own, in Chapter 4 – have attended to the way in which his earliest domestic travel text, *The Pennyles Pilgrimage*, is fabricated out of the materials of other models and discourses, such as the pilgrimage and the royal progress.[32] But Taylor was ultimately more ambitious and original than either of these models enabled him to be. He looked as much to the writing of Thomas Nashe as to that of Coryate, and he experimented with a range of existing genres.[33] Moreover, he increasingly situated travel not as an heroic or extraordinary event, but as rather more mundane, a fundamental part of wider national systems of industry and exchange.

---

[30] See esp. Capp, *World of John Taylor*, pp. 13–14, 18; Joanne E. Gates, 'Travel and Pseudo-Translation in the Self-Promotional Writings of John Taylor, Water Poet', in *Travel and Translation in the Early Modern Period*, ed. Carmine G. Di Biase (Amsterdam and New York, 2006), pp. 267–80; Michelle O'Callaghan, *The English Wits: Literature and Sociability in Early Modern England* (Cambridge, 2007), pp. 57–8.

[31] *Taylors Travels … from London to Hamburgh in Germanie* (1617), in *Workes*, III.77–89; *Taylors Travels to Prague in Bohemia* (1621), in *Workes*, III.90–100.

[32] See above, pp. 161–4.

[33] For Taylor's admiration of Nashe, see esp. *Crop-eare Curried* (1645), p. 3.

One of his most original pamphlets of this period describes the 'endlesse Journey' of an object rather than a person. In *A Shilling or, The Travailes of Twelve-pence* (1621), a text which prefigures a minor genre of the eighteenth and early nineteenth centuries, a shilling coin describes its movements.[34] The coin facilitates a range of market transactions in the city, and passes back and forth through an alehouse as farmers, brewers and artisans mix in the country. Although much of the narrative centres on London, the coin's radically peripatetic movements effectively render place redundant, imagining instead a limitless space of economic exchange. Coryate's 'progresse', Taylor proclaims, 'was but a walke in regard of my *Shillings* perambulations'.[35] In the country, for instance, the coin proclaims:

> Look on the hearbs, the flowr's, the fruits, the trees,
> Fowles of the ayre, the painefull lab'ring Bees,
> And aske their Owners why they breed and spring,
> His answere is, they must him *money* bring.
> Note but the toyling Plow-man, he is sowing,
> He's hedging, ditching, taking, reaping, mowing,
> Goes to bed late, and rises before day,
> And all to have my company, hee'll say.[36]

While Taylor treats all the activity with a measure of ironic detachment, in accordance with traditionally moralized representations of the pursuit of gain, the only truly incomprehensible attitude for him is that of a miser. Critically, a miser disrupts the circulation of wealth, and as a result the coin causes him to

> sell his soule to hell,
> because I here on Earth with him should dwell.
> And eighteene yeeres he kept me day and night
> Lock'd in a Chest, not seeing any light.[37]

Although the point is made experientially rather than theoretically, the poem acknowledges contemporary uncertainties about money, which on the one hand bound people together in complex interrelationships of credit and exchange, and on the other hand functioned as a 'solvent of traditional social arrangements'.[38] Money, Taylor recognizes, is at once an agent of

---

[34] On the later tradition, see esp. Aileen Douglas, 'Britannia's Rule and the It-Narrator', *Eighteenth-Century Fiction*, 6 (1993), 70–89; Christopher Flint, 'Speaking Objects: The Circulation of Stories in Eighteenth-Century Prose Fiction', *PMLA*, 113 (1998), 212–26.
[35] *Workes*, I.65.   [36] *Ibid.*, I.72.   [37] *Ibid.*, I.69.
[38] Appleby, *Economic Thought*, p. 201. For a study of credit relationships, see Muldrew, *Economy of Obligation*.

connection and transformation. Above all, though, it is an index of mobility; indeed, by focusing on the coin, rather than its owners, Taylor is able to concentrate on – and, by implication, align himself with – the fundamental energies driving the economic system. For the shilling, as for the poet, stasis is rendered as constraint.

Other pamphlets produced by Taylor in these years provocatively revise existing literary traditions under the weight of this emergent socio-economic vision. *The Praise, Antiquity, and Commodity, of Beggery, Beggers, and Begging* (1621), for instance, translates contemporary diatribes against beggars and vagrants into a different register. Here the beggar is 'an enemie to Idlenesse', and emerges by virtue of his 'right perpetuall motion' as emblematic of a dynamic society.[39] *Taylors Pastorall* (1624), meanwhile, is not a pastoral at all; indeed, as a study of 'the Noble Antiquitie of Shepheards, with the Profitable use of Sheepe' it is more obviously aligned with the georgic mode. Significantly, Taylor was not ignorant of the conventions of pastoral; like many aspiring poets, in fact, he had tried his hand at a pastoral complaint in his first published work.[40] Therefore, despite his protestations *Taylors Pastorall* is not an 'unlearned' work; it just applies its learning in novel ways. In the course of the pamphlet, characteristically sliding from verse to prose and back again, Taylor skips from a review of the literary tradition within which 'learned Poets of all times' have celebrated 'The harmlesse lives of rural shepheards Swaines', to an analysis of the uses and profitability of sheep. In a consideration of the 'infinite numbers of people rich and poore' who have derived 'their whole dependance from the poore sheepes back', he sketches the unravelling economic process generated out of wool: 'No Ram no Lambe, no Lambe no Sheepe, no Sheepe no Wooll, no Wooll no Woolman, no Woolman no Spinner, no Spinner no Weaver, no Weaver no Cloth, no Cloth no Clothier, no Clothier no Clothworker, Fuller, Tucker, Shearman, Draper, or scarcely a rich Dyer'.[41]

This attention to economic circulation is developed in a pamphlet which contains a narrative of the most ambitiously absurd of all Taylor's journeys, made in a brown-paper boat, using stockfish (cured cod) bound to canes as oars, down the Thames from London to Queensborough. The enterprise was effectively hopeless, sustained over the course of thirty-six hours mainly by the aid of inflated bullocks' bladders. The resultant narrative, meanwhile, is surprisingly modest, finished in just over 150 lines of verse and published at the end of *The Praise of Hemp-seed* (1620). In a preface to this

[39] *Workes*, I.99.   [40] *The Sculler Rowing from Tiber to Thames* (1612), in *Workes*, III.27–8.
[41] *Workes*, III.49, III.51, III.54.

pamphlet, Taylor invokes the model of the mock-encomium, citing as models *Nashe's Lenten Stuff* (with its praise of the red herring of Great Yarmouth) and Sir John Harington's *Metamorphosis of Ajax*.[42] Yet *Hemp-seed* stretches at the constraints of this genre, expressing genuine wonder at the various industries underpinned by hemp, and following the production of rope and sail-cloth into a celebration of the growth of navigation and international trade. Further, as Katharine Craik argues, its perception of 'the dignity involved in domestic industry' admits an associated defence of popular literature as similarly 'ennobled by labour'.[43] Within this context, the narrative of Taylor's adventure in the brown-paper is positioned not purely as mock-heroic or farce, but as a legitimate form of labour. This point is underscored by a concluding encomium, which is in no way ironic, on the 'noble *Thames*'. Here, the river not only provides the site of Taylor's misjudged adventure, but typifies the pamphlet's guiding principle:

> If like a Bee I seeke to live and thrive,
> Thou wilt yeeld hony freely to my hive,
> If like a drone I will not worke for meate,
> Thou in discretion gives me nought to eate
> Thou the true rules of Justice doth observe,
> To feed the lab'rer, let the idle sterve.[44]

Travel on adventure is here positioned in relation to Taylor's travel in his daily course of work as a waterman. In each case, acts of labour lead directly to reward, demonstrating that to be mobile is to be industrious.

The journey in the brown-paper boat is most commonly linked to a tradition of bizarre or wondrous voyages, stretching back through Coryate to the likes of William Kemp, who morris-danced from London to Norwich. While these connections are undeniable, there is a danger in removing such texts from their social and economic contexts, in favour of a depoliticized literary tradition. As I suggested in Chapter 4, Kemp's pamphlet is itself engaged with debates over popular mobility.[45] For Taylor, meanwhile, such debates were simply unavoidable to his construction of authorship and selfhood, and he returned to them repeatedly. In 1619 he proposed a loose theory of 'Adventures upon Returnes', in response to those who 'do speak harshly, and hardly of mee and of divers others, who have attempted and gone dangerous voyages by sea with small Wherries or Boats, or any other adventure upon any voyage by land'. He argued, not entirely facetiously, that 'all men in the world are Adventurers upon Returne', taking risks of

---

[42] *Ibid.*, III.62.   [43] 'John Taylor's Pot Poetry', *The Seventeenth Century*, 20 (2005), 194, 192.
[44] *Workes*, III.81.   [45] See above, pp. 161–4.

various kinds – physical, economic, spiritual – in pursuit of a living.[46] This argument seeks to strip adventurous voyages of their wonder, bringing them into alignment with the quotidian challenges undertaken by labouring men and women throughout English society. Far from being either 'sport[s]' undertaken merely for the sake of entertainment, or acts of heroism pursued in the interests of the nation, they are figured more simply – and fundamentally – as forms of work.[47]

THE INDUSTRIOUS TRAVELLER

For all the apparent assurance of his early celebrations of industry and exchange, Taylor's literature of domestic travel remained, throughout his career, a novel enterprise. He registers an awareness of this novelty at a semantic level in 1641, reflecting on a 'painefull travell, Joruney [*sic*], Voyage, Perambulation, and Perigrination, or what you please to call it'.[48] In a later pamphlet he assesses the applicability of various extant textual models, as he proposes:

> To write my acts my selfe, as 'tis most fit,
> *Cæsar* himselfe his Commentaries writ:
> And solid *Johnson* made his Muse his Cock
> To crow his savoury Voyage up Fleet Dock:
> So I do hold it worthy imitation,
> To follow them, and write mine own Relation.[49]

The selection is characteristically quirky: the commentaries of an imperial conqueror set alongside the journey through London's Fleet Ditch narrated in Ben Jonson's mock-heroic poem, 'On the Famous Voyage'. Yet it is nonetheless striking that, at the age of seventy-two, Taylor should still be struggling to define a generic, and cultural, place for his work. The collection of travel pamphlets that Taylor produced is accordingly diverse. Notably, Taylor experimented with different ways of adding interest or value to the narration of his own movement. The bizarre challenges of early texts give way in most later pieces either to a concern with the improvement of transportation, or to an excess of 'pleasant passages' akin to the style of a jest-book.[50] Throughout, however, there is one principle of coherence. In

---

[46] *A Kicksey Winsey, or A Lerry Come-Twang* (1619), in *Workes*, II.42.
[47] *Ibid.* II.40. Cf. Laurie Ellinghausen, 'The Individualist Project of John Taylor "The Water Poet"', *Ben Jonson Journal* 9 (2002), 147–69.
[48] *John Taylors Last Voyage* (1641), sig. B2v.   [49] *A Late Weary, Merry Voyage, and Journey* (1650), p. 12.
[50] *Part of this Summers Travels* (1639), t.p.

the course of his travel-writing career, Taylor fashioned himself as a legitimate centre of interest, cajoling his audience into accepting his conjoined labours, as traveller and author, as being worthy of reward. For all the apparent uncertainty of the invocation of Caesar and Jonson, therefore, I would suggest that Taylor is well aware of what defines his project. He was a commoner and a labourer, but one with unique powers of expression, setting out 'To write my acts my selfe'.

Taylor began to clarify the relation between travel and authorship on his first significant journey after the 'Pennyles Pilgrimage' to Edinburgh. In 1622 he travelled in a wherry from London, up the east coast as far as the mouth of the Witham River in Lincolnshire, then inland via the Trent, the Humber and the Ouse, to York. Having reached his destination, Taylor sought out the Lord Mayor and told him 'What labour, and what dangers manifold, / My fellow and my selfe had past at Seas'. He then presented the Lord Mayor with a 'booke of all my Workes together', bound in 'red guilded leather', and offered to 'give' him the wherry in which he had travelled from London.[51] The models for Taylor's actions are not hard to locate. A footnote suggests that the boat might be 'as good a munument' as Coryate's shoes, which were famously displayed in the church of his native village of Odcombe.[52] Furthermore, Richard Ferris, who rowed by sea from London to Bristol in 1590, had his boat carried in a procession through Bristol before being 'feasted most royally' by civic leaders, while Kemp had his shoes displayed in the Norwich town hall after being granted a generous annuity by that town's mayor.[53] Yet Taylor's presentation of his 'Workes' – eight years before the still more audacious printing of a collected volume of his pamphlets – signals a peculiar circularity to Taylor's enterprise. He is not a traveller who writes, nor a writer who travels; rather, the roles are inseparable and interdependent. The performance of travel provides a rationale for Taylor's entrance into authorship, reminding readers of his social status while simultaneously making a unique claim to authority.

Taylor's encounter with the Lord Mayor of York also demonstrates the ways in which he was rethinking traditional structures of patronage, moving instead towards freshly mercantile relationships. Significantly, the Mayor himself resists Taylor's attempt to establish a patronage relationship. The pamphlet records his response to the gift of the 'Workes' in a truncated line

---

[51] *A Very Merrie Wherrie-Ferry-Voyage* (1622), in *Workes*, II.14.
[52] *Workes*, II.14. See Richmond Barbour, *Before Orientalism: London's Theatre of the East, 1576–1626* (Cambridge, 2003), p. 116; O'Callaghan, *English Wits*, p. 115.
[53] *The Most Dangerous and Memorable Adventure of Richard Ferris* (1590), sig. B2r; *Kemps Nine Daies Wonder* (1600), sigs. D1r–v, D2r.

of verse – 'Which he did take' – and an explanatory footnote: 'Heere I make a full point, for I received not a point in exchange.' Moreover, he treats Taylor's offer of the boat as a commercial transaction, inspecting it in action before eventually refusing to accept it. As much as he seeks to blame the Lord Mayor for a breach of decorum, however, Taylor himself contributes to a renegotiation of his status. When the Lord Mayor has rejected the boat, Taylor immediately sells it instead to 'honest *Mr. Kayes* in Cunny street', who 'entertain'd me well, for which I thanke him, / And gratefully amongst my friends I'l ranke him'.[54] Mr Kayes, an innkeeper, appears to have accepted on the one hand the equivocal nature of own his role as both patron and customer, and on the other hand the fine distinction between Taylor and any other common trader. In recompense, following a pattern established in *The Pennyles Pilgrimage*, Taylor inscribes him as a 'friend', offering the scene as an image in miniature of the author-traveller locating, and in turn rewarding in print, his audience. It is in part a business transaction, just as Taylor concedes that his journey is fundamentally a commercial venture. As he had told the suspicious constables who detained him at Cromer, Norfolk, earlier on the trip, he was little different from any other common trader: 'bound' to York 'upon a Mart'.[55]

   This act of authorial self-fashioning also required a subtle renegotiation of Taylor's relation with the readers of his pamphlets. From the outset of his career Taylor, like many of his peers, was fascinated by the complex business of print, which was sustained in part by traditional systems of patronage and in part by the more abstract forces of the market. His unease is registered in the dedications of early works, which range from earnest addresses to men of higher status, through to mock-dedications, on the model of Nashe.[56] For his travel pamphlets, he developed a novel form of publication by subscription.[57] Though details of this practice are unclear, Taylor appears to have procured sponsors, numbering perhaps in the thousands, before his journeys. Some may have paid him in advance, to help him to fund a trip; however, it appears that most withheld payment until his return, when Taylor presented them with a copy of his pamphlet. At the outset, a subscriber would sign a 'bill', which may have been as informal as that he

---

[54] *Workes*, II.14.   [55] *Ibid.*, II.9.

[56] On Nashe's relation to patronage, see Lorna Hutson, *Thomas Nashe in Context* (Oxford, 1989), pp. 197–214.

[57] See Capp, *World of John Taylor*, pp. 62–6; and Alexandra Halasz, 'Pamphlet Surplus: John Taylor and Subscription Publication', in *Print, Manuscript, and Performance: The Changing Relations of the Media in Early Modern England*, ed. Arthur F. Marotti and Michael D. Bristol (Columbus, Ohio, 2000), pp. 90–102.

prints at the beginning of his account of one of his last tours, described as 'A
Taylors Bill, with few or no *Items*':

> Now in the seventy fourth yeare of mine Age,
> I take an *English* and *Welsh* Pilgrimage:
> From *London* first I bend my course to *Chester*,
> And humbly I to all men am Requester;
> That when I have past over Hills and Dales,
> And compast with my Travels famous *Wales*,
> That when to you that I a Book do give,
> Relating how I did subsist and live,
> With all my passages both here and there,
> And of my Entertainment every where.
> Write but your Names and Dwellings in this Bill,
> I'le finde you, for the Book give what you will.[58]

The value of the pamphlet, within the terms of this contract, is its record of
a journey. For Alexandra Halasz, it stands as 'the commodified form of the
labor expended' by Taylor, as traveller and author, in his ventures.[59] This
model of authorship allows Taylor to evade issues that pressed heavily on
prospective authors who were uneducated and socially unelevated. In
practical terms, he gains access to the press because sponsorship allows
him to shoulder the costs of publication. In textual terms, the express
purpose of his pamphlets as tokens, providing proof of his travels, allows
him to dodge questions of quality or value. Like a letter-writer, Taylor
relates his experiences, in a manner that is figured as primarily documentary.
If his pamphlet also commands returns from those who had not previously
agreed to sponsor the author, thereby situating Taylor independently
within the marketplace of print, this might be seen as incidental, even
accidental.

The intertwined projects of travel and authorship are united by Taylor's
discourse of friendship. In York, the innkeeper who purchases his boat is
'ranke[d]' among the author's 'friends'. Similarly, his pamphlets consistently proclaim a goal to 'get money, and to try my friends', or 'to make use
of some friends, and devise a painfull way for my subsistence'.[60] For all its
debts to the hierarchical relations of a patronage system, this discourse has
an edge of social radicalism. However speculatively and playfully, Taylor
situates himself at the centre of a system in which an individual's value is
determined, above all, by his or her response to the culturally ambiguous

---

[58] *A Short Relation of a Long Journey* (1653), p. 3.   [59] 'Pamphlet Surplus', p. 96.
[60] *Kicksey Winsey*, in *Workes*, II.39; *John Taylors Wandering, to See the Wonders of the West* (1649), t.p.

figure of the 'water-poet'. Taylor's responsibility is to repay his friends in print: at once through the presentation of a pamphlet and through recognition within that pamphlet. For instance, having reached Christchurch, at the mouth of the Avon in Hampshire, in 1623, he pauses in his narration to acknowledge patrons and hosts alike:

> My love, my duty, and my thankfulnesse,
> To Sir *George Hastings* I must here expresse:
> His deedes to me, I must requite in words,
> No other payment, poore mens state affords.
> With fruitlesse words, I pay him for his cost,
> With thanks to Mr. *Templeman* mine Host.[61]

Much space within his travel narratives, in fact, is devoted to providing details of the material hospitality he has received, including information about the location of inns, the monetary value of meals and accommodation, and the identities of his hosts.[62] Moreover, Taylor accepts that the material nature of these responses will be determined by an individual's social status, and he makes allowances accordingly; hence Sir George Hastings and Mr. Templeman – the latter, presumably, an innkeeper – are acknowledged, with a rough degree of equality, for their support. Similarly, the level of sponsorship, and even the cost of his pamphlets, appear to have been determined in part by a sponsor's ability to pay. By contrast, Taylor's scorn is reserved only for those who snub – or, more correctly, *devalue* him – either materially or immaterially. This list includes those who renege on their promises of sponsorship, innkeepers who overcharge him, and the man in Hull who 'Talk'd very scurvily' when Taylor accepted an invitation to sit at church 'in a worthy Towns-mans Pue'.[63]

The discourse of friendship also diverges from existing models of patronage by virtue of its insistence on a dynamic of labour and reward. After his early efforts to found an authorial career upon principles of labour, as considered above, Taylor set out to develop textual and discursive models within which travelling and travel-writing alike are clearly situated as forms of work. Indeed Taylor delights in a creative confusion of his own cognate labours. Comparing himself at one point with chorographers, he reflects on a journey down the Thames that, 'As they before these Rivers bounds did show, / Here I come after with my Pen and row'.[64] And, later in his career,

---

[61] *A Discovery by Sea, from London to Salisbury* (1623), in *Workes*, II.25–6.
[62] Cf. Craik, 'John Taylor's Pot-Poetry', 197.
[63] *A Very Merrie Wherrie-Ferry-Voyage*, in *Workes*, II.13.   [64] *Taylor on Tame-Isis*, sig. A5v.

he concludes a pamphlet with the comment, 'With feet and pen, my walke and worke is done, / And (*Cæsar* like) the Conquest I have won'.[65] In this respect, the enterprise of travel also afforded Taylor a convenient pun, which he was characteristically delighted to exploit. For, while 'travel' had traditionally referred to journeys beyond the nation's boundaries, 'travail' had always been a condition of life for those of middling and low degree. The spelling of these two words is commonly confused in early modern usage; Taylor, however, wilfully erodes the distinctions, knitting together the concepts of travel and labour. For instance, the title-page of *The Pennyles Pilgrimage* proclaims an account of how Taylor 'travailed on foot, from *London* to *Edenborough*', and in the course of the account he reflects on 'neere being dead with extreme travell'.[66] In another text, 'travel/travail' becomes a fundamental principle of existence:

> At Travellers, let no man carpe or cavill,
> Our Mothers (at our births) were all in travell.
> And from our birth unto our buriall,
> In divers Functions we do travell All.
> The Footmans feet, the Statesmans working braine,
> In travell, labour, and continuall paine
> Do spend themselves, and all their courses bend
> For private ends (to no end) till they end.[67]

By conflating the 'travell' of 'The Footmans feet' and 'the Statesmans working braine', Taylor claims an essential dignity for the business of travel. For Taylor himself, as for the footman, travel is a purposeful and socially valuable activity, distinct at once from the pleasure-seeking tours of an aristocrat and the mere 'wandring' of a beggar. Unlike the beggar, Taylor does not try to escape the 'curse' that 'was laid on all the race of man, / That of his labours he should live and eate, / And get his bread by travell and by sweate'.[68]

Although he never claims to speak for anybody other than himself, this position also aligns Taylor with the countless people for whom travel within England demonstrably *was* travail. By comparison with the work of the nation's myriad petty traders and itinerant labourers, his own journeys were at once utterly different and uncannily similar. Whereas carriers attracted business by virtue of their regularity and reliability, Taylor traded on his

---

[65] *A Late Weary, Merry Voyage*, p. 24.
[66] *Workes*, I.122, I.128. In each case, the spelling exactly duplicates the original text (*The Pennyles Pilgrimage* (1618), t.p., sig. D1r–v).
[67] *A Late Weary, Merry Voyage*, p. 9.
[68] *The Praise, Antiquity, and Commoditie of Beggerie, Beggers, and Begging*, in *Workes*, I.99, I.102.

idiosyncrasy and unpredictability. His journeys, and his observations on them, were unique. Yet, like that of a pedlar or a chapman, Taylor's travel was a form of business; it was a method he devised in order to sell his labour, either to sponsors in London, supporters along his routes, or purchasers of his pamphlets. The essential difference between him and a pedlar is that whereas the latter carried goods, Taylor's only commodity was his self: a product he peddled assiduously, at once generating demand and managing circulation, through the vehicle of print. It is on this basis, as a mobile commoner, perceiving the nation as a site of labour and mobility, that he attends to the business of representing the land through which he passes.

TAYLOR'S NATION: THE SPACES OF CIRCULATION

It is entirely possible to represent England as a land of novelties and wonders. Seventeenth-century antiquarians and natural historians, for example, were alike committed to a project of discovery, revealing new facts about the landscape and history of their nation.[69] But Taylor was by comparison uninterested in novelty. Instead, he concerned himself with essentially familiar spaces and experiences, developing new ways of envisaging the inland as a space of labour and opportunity. While his construction of this vision was neither straightforward nor methodical, he presents nonetheless some of his era's most perceptive analyses of economic process, and most prescient arguments for economic improvement. Through his definitive attention to the commoner laboriously traversing the land, I want to argue, Taylor radically revises prevailing conceptions of the functions of human and mercantile mobility within England.

On several occasions through the course of his career, Taylor weighed his own project against that of chorographers, who set out to describe either the country as a whole, or its constituent counties, in maps and words. He made clear that he had read William Harrison, William Camden, John Speed, as well as Michael Drayton's *Poly-Olbion*, and he often acknowledges information borrowed from this reading.[70] On his final journey, for instance, he observes merely that '*Lewes* is an ancient Town, as may be seen / In

---

[69] See esp. Graham Parry, *The Trophies of Time: English Antiquarians of the Seventeenth Century* (Oxford, 1995); Stan A. E. Mendyk, *'Speculum Britanniae': Regional Study, Antiquarianism, and Science in Britain to 1700* (Toronto, 1989).

[70] For his list of reading in what he categorizes as 'Histories', see *Taylors Motto* (1621), in *Workes*, II.57. On Drayton, see *Taylor on Tame-Isis*, sig. A5r.

Cambden, page three hundred and thirteen'.[71] Considering his own pamphlets, he is, overtly at least, somewhat defensive. At the beginning of *John Taylors Wandering, to see the Wonders of the West*, for instance, he writes:

> My Reader must not her[e] expect that I
> Will write a treatise of Geography:
> Or that I meane to make exact Relations
> Of Cities, Townes, or Countries scituations;
> Such men as those, I turne them o're to reade
> The learned *Cambden*, or the painefull *Speed*.[72]

Taylor astutely acknowledges here that, whereas chorographers present panoptic surveys of the land and its history – attempting, as he writes, 'exact Relations / Of Cities, Townes, or Countries scituations' – his own work operates according to different principles. His perception of the nation, that of the landless traveller, is infinitely more sketchy, casual and occasional. It is not, however, entirely without method.

Taylor's texts are itineraries. One after another, they begin with specificities of time and place, often worked into the opening lines of poems. His description of his journey to Salisbury, for example, begins:

> As our accounts in Almanacks agree,
> The yeere cal'd sixteen hundred twenty three:
> That Julyes twenty eight, two houres past dinner,
> We with our *Wherry*, and five men within her,
> Along the christall Thames did cut and curry,
> Betwixt the Counties, Middlesex and Surry.[73]

Throughout, the texts are replete with place-names, distances and dates. For example, he calculates that in his 1649 wanderings in the West Country he traversed 546 miles in six weeks, out of which he rested eighteen days.[74] On other occasions, such as his trip to visit the imprisoned Charles I on the Isle of Wight in 1648, he simply lists his stages:

I came from the Island on Tuesday the 7. of *November*, and landed at a place called Hell Head, from thence I came 3 miles to *Titchfield*, on Wednesday I came 4 miles to *Wickham*, Thursday to *Warnford*, (7 miles) Fryday I footed it 17. miles to *Alton*, and to *Farnham*, Saturday to *Guilford*, and to *Cobham* 18. miles, and Sunday 6 miles to *Kingston*, and on Munday the 13. of November, I came to *London* 10. Miles'.[75]

[71] *The Certain Travailes of an Uncertain Journey* (1654), p. 14. The reference is correct; Taylor is using Philemon Holland's 1610 English translation of the *Britannia*.
[72] *John Taylors Wandering*, p. 2.   [73] *Discovery by Sea*, in *Workes*, II.21.
[74] *John Taylors Wandering*, p. 21.
[75] *Tailors Travels from London, to the Isle of Wight* (1648), p. 13.

Unlike the chorographers, he is relatively unconcerned here with what makes Guildford, for instance, different from Cobham. His attention is refocused; indeed, while maps and chorographies, as Anne Wallace observes, seek to make 'the process of travel literally unreadable', Taylor determinedly reverses this process, prioritizing the spatial experience and knowledge of the traveller.[76]

This model invokes, yet distinctly modifies, existing printed itineraries of English travel. As discussed in Chapter 2, itineraries of journeys along the nation's major roads became increasingly common from the late sixteenth century.[77] These documents are typically in tabulated form, devoid of any detail beyond a list of places and the distances between them. They concentrate on journeys along what we would call arterial roads, which generally meant those that were in the process of being distinguished as post-roads, and are concerned simply to break certain common journeys down into manageable and relatively regular stages, suggesting to the reader a series of prominent places linked by an unravelling ribbon of miles. Taylor's determinedly personalized itineraries, by contrast, prioritize the process and vicissitudes of travel. His texts usually provide fulsome details of his forms of transportation, methods of route-finding, and places of accommodation. To take one example, on 28 June 1649 he hired 'an old drunkard' to guide him eight miles from the Wiltshire village of Purton to Malmesbury, and from there he 'hired a Horse for 2s. seven miles, and footed it seven miles more that day to the famous, renowned, ancient, little pritty City of *Bathe*'.[78] The subject of so many tourist descriptions in the early modern period, Bath is here subordinated to the individual traveller's experience. It is a 'little pritty Citty', lending shape to an eventful journey. Within this model of travel, moreover, pace becomes more important than place. In the West Country, he surely wants his reader to calculate that traversing 546 miles in twenty-four days equates to 22.75 miles per active day (albeit not all of it on foot), at the age of seventy. In his journey along the nation's principal southern and western river systems in 1641, he identifies pace still more clearly as an index of authorial achievement, stating that 'in lesse then twenty dayes labour 1200. miles were past to and fro in most hard, difficult and many dangerous passages'.[79]

Furthermore, while destinations provide a framework to most of his journeys and a foundation for many of his bets, his pamphlets consistently

[76] *Walking, Literature and English Culture: The Origins and Uses of Peripatetic in the Nineteenth Century* (Oxford, 1993), p. 39.
[77] See above, pp. 76–7.   [78] *John Taylors Wandering*, p. 3.
[79] *John Taylors Last Voyage*, sig. B3v.

posit a self-consciously wayward model of both travel and writing. On Saturday 7 September 1650, for example, he was 'determined' to see Stourbridge Fair, the greatest of all the nation's fairs, on the outskirts of Cambridge: 'but by fortune I espyed an empty Cart returning towards London 17 miles to a Towne call'd *Baldock*; by which meanes I left *Cambridge* without taking my leave of Mr. *Brian*, for which I crave his and his Wives pardon'.[80] This is an instance at once curious and characteristic; the professional traveller misses his purported goal, then unashamedly admits his failure to the reader. As Taylor acknowledges, the demand of the traveller, for cheap mobility in his general direction, supersedes the text's pretensions to a mode of conventional geographical description. While Stourbridge Fair will continue to function without him, for this traveller and this text the site remains effectively meaningless, displaced from his itinerary by the chance arrival of an empty cart. Within this form of travel-writing, the digression and the anecdote become fundamental structural devices. Coryate was an important model in this respect, since he had helped to give shape to 'a tradition of demotic and burlesque pedestrian travel'.[81] In *The Pennyles Pilgrimage*, Taylor concedes that he has included 'a few additions of my owne devizing, / (Because I have a smacke of *Coriatizing*)'.[82] This is in part a dig at his rival; Taylor suggests that while Coryate passed off his 'additions' as serious and factual, he will himself lay bare the arts of the travel writer, drawing his reader along with him. Yet, as Michelle O'Callaghan argues, '"Coriatizing" is more than telling tall tales; it signifies an errant, improvisatory narrative mode and the novel conceptual freedoms available to the independent traveller.'[83]

This approach typically has a levelling effect on narrative episodes, draining even accounts of genuine dangers of any special significance. For instance, Taylor's description of the storms that threatened his wherry at sea off the south coast in 1623 are set alongside anecdotes of altogether less troubling events, which appear more fully to engage his attention. Thus, having survived the storms, he lands safely at Goring-on-Sea in Sussex, only to attract the attentions of 'an Host of Fleas' in his bed and an officious constable:

> Who ask'd my Trade, my dwelling, and my name:
> My businesse, and a troope of questions more,

[80] *A Late Weary, Merry Voyage*, pp. 23–4.
[81] O'Callaghan, *English Wits*, pp. 142–3. Cf. Anthony Parr, 'Thomas Coryat and the Discovery of Europe', *Huntington Library Quarterly*, 55 (1992), 591.
[82] *Workes*, I.133.   [83] O'Callaghan, *English Wits*, p. 143.

And wherefore we did land upon that shore?
To whom I fram'd my answers true, and fit,
(According to his plenteous want of wit)
But were my words all true, or if I li'd,
With neither I could get him satisfi'd.
He ask'd if we were Pyrats? We said no,
(*As if we had, we would have told him so.*)
He said that Lords sometimes would enterprise
T'escape, and leave the Kingdome, in disguise:
But I assur'd him on my honest word,
That I was no disguised Knight or Lord.[84]

Comic accounts of discomforts or temporary blockages, such as this one, become one of Taylor's textual signatures. They typify his commitment to demonstrating that England is essentially open to the traveller, for all the minor challenges that may confront him along the way. In a similar instance the previous year at Cromer, he had seized an opportunity for self-promotion, producing copies of his books in order to prove his identity to justices of the peace.[85] Here, more typically, the threat to the journey simply evaporates. When the constable commands a walk of six miles to meet the nearest 'Sir *John*, or else Sir *Giles*', Taylor replies that he is 'loth to goe so farre'. When the constable hides the wherry's oars in an attempt to detain the party, a ploughman helpfully locates them in a nearby field. Eventually, inevitably, the journey continues: 'madly, gladly', Taylor declares, 'out to Sea we thrust'.[86]

Such narrative is informed by traditions of mock-heroic and burlesque, but adapts these resources to a distinctive purpose. Elsewhere, Taylor accuses foreign travellers, including Coryate, of relying on discourses of heroism and wonder:

Of men with long tailes, faced like to hounds,
Of oysters, one whose fish weigh'd forty pounds,
Of spiders greater then a walnut shell
Of the *Rhinoceros* thou wouldst us tell.[87]

Within this context, Taylor's own mobilization of the mock-heroic indicates at once a rejection of discourses of the outlandish, and an associated commitment to fashion in response a discourse of the inland, or the domestic. This discourse prioritizes demonstrable products of human endeavour over artefacts of history or peculiar manifestations of nature.

---

[84] *Discovery by Sea*, in *Workes*, II.24–5.   [85] *A Very Merrie Wherrie-Ferry-Voyage*, in *Workes*, II.9.
[86] *Discovery by Sea*, in *Workes*, II.25.   [87] *Praise of Hemp-seed*, in *Workes*, III.68.

Its heroism, therefore, is that of common people producing economically valuable items. Encountering an unusual coal-mine in Scotland, for instance, he observes:

which (if man can or could worke wonders) is a wonder: for my selfe neither in any travels that I have beene in, nor any History that I have read, or any Discourse that I have heard, did never see, read, or heare of any worke of man that might parallell or bee equivalent with this unfellowed and unmatchable work.[88]

Though notably cautious in his invocation of a discourse of wonder, Taylor nonetheless stretches its parameters in order to incorporate remarkable instances of human intervention in a natural landscape. Such descriptions punctuate his works, often providing considerable detail of local industries. His outline of pilchard fishing out of Mevagissey, in south Cornwall, to take one example, includes calculations of the number of men employed, the quantity of salt required, and other details which help to establish an image of a local economy in action.[89] Elsewhere he contributes to one of the central economic debates of his age, considering schemes to provide work for the poor.[90] His governing principle, which covers both his own labours and those he observes, is that 'painfull industry' and 'worthy endeavours' will be rewarded with 'Gods blessings'.[91]

Crucially, Taylor perceives such economic activity, like his own idiosyncratic project, to be dependent on mobility. As discussed in Chapter 1, his most important work in this regard relates to the improvement of rivers; he reflects, at one moment, that he bears 'a naturall affection to Portable Rivers, and a setled inclination and desire of the preservation and use of them'.[92] And, as noted in Chapter 2, his publication in 1637 of *The Carriers Cosmographie* provided the first printed guide to private carriers operating on regular routes from London into the provinces. What these various projects and publications share with his travel pamphlets is a fundamental vision of connectedness. Taylor perceives all places, both within England and beyond, as potentially connectable with all other places. Some, he acknowledges, are better placed than others. London, the point at which all his journeys begin and end, was assuming an increasingly pivotal position in trade networks, and Taylor is keenly aware of this development. But regional centres are also assessed with an educated eye. Gloucester, for instance, 'is scituated in as convenient a place as any other within this

---

[88] *Pennyles Pilgrimage*, in *Workes*, I.132.   [89] *John Taylors Wandering*, pp. 17–18.
[90] See, for example, *A Very Merrie Wherrie-Ferry-Voyage*, in *Workes*, II.13; and *Discovery by Sea*, in *Workes*, II.26–7.
[91] *Pennyles Pilgrimage*, in *Workes*, I.133.   [92] *John Taylors Last Voyage*, sig. A5v.

Kingdome', while King's Lynn benefits from its position at the head of a system of inland waterways.[93] By contrast, the inhabitants of Salisbury have failed to maintain their town's natural advantages, allowing the channel of the Avon to become unpassable. Within this context, one function of Taylor's own travelling is to demonstrate the relation between the specific journeys of individuals and a wider appreciation of national space as itself shaped by human mobility.

By extension, his texts serve as arguments in favour of the free circulation of people and goods. Early in his career, especially in a text such as *The Pennyles Pilgrimage*, he represents his own mobility as being facilitated by traditional codes of hospitality. In later works, however, as his reliance on 'friends' becomes more openly commercialized, freedom of movement emerges as a social and economic imperative. Hence he describes, in 1649, demanding lodging in an alehouse, in accordance with contemporary laws governing inns and alehouses.[94] On the same journey, at a time of obvious political tension, he found that the 'very strict examination of persons' at military garrisons was threatening 'a Travellers liberty'.[95] Indeed that notion of liberty – the idea that national space was essentially open to the traveller, regardless of whether he was a celebrity voyager or a more common trader – is never more powerfully expressed in the seventeenth century than it is in Taylor's works. In Michel de Certeau's analysis of uses of space in the modern city, the manifold itineraries of individuals, exercising practices of 'everyday creativity', are seen to construct a spatiality of encounter and immediacy, at odds with orthodox models of order.[96] Taylor was perhaps the first Englishman to translate a comparable appreciation of his nation's space into print, effectively claiming for the commoner an integrity that had previously been unimaginable. While, as I suggested in Chapter 2, texts such as almanacs suggested that the movement of pedlars and other petty traders might be regular and orderly, Taylor takes a crucial step further by figuring commoners as independent and constructive in their engagements with national space. Indeed the act of wandering, traditionally stigmatized in social and legal discourse, is refashioned by Taylor as at once creative and dynamic. For Taylor, England is constitutionally, and must remain, open to the common carriers, the industrious workers, and even to the immigrants who bring new skills and expertise into the country.[97]

---

[93] *Ibid.*, sig. B6r; *A Late Weary, Merry Voyage*, pp. 22–3.   [94] Cf. above, p. 127.
[95] *John Taylors Wandering*, pp. 17, 15.
[96] *The Practice of Everyday Life*, trans. Steven Russell (Berkeley, 1984), pp. xiv, 91–110.
[97] On immigration, see his discussion of the Dutch community in Norwich, in *A Late Weary, Merry Voyage*, pp. 17–18.

Taylor's achievement was not without contradictions and equivocations. Others have commented on the tensions in his work between a profound attachment to values of socio-political hierarchy and a passionate admiration for individual endeavour. 'In his individualist project,' Laurie Ellinghausen argues, 'Taylor unwittingly participated in the revolutionary pressures that he feared.'[98] Given his status, as a 'mechanicke Waterman' seeking to fashion a public identity, these contradictions were inevitable, and perhaps even necessary. He was not an economic theorist; he was a practitioner, whose experiences of the nation, for all their essential idiosyncrasy, correlated with those of the countless others involved in the business of domestic travel. His insights into the functions of mobility and the need to promote traffic were both original and important, yet so were the singular ways in which he worked and wrote. In his insistence on the value of labour, and his commitment to the land as space open to the forces of industry, he emerges as his century's preeminent poet of traffic.

In the decades after Taylor's death, traffic finally began to receive some attention from economic theorists. Thomas Hobbes, for instance, invokes the model of circulation in a discussion of the sovereign's right 'to appoint in what manner, all kinds of contract between Subjects, (as buying, selling, exchanging, borrowing, lending, letting, and taking to hire,) are to bee made'. His marginal note underscores his appreciation of the importance of circulation: '*Mony the Bloud of a Common-wealth*'.[99] Others sought to loosen the sphere of economics from that of government. Sir Dudley North, who would be treated by subsequent generations as perhaps the most important economic theorist of the seventeenth century, argued for the values of what he termed 'the free Market of things'.[100] Moreover, unlike any previous theorist, he 'made no distinction between domestic and international trade', and as a result he was able to incorporate the former, for the first time, into the realm of theoretical debate.[101] 'A Nation in the World, as to Trade,' he argued, 'is in all respects like a City in a Kingdom, or a Family in a City.' Within this model, trade is perceived not merely as a mechanism for the circulation of a fixed sum of wealth, but as an agent of economic expansion and individual advancement. A family, just

[98] 'The Individualist Project of John Taylor', 164; cf. Capp's analysis of Taylor's 'lasting unease about his social and cultural identity' (*World of John Taylor*, p. 54).

[99] *Leviathan*, ed. Richard Tuck (Cambridge, 1991), p. 174.

[100] *Discourses Upon Trade* (1691), sig. A5r.

[101] Richard Grassby, 'North, Sir Dudley', *ODNB*. See further Grassby, *The English Gentleman in Trade: The Life and Works of Sir Dudley North, 1641–1691* (Oxford, 1994).

like a country, 'never thrives better, then when Riches are tost from hand to hand'.[102]

Like Taylor, North was a practitioner; from a relatively modest beginning, in material terms, he became one of the most successful merchants of his age. As such, his work might be placed not only in a canon of economic theory, but equally in a trajectory that may be traced back to the beginning of the century, when Taylor himself began his career by trying to make sense of the various economic processes with which he was engaged. This trajectory includes much of the material considered in earlier chapters: discourse on the improvement of rivers and roads, for example, or guides for those who were involved in the practical business of internal trade. And it leads, ultimately, to Defoe. Defoe's *Tour thro' the Whole Island of Great Britain*, to which I turn in the Epilogue, is in many respects a product of a different age, removed from the quirky innovations and experimentations of a writer such as Taylor. In other respects, however, the *Tour* adapts and clarifies key strands of analysis evident throughout the early modern period, and traced through the course of the present book.

---

[102] *Discourses Upon Trade*, pp. 14, 15.

Epilogue: Defoe's Tour

By the end of the seventeenth century, the tour had emerged as an acceptable, even a conventional, form for spatial representation. As considered in Chapter 5, Celia Fiennes was one of a number of domestic tourists keen to record her experiences, while other writers appear to have adopted the tour as a model despite not having actually travelled themselves. This pattern continued into the early decades of the eighteenth century. The publication of John Leland's *Itinerary* in 1710–12 undoubtedly fuelled interest in tours, while John Macky's *Journey through England* (1714–23) was the most ambitious exercise yet in shaping domestic travel-writing for the press. More specialized works included William Stukeley's *Itinerarium Curiosum, or, An Account of the Antiquitys and Remarkable Curiositys in Nature or Art, Observ'd in Travels thro' Great Brittan* (1724). Associated developments in fiction, meanwhile, were critical to the emergence of the novel. Late seventeenth-century works such as Richard Head's fictional criminal autobiography, *The English Rogue* (1665), and John Dunton's *A Voyage Round the World* (1691), provided a foundation for the subsequent achievements of authors such as Daniel Defoe, Tobias Smollett and Laurence Sterne.[1]

Detailed attention to such developments would stretch the bounds of this book. On one hand, the rough temporal end-point of 1700 is somewhat arbitrary: one date of several which tends to be taken to designate the end of the early modern period. On the other hand, however, there are good reasons at least to pause at this point. Not only did the English acquire a new monarch, Anne, in 1702, they officially assumed a new national identity, as Britons, in 1707. Less tangibly, but no less importantly for the present project, I believe that the prevalence of the tour as a structuring device in texts around the turn of the eighteenth century is a sign of a transformation in the literature and culture of domestic travel. It signals an

---

[1] On Dunton as a travel-writer, see Melanie Ord, *Travel and Experience in Early Modern English Literature* (Basingstoke, 2008), pp. 155–85.

end to the long era in which domestic mobility was overwhelmingly perceived as problematic, threatening orthodox values of place and settlement. This book has been concerned with this context, and with struggles across the period to imagine new relations between English subjects and the spaces of their nation. While these struggles were by no means over by 1700, and while tensions between settlement and mobility, place and space, inform representations of the land through to the present day, it is fair to say that something had changed. There was a distinct shift in the intangible codes governing what could be said, and how it could be said. That, at least, has been the underlying narrative of the book.

Within this context, the main purpose of these final pages is not to move the argument forward temporally, but rather to focus on one crucial text from the early eighteenth century as a way of reflecting on the processes of contestation and change I have traced throughout the preceding centuries. The text at hand was written by a man whose career straddled the seventeenth and eighteenth centuries, and whose arguments of 1697 about the improvement of the nation's roads have already been considered.[2] Defoe continued his work as a proponent of economic reform into the following century, particularly in his role as editor, and virtually sole author, of *The Review* (1704–13). His *Tour thro' the Whole Island of Great Britain* was a late work, published in three volumes between 1724 and 1726, and assumes a central position within a vital period of Defoe's career, which produced a series of important works of fiction and non-fiction. Other critics of the *Tour* have attended to its innovative conception of nationhood: based on Britain's geography and realized in its web of trade networks.[3] Some, also, have considered his struggle to incorporate Scotland into his perception of the nation.[4] Here, I want to consider particularly the extent to which, in the *Tour*, nationhood is at once founded upon and enacted through instances of individual mobility. In a powerful engagement with centuries of debate over popular mobility, I suggest, the author's journey is aligned with, and

[2] See above, pp. 89–90.
[3] Terence N. Bowers, 'Great Britain Imagined: Nation, Citizen, and Class in Defoe's *A Tour Thro' the Whole Island of Great Britain*', *Prose Studies*, 16 (1993), 148–78; Christopher Parkes, '"A True Survey of the Ground": Defoe's *Tour* and the Rise of Thematic Cartography', *Philological Quarterly*, 74 (1994), 395–414. See also Betty A. Schellenberg, 'Imagining the Nation in Defoe's *A Tour Thro' the Whole Island of Great Britain*', *ELH*, 62 (1995), 295–311.
[4] See esp. Alistair M. Duckworth, '"Whig" Landscapes in Defoe's *Tour*', *Philological Quarterly*, 61 (1982), 458–9; Parkes, '"A True Survey of the Ground"', 402–3; Pat Rogers, 'The Making of Defoe's *A Tour Thro' Great Britain*', *Prose Studies*, 3 (1980), 129–32; Schellenberg, 'Imagining the Nation', 305–6. More generally, on Defoe's relation to Scotland, see John Kerrigan, *Archipelagic English: Literature, History, and Politics 1603–1707* (Oxford, 2008), pp. 326–49.

becomes emblematic of, wider patterns in the mobility of people, commodities and information.

Defoe is forthright about the way in which he transforms the experience and knowledge of Britain derived from numerous journeys, conducted over many years, into the textual form of thirteen 'circuits'.[5] Although the circuits are described in the form of letters, one of their most striking characteristics, especially in comparison with travel-writing of the preceding centuries, is their suppression of the vicissitudes of individual experience. For instance, encounters with guides and experiences in inns, which had been staples of seventeenth-century narratives of travel, are rarely mentioned. This is in part attributable to Defoe's effort to downplay the difficulty of travel, so as to 'create an image of Britain as a country without internal barriers'; however, it also indicates the degree of artifice upon which the text is based.[6] As he writes at the beginning of 'Letter 10', introducing his description of the north-east of England:

as I do not write you these Letters from the Observations of one single Journey, so I describe Things as my Journies lead me, having no less than five times travelled through the North of *England*, and almost every time by a different Rout; purposely that I might see every thing that was to be seen, and, if possible, know every thing that is to be known. (II.664)

He emphasizes here, as throughout, spatial coverage: almost, though never entirely, to the point of omniscience. The structure of the circuits, therefore, represents his effort to translate this wealth of information onto the page, creating a method of spatial description in which 'every route is related to the others', and every place is positioned within wider spatial grids.[7]

This approach informs Defoe's interests, and consequent selection of information, as he travels through the country. Like Fiennes, and other travellers of the seventeenth century, he admits the promptings of 'curiosity'.[8] In Suffolk, for instance, he travels to a site of Marian martyrdom, 'principally to satisfy my Curiosity', while in Staffordshire he notes that the park and gardens at Ingestre 'are very well worth a Traveller's Curiosity' (I.48; II.478). More commonly, however, he positions such established places of interest for the tourist as mere diversions. Stories that attract travellers to sites of supposed Arthurian interest, for example, are dismissed as 'no better than a FIBB', while Guy of Warwick he leaves disdainfully 'to the curious Searchers into

---

[5] *A Tour Thro' the Whole Island of Great Britain*, ed. G. D. H. Cole, 2 vols. (London, 1927), esp. I.5.
[6] Bowers, 'Great Britain Imagined', 158.   [7] Parkes, '"A True Survey of the Ground"', 400.
[8] See above, pp. 179–80, 204.

Antiquity' (I.185; II.483). He even manages to brush past Canterbury Cathedral, acknowledging it merely as 'a Noble Pile of building' (I.117). Instead, as he repeatedly reminds his reader, his central concern throughout the *Tour* is with 'the present State of Things' (I.69). This attention to social and economic practice prompts him in turn to revise the touristic discourse of 'wonder', evident in travel-writing of the preceding century. Hence he relentlessly demolishes the 'wonders of the Peak [District]', which he figures as something of a literary hoax perpetrated to attract travellers to a mere 'houling Wilderness' (II.567). By contrast, he asserts that '*Liverpoole* is one of the Wonders of *Britain*, and that more, in my Opinion, than any of the Wonders of the *Peak*' (II.664). Commenting on Liverpool's rapid growth, Defoe comments: 'that it still visibly encreases both in Wealth, People, Business and Buildings: What it may grow to in time, I know not' (II.665).

In this instance, as throughout the *Tour*, wonder is predicated not on timelessness but on change. Indeed Defoe is fascinated by the way in which the dynamic nature of Britain undermines his entire project: 'for the Face of Things so often alters, and the Situation of Affairs in this *Great British* Empire gives such new Turns, even to Nature it self, that there is Matter of new Observation every Day presented to the Traveller's Eye' (I.2). The very act of description, therefore, risks redundancy at every stroke. Yet this quality of his nation paradoxically drives the work onward, providing an ideological framework for a new form of geographical description. Above all, as Pat Rogers observes, Defoe 'has a marvellously acute sense of *process*', which centres attention on instances of 'increase'.[9] And the greatest determinant of increase – as, for that matter, of its antithesis – is trade. In Lancashire, for example, he comments:

The *Manchester* Trade we all know; and all that are concerned in it know that it is, as all our other Manufactures are, very much encreased within these thirty or forty Years … and as the Manufacture is encreased, the People must be encreased of course. (II.670)

By contrast, Southampton is described as 'a truly Antient Town, for 'tis in a manner dying with Age; the decay of the Trade is the real decay of the Town' (I.141). His attention is also drawn to specialized fairs, as the nation's most visible realizations of internal trade. In Staffordshire, for example, he was 'surpriz'd in a most agreeable manner' to discover 'a prodigious Number of Horses' brought to a fair at Penkridge (II.477). At Weyhill,

---

[9] 'Literary Art in Defoe's *Tour*: The Rhetoric of Growth and Decay', *Eighteenth-Century Studies*, 6 (1972–3), 175–7. Rogers notes that the word 'increase', as noun or verb, 'appears at least 140 times in the text, an extraordinarily high figure compared with its frequency in ordinary discourse' (177).

Wiltshire, he saw a similarly 'prodigious' quantity of sheep, at what he believed to be 'the greatest Fair for Sheep ... that this Nation can shew' (I.290).

These developing trade networks, in Defoe's view, were reorienting relations between localities and the nation. The *Tour* has little time for traditional spatial models of regional self-sufficiency; rather, its consistent attention to local agricultural and industrial specializations implies a nation within which particular places are all bound into, and in part given meaning by, economic relationships with other places. Indeed a proper study of local conditions, Defoe had learned from the new philosophy of the previous century, might well lead to a better exploitation of natural resources.[10] And at the centre of this model was London. One recurrent argument in the *Tour*, in fact, is that the people of 'every Part' of Britain 'are employ'd to furnish something ... to supply the City of *London* with Provisions' (I.12). The entire population, he claims, is thus bound with London in a relationship of 'general Dependance' (I.3). In the course of the text he acknowledges that the growth of London has had negative effects on towns that once enjoyed greater regional prominence, such as Southampton or Ipswich. London, he writes, is a 'great and monstrous thing', that 'sucks the Vitals of Trade in this Island to itself' (I.325; I.43). But in general the text simply assumes that connectedness with London is essential to any place in Britain. Indeed he concerns himself extensively with the mechanics of connection, particularly by devoting a lengthy appendix to the second volume to the improvement of roads. Thanks to the introduction of turnpike roads, he expresses a hope 'that the Roads in most Parts of *England* will in a few Years be fully repair'd, and restor'd to the same good Condition, (or perhaps a better, than) they were in during the *Roman* Government' (II.530). Given the awe which the Roman roads had inspired in previous observers, the parenthetic comment underscores Defoe's extraordinary optimism.[11]

In other works Defoe theorized his nation's systems of trade, seizing in particular on the figure of circulation. In 1709, for instance, he declared that:

The Circulation of Trade in *England* is the Life and Being of all our Home Trade – By this means one Man employs a Thousand – And all the Thousand employs him – And the Wealth that rolls from hand to hand, insensibly growing as it goes, is inexpressible.[12]

---

[10] See Ilse Vickers, *Defoe and the New Sciences* (Cambridge, 1996), pp. 151–76.
[11] On the Roman roads, see above, pp. 71–4.
[12] *Review*, 9 July 1709; quoted in David Trotter, *Circulation: Defoe, Dickens, and the Economies of the Novel* (Basingstoke, 1988), p. 4.

As has become apparent in previous chapters, circulation emerges across the early modern period as perhaps the most important metaphor for the activities of internal trade. For Defoe, as David Trotter has argued, it provided 'the condition' of his 'understanding of the "economic", that which enabled him to grasp the sequences of manufacture and exchange as a system'.[13] It was also a metaphor that he could adapt and refine. Hence, in *A Brief State of the Inland or Home Trade*, published several years after the *Tour*, Defoe theorized the significance of the capital, arguing that 'here the main Stream will run as to the Center, as the Rivers to the Ocean, and as the Blood to the Heart'.[14] This instance posits the nation as a 'coherent and dynamic system', with London as its central, driving force.[15] Networks of rivers and roads – and also coastal trade routes, which he consistently notes in the *Tour* – are therefore positioned as 'Veins and Arteries' which transmit the lifeblood of the nation. In practical terms, blood is equated immediately with commodities; however, in the wider economy of the *Tour* it is also aligned with other kinds of mobility, including that of people and news.[16] Ultimately it comes to represent the mysterious mobility of money: rolling 'from hand to hand, insensibly growing as it goes'.

Within the *Tour*, however, the central index of this underlying economic theory is not money, nor any particular product, but the author himself. Defoe shapes his journeys as physical realizations of an economy of circulation. Hence the presentation of the text as epistolary, as though he is transmitting information from across the nation to its centre. Hence the consistent representation of travel as an unproblematic sweep across the face of the land. And hence also the arrangement of the circuits, most of which position London as the central point. Consequently, when he states that he writes 'in the Person of an *Itinerant*', he implicitly confronts centuries of antagonism towards commoners moving through the nation (I.325). His movement is never considered as pointless; he has, he declares, 'Travell'd *critically*', and this produces 'an Account of Things fit for the Use of those that shall come after' (I.3; I.251; my italics). These strategies, as Rogers argues, suggest 'a sense of space as something mastered, easily comprehensible, already named and measured'.[17] In turn, they invite comparison with the movements of the multitude of commoners who travelled the roads and

---

[13] *Circulation*, p. 3.

[14] (1730), p. 17; quoted in Geoffrey M. Sill, 'Defoe's *Tour*: Literary Art or Moral Imperative?', *Eighteenth-Century Studies*, 11 (1977), 81.

[15] Bowers, 'Great Britain Imagined', 169.   [16] Trotter, *Circulation*, p. 6.

[17] 'Speaking Within Compass: The Ground Covered in Two Works by Defoe', *Studies in the Literary Imagination*, 15 (1982), 109.

rivers of Britain daily, in the course of their various forms of business. Like that of Defoe himself, their independent movements are assumed to be at once purposeful and dynamic.

As this brief analysis of Defoe's *Tour* demonstrates, to write about subjects moving through a land is to write about the social and spatial constitution of that land. As we have seen throughout this book, it is entirely possible to write about travel in a manner that reinforces, rather than challenges, discourses of property and placement. Significantly, this is how the nearest rival to the *Tour*, Macky's *Journey through England*, works. This text, as others have also suggested, serves as 'a mere listing of discrete places', centring attention on properties and their owners.[18] Defoe, by contrast, configures nationhood on the basis not of placement but of connectedness. Just as a study of the Roman roads might offer 'so lively a Representation of the antient *British*, *Roman* and *Saxon* Governments', so Defoe seeks to represent his own nation by exploring its systems of spatial connections (II.485). His version of nationhood, as Christopher Parkes argues, is thereby loosened from concerns of history and genealogy, and imagined instead 'as a set of lines on the map'.[19] It realizes, as much as was possible, the seductive vision of John Adams's 1677 line-map, criss-crossed with straight lines linking dozens of the nation's settlements.[20] Within this structure, community and national identity are a matter of 'complex interdependency', among men and women committed to the pursuit of profit.[21] As he writes, approvingly, of a ride through Norfolk: 'we saw no idle Hands here, but every Man busy on the main Affair of Life, that is to say, getting Money' (I.72).

The eighteenth century brought its own inflections to struggles over space, which in many respects were as repressive as anything that had come before. The history of Defoe's own text, after his death, underscores this point, since subsequent editors (most notably, the novelist Samuel Richardson), markedly refocused its gaze onto matters of property and aesthetics.[22] At the other end of the social spectrum, meanwhile, legal and literary treatments of commoners on the road could be as harsh as ever. But Defoe is instructive in the present context because he articulates – and, as a traveller, physically enacts – a vision of human mobility and national space that had previously been evident mainly at the level of shadowy fantasy. This vision may be glimpsed, for instance, in discourse

---

[18] Bowers, 'Great Britain Imagined', 170; see also Rogers, 'Literary Art', 154–5.
[19] '"A True Survey of the Ground"', 403.   [20] See above, pp. 83–5; Fig. 2.4.
[21] Bowers, 'Great Britain Imagined', 170.   [22] Schellenberg, 'Imagining the Nation', 307.

on the improvement of rivers and roads. It is realized, albeit in a less methodical manner, by Fiennes. And, perhaps most notably of all, it gives shape and direction to the extraordinary career of John Taylor, whose various writings on travel and mobility have demanded attention so often throughout this book. While Defoe writes in a manner effectively unconstrained by the debates over mobility that had shaped discourse on internal travel for so long, Taylor and his peers had no such liberty. As I have argued, their works were informed by struggles against powerful orthodoxies, and they sought in various ways, and through various generic forms, to make sense of different experiences of mobility. Their disparate achievements, which collectively made Defoe's career possible, confronted and undermined prejudices against mobility, repositioning the peripatetic subject within the English nation.

Index

Adams, John 83–5
    Angliae totius tabula 109
Agnew, Jean-Christophe 10
Alford 203
antiquarianism 181–2, 183, 196
Appleby, Joyce Oldham 10
Artificers, Statute of 8
Arundel Castle 197
assize judges 147
Awdeley, John 98, 99

Bacon, Francis 182
Barnet 135, 139
Barrell, John 199–200
Baskerville, Thomas 206
Bath 196
Beier, A. L. 93
Benedict, Barbara M. 177
Bergeron, David 158
Berry, William
    The Grand Roads of England 109
Beverley 6
Bevis of Southampton 197
Bispham, Thomas
    Iter Australe 186
Blith Abbey 203
Bosworth 191
Botero, Giovanni
    Cause of the Greatness of Cities 47
Brathwaite, Richard
    Barnabae Itinerarium 212–13
Brereton, Sir William 194, 206
bridges 5
Bristol 221
Brome, James
    *Travels Over England, Scotland
        and Wales* 175
Brome, Richard 131–2
Browne, Anthony, first Viscount Montague 153
Browne, Edward 175, 197–8, 199
Browne, William 33

Bunyan, John 117–20
    Grace Abounding 117
    The Heavenly Foot-man 117
    The Pilgrim's Progress 117–20
Burghley House 204
burlesque 187–90
Burton, William (c.1545–1645)
    Description of Leicester Shire 32
Burton, William (1609–57) 71, 72, 74
Byshop, John 44–6

Callis, Robert 27, 47
Camden, William 178
    Britannia 32, 71, 72, 178–9
    'De Connubio Tamae et Isis' 36–7
canals 51–2
Canterbury Cathedral 178, 195, 238
Carew, Thomas
    'To my friend G. N. from Wrest' 58–9
Carr, Richard
    A Description of all the Postroads in England 109
Carter, Paul 22
cartography 29–32
Casey, Edward S. 193
Cecil, William, Lord Burghley 149, 150
Certeau, Michel de 12, 232
chapmen and chapwomen 74, 94, 101–11
character books 123
Charles I, King 164–71
Charles II, King 171–2
Chartres, John 127, 215
chorography 29–31, 32–3, 178–9, 224, 227
Churchyard, Thomas 154–5, 157–61
    *A Discourse of The Queenes Majesties
        Entertainement in Suffolk and Norffolk* 158
    The Worthines of Wales 159–61, 171
Cirencester 6
The City and Country Chapmans Almanac 110
Clarkson, Laurence
    The Lost Sheep Found 113–14
Cleveland, John 165–6

Coker, John
  Survey of Dorsetshire 32, 33
Colchester 205
Cole, Mary Hill 148
Coleshill 199
Collinson, Patrick 145
Coppe, Abiezer 113
Corbett, Richard
  'Iter Boreale' 186, 189–90, 191
Coryate, Thomas 180, 221, 229, 230
  Coryats Crudities 180, 187–8, 216
Cotton, Charles 65, 187, 188–9
Craik, Katharine 219
curiosity 177, 179–80, 185, 191–2, 204, 237–8

Dart, River 39
Defoe, Daniel 2, 15, 212
  A Brief State of the Inland or Home Trade 240
  Essay Upon Projects 89
  The Review 236
  Tour thro' the Whole Island of Great Britain
    236–41
Dekker, Thomas 92–3, 96–8
  O Per Se O 97–8
  1603. The Wonderfull Yeare 100–1, 139
Delano-Smith, Catherine 76
Denham, Sir John
  Cooper's Hill 60–5
Donne, John 22
Drayton, Michael
  Poly-Olbion 41–3, 72–4
Dudley, Robert, Earl of Leicester 152
Dugdale, William 71
Dunton, John
  A Voyage Round the World 235

Edwards, Philip 119
Eedes, Richard
  Iter Boreale 185
Ellinghausen, Laurie 232
Elsky, Martin 55–6
Ely 203
Emmison, F. G. 118
Erdeswicke, Sampson
  Survey of Staffordshire 32
Evelyn, John 181, 194–5, 199
Everitt, Alan 9
Exeter 209

fairs
  see markets
Family of Love 112
Ferris, Richard 161, 221
Fiennes, Celia 195, 197, 199, 201–9
Five Mile Act 112

Flecknoe, Richard
  The Diarium, or Journall 188, 189
Fletcher, John
  and Philip Massinger, *Beggars Bush* 130, 131
Foucault, Michel 12, 48
Fox, George
  Journal 114–17
Fumerton, Patricia 11, 93

Gascoigne, George 152
Geertz, Clifford 147
georgic 160–1, 218
Glastonbury 194
Gloucester 231
Grand Tour 179–80, 181
Greene, Robert 96, 99–100
  The Black Book's Messenger 100
Greenwich 36
Gregory, Derek 12
guides 188–9
Guy of Warwick 191, 197, 237

Habermas, Jürgen 145, 169, 172–3
Hakluyt, Richard
  Principal Navigations 215
Halasz, Alexandra 223
Hammond, Lieutenant 175, 195–6, 198, 199
Harington, Sir John 104
Harman, Thomas
  A Caveat for Common Cursitors Vulgarly Called
    Vagabonds 95–6, 98
Harrison, William 8, 147
  'Description of Britain' 24–6, 29, 49, 71
  'Description of England' 24, 76, 124–5, 179, 213
Hartlib, Samuel 183
Hattaway, Michael 136
Head, Richard
  The English Rogue 100, 235
Helgerson, Richard 10, 31, 41
Hely, James 47–8, 53
Hentzner, Paul
  Itinerarium 182
Heywood, Thomas
  If You Know Not Me, You Know Nobody 104
highwaymen 100
Hobbes, Thomas 233
Horace 186
Howell, James 47, 180–1

improvement 204–5
industry, description of 204–5, 206, 231
Ingestre 207
inns and alehouses 122–42, 163–4, 189–90, 206
  definitions of 124
  laws concerning 116, 127, 128, 232

Ireland 39–40
Irenodia Cantabrigiensis 165–6
Isis, River 36–7
itineraries 76–7, 192–3, 227–8

James I, King 8, 57
James, Richard
    Iter Lanacastrense 71–2, 191–2, 195
jestbooks 123
Jonson, Ben
    The New Inn 134–42
    'On the Famous Voyage' 220
    'To Penshurst' 56–8
    'To Sir Robert Wroth' 55
journals 175, 192–208
journey poems 185–92, 212–13

Kemp, Will
    Kemps Nine Daies Wonder 161–4
King, Gregory 110
King's Lynn 232
Klein, Bernhard 31, 42

Land's End 115
Landry, Donna 200
Lea, River 33–4, 55
Lefebvre, Henri 11–12, 32, 68, 122
Leinwand 130, 131
Leland, John 1–2
    Cygnea Cantio 35–6
    Itinerary 1, 3–7, 235
Lenton, Francis 127
Leslie, Michael 152–3
Liverpool 238
locks 26, 27, 44–5
London 77, 99, 214, 231, 239, 240

McGee, C. E. 154
Mace, Thomas 87
Macky, John
    Journey through England 235, 241
Maidstone 205
Malvern Hills 199
Manley, Lawrence 99
markets (and fairs) and market towns
    changing conceptions and status of 10, 215
    descriptions and lists of 109–10, 238–9
    traditional status of 213–14
    see also trade, internal
Marprelate, Martin 112
Marvell, Andrew
    Upon Appleton House 59–60
Massinger, Philip
    A New Way to Pay Old Debts 132–4
    see also Fletcher, John

Mather, William 87
Mathew, Francis 51, 53
    Of the Opening of Rivers for Navigation 46
Medway, River 37–8, 56
Mennes, John
    'To a friend upon a journey to Epsom Well' 190
mercantilism 215
Mevagissey 231
Midlands Revolt 103
migration, internal 9
Misson, Francis
    Mémoires et observations faites par un voyageur
      en Angleterre 182
Mompesson, Sir Giles 133
monasteries 124
Montrose, Louis Adrian 152
Moryson, Fynes 182

Nashe, Thomas 99
Nedham, Marchamont
    Mercurius Britanicus 169–70
Newcastle-under-Lyme 205
new philosophy 182–5
New River Scheme 53, 54
news 168–71
Norden, John 179
    England: An Intended Guyde for English
      Travailers 82–3
North, Sir Dudley 233–4
Norwich 205–6, 221
Nottingham 194–5

O'Callaghan, Michelle 229
Ogilby, John 77–82, 106–10
    Britannia 79–82, 106
    English Travellers Companion 106
    Itinerarium Angliae 106
    Mr Ogilby's Pocket Book of Roads 106–9
    Mr Ogilby's Tables of his Measur'd Roads 106
Overbury, Sir Thomas 103, 127
Oxford 208

Palmer, Daryl W. 157
Parkes, Christopher 241
Parr, Anthony 180
Peacham, Henry 181
Peak District 197–8, 238
pedlars 94, 101–11, 112
Pepys, Samuel 196
Peterborough 203
Petty, William 110
pilgrimage 177–8
Plot, Robert 182
    Natural History of Oxford-Shire 183
Pontefract 205

Poor Laws 8, 94, 141
posts and postal system 77, 79–81, 106, 147, 170, 172
progresses 145–73
    as model for popular authors 157–64
    Elizabethan 147–57
        Bisham, 1592 150, 152
        Bristol, 1574 154–5
        Cowdray, 1591 153–4
        East Anglia, 1578 148–9, 150, 154–5
        Elvetham, 1591 148, 150, 151–2
        Kenilworth, 1578 151, 152
        Rye, 1573 156
        Sandwich, 1573 154
        Stafford, 1575 155
        Sudeley, 1591 152, 156
        Theobalds, 1591 152
        Worcester, 1575 155–6
        see also Charles I, King, Churchyard,
            Thomas, Gascoigne, George, Sidney, Sir
            Philip
    Jacobean 149, 156
Procter, Thomas, 87
prospects 199–200, 202–3
Pyott, Edward 115, 117

Quakers 114–17
Quint, David 38

Ray, John 182–3, 194
Raylor, Timothy 187
Raymond, Joad 169
Reading 6
Reynolds, John 103–4
Richards, William
    Wallography 188
Richardson, Samuel 241
rivers 5, 21–66
    difficulty of travel on 26–7
    improvement of 21–2, 27–8, 46–51
    and internal trade 21–2
    laws relating to 26–7, 46
    navigable and non-navigable 23–7, 47
roads 67–121
    definition of 67
    improvement of 86–90, 239
    laws relating to 70, 75–6, 86–7, 116–17
    mapping of 77–85, 106–9
    Roman 71–4
Robin Hood's Well 198
Robinson, Henry 51–2
Rogers, Pat 238, 240
rogue literature 93–101
Rollison, David 6, 211
Rowse, A. L. 29
Royal Society 110, 182

S., R. 48
St Austell 207
Salisbury 232
    Cathedral 194
Saxton, Christopher 24–5
    Atlas 31–2, 149
Scattergood, John 5
Schama, Simon 47
Schwyzer, Philip 4, 7
Scotland 15
Shakespeare, William
    1 Henry IV 52, 129–30
    The Merchant of Venice 215
    The Taming of the Shrew 130–1
    The Winter's Tale 104–5
Sidney, Sir Philip
    The Lady of May 153
Slack, Paul 95
Southampton 238
souvenirs 207–8
Speed, John 49
Spenser, Edmund 35
    Colin Clouts Come Home Againe 40
    Faerie Queene 35, 37–41
    'Prothalamion' 35
Spufford, Margaret 104
stages and stage coaches 77
Stoke Edith 203
Stonehenge 194, 196, 197
Stow, John 76
Stukeley, William
    Itinerarium Curiosum 235
Sullivan, Garrett A. 69
Summit, Jennifer 6

Tarlton, Richard 127–8
Taylor, John 15, 49–51, 53, 167–8, 211, 216–33
    The Carriers Cosmographie 105
    *John Taylors Wandering, to see the Wonders of the
        West* 227
    The Pennyles Pilgrimage 161–4, 216, 221, 222,
        225, 229, 232
    *The Praise … of Beggery, Beggers,
        and Begging* 218
    The Praise of Hemp-seed 218–19
    A Shilling or, The Travailes of Twelve-pence 217–18
    *Tailors Travels from London to the Isle
        of Wight* 168
    Taylor on Tame-Isis 49–50
    Taylors Pastorall 218
Thames, River
    navigation on 44–6, 49–50
    poetry of 35, 37–8, 40, 44–6, 49–50, 61–2, 219, 224
Thomas, Max W. 162
tinkers 101–11

tourism, domestic 174–209, 235–42
  anxiety about 174–5, 177, 187
  and consumption 206–8
  definition of 174
  development and justification of 180–5,
    201–2, 206
  and national identity 196–200, 208–9
  values and objectives of 195–7, 203–6
trade, internal 210–34
  celebrations of 161, 212, 238–40
  forms and development of 9–10, 14, 102–3, 125,
    210–11, 214–15
  state efforts to control 155–6, 213–14
  see also markets (and fairs) and marketing
traffic
  see trade, internal
Trapnel, Anna
  Anna Trapnel's Report and Plea 112–13
Tricomi, Albert H. 133
Trotter, David 240
Turner, Sir Edward 21
Turner, James 119

vagrancy 8, 91–120, 125
  category of 91–3
  laws concerning 93–5, 101–2, 116
Vallans, William
  A Tale of Two Swannes 33–5

Van Es, Bart 39
Vaughan, Henry
  'The King Disguised' 166–7

Wall, Wendy 157
Waller, Edmund 52–3
Waltham Lock 33–4
watermen 28–9, 44–54, 59
  Watermen's Company 28
Weever, John
  Ancient Funerall Monuments 181–2
weirs 26, 27, 44–5
wells, holy 178, 195
  St Winifred's Well 192
Wells, Jeremiah 188
Westcote, Thomas
  A View of Devonshire in 1630 33
Wharfe, River 59–60
Wilton 199
wonder 197–8, 230, 238
Woodbridge, Linda 98, 104
Wrightson, Keith 8
Wytham, River 42

York 221

Zacher, Christian Z. 177
Zaret, David 150